The Far Islands

The
Far Islands
and
Other Cold Places

Travel Essays of a Victorian Lady

by ELIZABETH TAYLOR

JAMES TAYLOR DUNN, *Editor*

ISBN 1-880654-11-3.

Library of Congress No. 97-65060.

Photographic and other credits:

Hudson's Bay Company Archives,
Provincial Archives of Manitoba,
for the photograph at pg. 55;

Føroya Landsbokavn, Tórshavn
for the photograph at page 220;

Dunn Family Papers,
Minnesota Historical Society,
for the front cover photograph and
the photographs and sketches
at pp. 6, 8, 10, 60, 74, 90, and 301;

and

James Taylor Dunn,
for the map at pg. 127,
and all other photographs.

Table of Contents

Part VI: The Faroe Islands (1895–1919)

Preface

In the 1880s residents of St. Paul, Minnesota, felt insulted. An article in *Harper's Weekly* said that Minnesota was a very cold place in winter, certainly too frigid for anyone to visit willingly. In an effort to counter that idea and develop tourism, city boosters determined to celebrate the cold through parades, an ice palace modeled on Montreal's, and all the skating, tobogganing and sleigh riding events which could be imagined. Elizabeth Taylor (1856–1932) grew up in that St. Paul, so when she was ready to see the world she was inspired by the cold and headed north.

After leaving St. Paul, Elizabeth Taylor's life became one of travel punctuated by short or long term periods of residence in Paris, Venice, Scotland, England, and the Faroe Islands of Denmark. She resided in the United States from 1908 to 1913, and returned home for good in 1924. Her only permanent home was to be her last, a cottage she named "Wake Robin," built on the Vermont property of friends. It was there that she died in 1932.

Following the death of Elizabeth Taylor her will directed that her papers be given to Blanche Dunham Hubbard on whose land "Wake Robin" stood. In 1948 Mrs. Hubbard's daughter-in-law Florence Hubbard gave the Taylor archive to James Taylor Dunn, historian and librarian, who is a great-grandnephew of Elizabeth Taylor.

This was a fortuitous decision as Mr. Dunn had long been interested in his Great-Aunt Lizzie's life and writings. Dunn put the papers in order and substantially expanded the collection by locating examples of her published work (totalling 39 articles) and adding letters she had written to others. Using the Taylor archive he then published articles concerning her travels and compiled a manuscript about her life in the Faroe Islands. In 1978 Dunn visited the Faroes where he was able to meet people and see places connected with the ten years that Elizabeth Taylor spent there.

James Taylor Dunn subsequently gave the Elizabeth Taylor archive to the Minnesota Historical Society of which he was chief librarian for seventeen years. These materials included her diaries, letters, sketchbooks, photographs, drawings, published articles, artifacts and notes. They all form part of the collection called the *Dunn Family Papers* which contains papers of many other family members. Mr. Dunn gratefully acknowledges the cooperation of the Minnesota Historical Society with the publication of this book generally, including the use of several unpublished works of Elizabeth Taylor. He also thanks Kathryn Ann (Katie) Johnson, cataloguer, and Dallas Lindgren, research expert, of the Minnesota Historical Society for their assistance over the years with the Elizabeth Taylor archive. Thanks are due to Dr. Arthur F. Nelson, professor emeritus of chemistry at St. Cloud State University, for his translations of several letters Elizabeth Taylor wrote in Danish to friends on the Faroe Islands. Finally, he is especially grateful for the helpful comments and suggestions from his wife, Márie Dunn-Bach.

There are also other individuals who have helped to rediscover the work and life of Elizabeth Taylor. Nancy Chapman Alden researched the Taylor travels in Europe and North America. Mrs. Alden, the wife of another great-grandnephew of Elizabeth Taylor, has also written articles about Miss Taylor, and has graciously shared her discoveries and information. Thanks also go to the late Pauli Hansen of Tórshavn, for years the pilot of the Danish royal yacht and to Oli Egilstrød of Eiði, both of whom assisted James Taylor Dunn in the Faroe Islands, for making their time his time.

The Far Islands

Introduction

"Those of Feroe must be praised above many other Nations in this, that a stranger travelling through the Land . . . is well received by them, and treated with the best they have."

LUCAS DEBES, 1670

It was in June, 1895, while traveling on the little steamer *Laura* en route from Scotland to Iceland to study eider-duck farms, that Elizabeth Taylor got her first glimpse of the Faroe Islands. Those were three seemingly endless days and nights in a "Chamber of Horrors" on the *Laura* where she was squeezed into an overcrowded and airless Ladies' Cabin amidst the groans and lamentations of the Danish passengers. The voyage, she said, was "fifty-six hours of about as bad an experience as I've ever had on board a ship." It did not dissuade her, however, from making a brief stopover and discovering that the Faroes were the destination she had been seeking.

"After breakfast, going on deck," she recorded in one little pocket notebook, "we saw the distant headlands of the Faroes. The misty clouds hung low, hiding the summits. Coming nearer we could see the grassy, steep slopes & precipitous basaltic cliffs. There was Lítla Dímun, a cone rising abruptly from the sea; a larger island, Stóra Dímun & other headlands lost to sight in the mist. Tórshavn came suddenly in view from around a curve of the land, sod-covered, barren hills beyond them, little streams trickling down from the heights, narrow stone-paved muddy lanes between the tar-pitched houses."

Her perceptive eyes caught scenes she wanted to sketch and sights she wanted to remember. "I am much pleased with the Faroese," she continued in a letter to a relative back in the States, "fine broad-shouldered men with a very becoming costume. They look much more like my ideas of the old Vikings than most of the Norwegians do. Some are exceedingly handsome, a ruddy blond with thick half-curling hair and very thick soft beards. There was much of that red-gold hair, brilliant in color, that one hears spoken of in the Norse Sagas."

This first visit to Tórshavn was too soon over, and she was off to Northern Iceland where she spent nine weeks traveling by pony and on foot, staying at local farmhouses, and enduring discomforts and dangers few would tolerate, least of all an American woman of genteel background. It was on board the *Laura*, returning to the Faroes from Iceland in September, 1895, that she met by chance a well-known British scholar who was the first director of Scandinavian Studies at the University of London. Later the encounter became perhaps the single most important incident in the life of this thirty-nine year old spinster, even though at the time all she wrote of "The Professor" was that he gave "promise of being very friendly." William Paton Ker, reserved, modest, a man of few words, and a bachelor, was forty. The friendship which later developed was all-important and very personal to this lonely American woman. In her eyes he became a sort of counselor, mentor, and guide, even though their contacts were few and far between. From time to time they discussed Norse *kvaedi*, or ballads, on which he was a recognized authority, and exchanged scientific information about birds and flowers. Miss Taylor always took "great pains with letters to him" getting information of importance to both of them and sending bits of folklore that might be of special interest. And she carefully edited and rewrote those letters, too, "so they are not slip-shod affairs." His letters to her, on the other hand, were in what she called his usual, sometimes irritating, "telegraphic-dispatch mode." She characterized him as "a very reticent and silent man." Before and during the difficult war years on the Faroes, Ker was able to be of considerable help financially which gave her great "peace of mind." In 1915 she wrote to a cousin in upstate New York about Professor Ker, "I have more and more affection for him as time goes by & think of him less. Which is a proper frame of mind. . . . And I believe the Professor truly cares for me & has *all the time*. This is a very comfortable conviction." In

4

1921 she made one of her last known references to their close yet distant relationship: "If it had not been for that blessed Professor," she wrote to another cousin, "I think I could never have weathered the war-gales in the Faroes."

But all of this was yet to be. Elizabeth Taylor's first letter to Ker, written in Tórshavn on September 18, 1895, enclosed the music for the Faroese "Bride's Song." "The Faroes I find delightful," she wrote, "in spite of the continued storms. . . . It is too late for flowers, and too early for weddings, but in spite of . . . these drawbacks I congratulate myself daily on my determination to make a longer stay here."

It was not until late in November, after exploratory trips to several islands, that Miss Taylor returned to Scotland and five years were to pass before she would see the Faroe Islands again. This first experience made a great impression on her, but little did she know at the time that before leaving the Faroes for good, she would have spent more than ten years on those remote and lonely islands.

❈❦❈

Elizabeth Taylor was born in Columbus, Ohio, on January 8, 1856, the fifth daughter of James Wickes Taylor who, after considerable journalistic work in that state, was from 1854 to 1856 the state librarian, appointed to write what is still a well-considered history of early Ohio. During that year, however, the Taylor family moved to St. Paul, following a number of her maternal aunts and uncles of the Langford family. In the fast-growing capital of the Minnesota Territory Taylor established a law office, and he served as a lobbyist for various railroad interests. Elizabeth, the youngest, was brought up in a house on Washington Street, in the then fashionable Irvine Park. She attended The Misses L. K. and Clara Wheaton's Select School for Girls at 5th and Franklin streets in the early 1870s where she was instructed in all that was thought necessary for the deportment of young girls of good families. And, in an interesting coincidence, two of the Wheaton sisters (Miss Emma and Miss Clara who had moved to San Francisco) became her aunts, as they became the first and second wives of her uncle Nathaniel Pitt Langford, the first superintendent of Yellowstone Park.

Elizabeth Taylor and her older sister Harriet (circa 1860).
Photograph by Whitney's Gallery, St. Paul, Minnesota.

Lizzie, as she was called within her family, was a maverick. She enjoyed interests few other young ladies of her background would then have even considered. She also had the advantage of an articulate and fascinating father who, finding himself blessed with a very unusual daughter, doubtless encouraged home reading and continuing self-education—what she later called "good home influences." In his essay on James Wickes Taylor, Theodore C. Blegen wrote:

> "Taylor was a true nature-lover, fond of wandering on field and road, having, indeed, something of a roving, almost a vagabond spirit. He was particularly fond of flowers and took great delight in picking prairie flowers, especially early in the spring. It afforded him great pleasure to share his flowers with others; he was often seen on the streets of Winnipeg with a great basket filled with nosegays carried unconventionally upon his arm, distributing them among his delighted friends."
>
> BLEGEN, 1915: 208

Picking spring flowers was a habit Taylor had earlier practiced in St. Paul where the hillside he frequented is still called "Crocus Hill."

In 1870 James W. Taylor was appointed American Consul at Winnipeg, Manitoba, a position he held until his death in 1893. As she grew into young womanhood Lizzie frequently visited her father in what was then a distant, pioneer outpost. Consul Taylor had to travel occasionally on official duties through then unsettled Canada. Lizzie was more times than not his traveling companion.

Together they shared many common interests, an enduring love for nature, for travel, for bird study and botany, for the out-of-doors, for fishing and writing. "What are storms and congestive chills and 'skeeters and black flies and punkies and short supplies, cold and wet, compared to the delight of being out-of-doors all the time on this beautiful river," she wrote in 1888 during her first solo camping trip into the far reaches of Canada's Nipigon River. The trip tested how well she could stand up under difficult conditions and away from the amenities of civilization. It was so successful that this affinity for the out-of-doors continued undiminished throughout her life.

"If I'd only been a boy," she sometimes complained, but, in spite of the numerous restrictions forced upon women of that period, she managed to do things not many men would have dared. She became a true collector of experiences. In 1889 she took a trip to Sitka, Alaska, for a summer of salmon fishing and sight-seeing, and ended up shipwrecked for five days after the paddlewheeler *Ancon* struck a reef. Three years later she eagerly braved the wilds of northern Canada and the censure of less venturesome stay-at-homes to become the only woman included by the United States government in a 1908 list of explorers in the American Arctic region. This summer-long trip took her several thousand miles north down the Mackenzie River to the Arctic Circle forts of the Hudson's Bay Company.

The Mackenzie River trip was probably the most arduous of all her travels. She had long dreamed of seeing the river and prepared for the trip through reading and conversations with those who knew the area. To be permitted, as a tourist, to accompany their summer supply mission she had to convince officials of the Hudson's Bay Company that she could withstand the vigorous journey. And the months from late May until late August, 1892 were certainly tough. From Edmonton she traveled by Red River cart to the landing where she boarded the first of the Hudson's Bay Company steamboats, the *Athabasca*. Passengers and cargo were transferred to sturgeon-head boats at the Grand Rapids, then to another steamboat (the *Grahame*)

On her trip to Alaska Elizabeth Taylor carried food, clothing, sketching and collecting materials, and fishing tackle. Here (in 1889) she sketched herself waiting at Port Townsend for the steamship Victoria.

which took them to Lake Athabasca, and finally, after a portage, they boarded the *Wrigley*, which took them to the Mackenzie River delta and back. There were often very brief stops enroute to deliver cargo to the forts, and longer halts as the men loaded and unloaded the boats. Rain and fierce mosquitoes were the major problems of the trip, yet Elizabeth Taylor did manage to do more sketches and collect more specimens than she did on other, easier journeys.

Elizabeth Taylor wrote and illustrated a series of four articles about the 1892 Mackenzie trip that were published a year later in *Outing* magazine, but she was far more proud, as an amateur botanist and zoologist, of being the first to discover a hitherto unknown herb and moth. The herb, a red-flowered member of the campion family, received the scientific name *Lychnis Tayloriae*. The lepidoptera collected on the Mackenzie expedition was named *Pseudosiona Taylori*.

A newspaper clipping of the period, apparently from Boston, described her as "a very attractive young woman no more than twenty-five or twenty-six [she was actually about ten years older]; small, a bright talker and thoroughly informed about the country she passed through" even when closely questioned by members of a scientific society. On the other hand, she had this somewhat less glamorized picture of herself: "There are times when I don't look badly—put me in a shaded light, under favourable circumstances & dressed up a little & I often look almost pleasing. But 99 times out of 100 I look ugly, worn & funny. . . . Perhaps the nose is the worst affliction, but it is not always red."

Other trips to northern climates followed. In Norway during 1893, this "girl Greeley" traveled with guide Ole and Freya, "a pretty, buff-colored pony of true Norse blood." They traversed the desolate waste of the Hardanger Vidda, the upland summer pastures, throughout its greatest length and over its highest ridges. Again delighting in the unusual, she boasted of being the first English-speaking woman to make this Hardanger trip.

Between those difficult yet rewarding explorations, and especially after the death of her father in 1893 when she was suddenly faced with having to survive on a very small income, she lived abroad, in "out of the way nooks most of the time, where living was cheap." Hoping to better her income through a certain affinity she had for art, she studied still life for a short time at Abbott H. Thayer's New Hampshire studio.

For several years in the 1880s she enrolled in classes at the Art Students' League in New York City where one of her teachers was Kenyon Cox. After her first summer in Europe (in 1890) she determined to follow the pattern of many American artists by studying art in Paris. Writing to her friend Fannie Burr, Elizabeth Taylor commented on the various Parisian schools. The famous Académie Julian

Elizabeth Taylor (second from right) in Paris (circa 1890) with other young artists. Ernest Thompson Seton is the tall man in the open doorway.

she found so crowded that students seated at their easels bumped each others' elbows. The Colarossi school charged less, but instruction seemed inadequate. She finally selected the classes of Charles Lazar, an American artist, where language would not be a problem, and she felt he could best help develop her skills.

While in Paris she met another artist whose interests paralleled her own. Ernest Thompson Seton had known her father in Canada, was already successful as an artist-naturalist, and shared her interest in making a trip on the Mackenzie River. And, in a strange link with home, his artist-roommate, Alexis Fournier, was from St. Paul. Seton wrote her a letter of recommendation to be used on her Canadian trip and gave advice on equipment; she told him how to obtain a pass on the Canadian Pacific railroad which was a welcome surprise as he later wrote in his autobiography, *Trail of an Artist-Naturalist* (1940).

After leaving Paris Elizabeth Taylor spent a winter, as other American artists did, in Venice. There she visited museums and wrote stories from Dalmatia and Montenegro for the *Brooklyn Eagle*. Whenever she traveled she tried her hand at sketching and writing. For some reason she had a low opinion of herself as an artist. "The truth is," she reported, "I haven't the remotest idea how to paint . . . though I can compose well & I think I have the right feeling for nature & all that, my attempts are absolutely beginnerish." Many years later her last teacher, an American based in England, Edward Ertz, was of a contrary opinion. He said "she could grasp the essentials and character of her subject and she had a fine color sense." What she called her "potboilers" were only occasionally sold, although Ertz urged her to enter her work in shows.

In addition, Elizabeth Taylor was technically knowledgeable, although self-taught, in the fields of ornithology, botany and ethnology. She collected for The Gray Herbarium of Harvard University, Cornell, the Catholic University and the Smithsonian Institution in Washington, D.C., The British Museum, and the Pitt Rivers Museum at Oxford University. At one point she hoped that a museum might subsidize her travels in the Faroes by advancing money (perhaps $300 to $500) with the expectation that she would collect specimens for their collections. She suggested the idea to David Starr

Jordan, who was by then the president of Stanford University. Jordan was willing to "speak in the highest possible terms" of her "intelligence and interests" but could not offer her any contracts. So it was that throughout her life it was always a struggle to scrimp and save to have enough to live on. "A grinding worry," she called it, "as to ways and means."

Elizabeth Taylor's major attempt to supplement her income, however, was writing for newspapers and magazines. Newspapers such as the *Buffalo Morning Courier* and the *Brooklyn Eagle*, and magazines such as *Frank Leslie's Popular Monthly Magazine*, *Popular Science News*, *Forest and Stream*, as well as a number of English publications were among those who published her accounts of travels into unfamiliar regions. Like her father, who wrote many essays for newspapers during his career, Elizabeth had a natural bent for writing and a mastery of plain English. The charm of her style, intimate, personal and self-revealing with pleasant touches of humor, exactly suited whatever subject she covered, whether it concerned fishing in Canada, eider-duck farms of Iceland, experiences in the Highlands of Scotland, or the celebration of a royal betrothal in Montenegro. The results invariably had an original point of view and, in the words of one English magazine editor, "simplicity & refinement & ease."

So by the end of the century this little five foot one inch woman—"dumpy and short waisted" as she described herself, frail and frequently ill, yet of amazing stamina, was, at the age of forty-four, on the eve of her greatest adventure. It was November 19, 1899, when she wrote to Fannie Burr, a friend and fellow art student from Connecticut, "I am going up to the Faroes, & even to think of it gives me a feeling of strength & enthusiasm."

On May 16, 1900, Elizabeth left Edinburgh for the Faroes. This time she decided that her trip, planned as an extended one, would have but one purpose: to collect as much detailed information about the Faroes and the Faroese as possible; to travel to as many islands as she could reach, studying birds and collecting plant specimens along the way. She wanted, most of all, experiences she could make use of in her writings and sketches that might come in handy as illustrations. She must, she told herself, write six letters for the American outdoors publication, *Forest and Stream* (five actually were published), the pay for which was to take care of the journey. "In order to secure material," she resolved, "I must see different islands and have certain experiences. . . . I must write about trout fishing, bird cliffs, whales, etc. & keep moving far more than I wish." Most of all, she felt a scrupulous obligation to be accurate.

After that she wanted to get together a "little book" about the Faroes in fifteen chapters. She would use the articles that she was going to write, and then try linking them. This book, which unfortunately never materialized, was an overriding obsession. For a number of years she reported on its progress and attendant frustrations in every letter she wrote to friends and relatives. "I wish I had the happy facility," she complained in one letter, "of writing with only slight experience. I 'wrastle' & have tough times & lots of them—and produce little." Among the many problems that troubled Miss Taylor, in addition to a lack of time for writing and sketching, was how to bring facts into her articles without their seeming like "useful information." In another letter she wrote, "Everyone seems to be dreadfully clever nowadays and the public wants things that are striking and a trifle sensational and picturesque, and I fear that is all beyond me."

It may be, too, that she perhaps kept putting things off. In fact she readily admitted such: "I am a slowminded person & I fear a lazy and procrastinating one." By 1906, in a letter to Professor Ker written from England she made one of many discouraging references to her projected book on the Faroes: it "is, as usual, having a vacation. . . . I suppose I must . . . pray that no clever writer will rush up there and do 'between steamers' what I have been trying to do in five years." She continued to refer to the planned publication in letters, and her papers show, through numerous scribbled memos and outlines, that it remained uppermost in her mind. Moreover, a number of inquiries from Ellery Sedgwick, editor of the *Atlantic Monthly*, and others from the Century Company, Appletons, and from Henry Goddard Leach of the *Forum* during the 1920s show that there were publishers who were definitely interested in being the first to see the manuscript. In one of his letters, editor Sedgwick called her writing "radiant with color." But time and failing health worked against her producing the Faroe book.

On board the steamer which brought Elizabeth Taylor to Tórshavn in May, 1900, was Montagu Villiers, newly-appointed consul of Great Britain, whose primary task was to help settle disputes over fishing rights. Mr. and Mrs. Villiers later became friends and invited Miss Taylor to spend the winter with them. She declined, however, because of the social life she would have to lead at the consulate. "I haven't party gowns, & they will entertain." Active partying in the capital city was the last thing she wanted. Her goal was to experience the life of local people, not that of other foreigners.

During that first five-year stretch on the Faroes, she stayed in many native homes, made numerous friends, and was beholden to a great number of Faroese not only for useful information but also for assistance in her island-hopping travels. Much of this is told in her published articles. Her initial host in Tórshavn was the head schoolmaster of all the Faroes, the *Hovedlaerer* Louis Bergh, who furnished her with introductions to a number of people, "clean farmers &c. who have a guest room, and will take me in." The most important of these was Hans Kristoffer Joensen of Miðvágur who looms large in her writings as "Hans Kristoffer" and to whose home in the "Ryggi" enclave of Miðvágur she frequently returned when in need of rest, relaxation, peace and quiet. Through the winter of 1900–1901 she was the guest at the governor's home in Tórshavn. Christian Baerentsen, the first and only native-born *Amtmand* of the islands, offered her free lodging if she would teach him and his family conversational English. "I couldn't go on such terms," she wrote. "I *must* work this next year or two & I could not do it if I was not paying. So we have compromised. I shall pay what I would in a simple Faroe home, enough to cover all possible expense to them. So both will be gainers. I get good quarters & better food than I otherwise would, and they get enough English, for nothing, for I can talk with them at meals, & for a while after dinner & supper—only in the dark days. I must have no interruption between 10 & 2, the hours when there is daylight."

Elizabeth was pleased with Amtmand Baerentsen's home. "The house," she said, "is on high land, well drained, & is by far the best in the Faroes—of solid hewn stone. . . . Rather cold, perhaps, but I can wear heavy clothes &c. . . ." "It is something of a risk to go into a strange family," she continued, "but I like the looks of the Governor & his wife, everyone thinks very highly of them & they are sincere & frank & kind, so I think with good feeling on both sides, we cannot go far amiss." She was particularly delighted with the governor as a source for local information and folklore. "The Amtmand knows lots of little Faroe incidents & doles them out from time to time."

That winter, however, did not turn out to be quite as euphoric as Elizabeth had hoped it would. The servants were "disorganized" and the nine children in the family, five of them babies, turned out to be "unruly." Also whooping cough, chicken pox, convulsions, and meningitis were intruders in the house during the time she was there, and "the poor baby died after four months of great suffering." Little wonder then, that amidst all that noise and confusion, she was unable to accomplish much, although during the winter she did manage to write one article, "A Night with the Mouse's Brother," which to her delight was accepted by the *Atlantic Monthly*. In February, however, she could take it no longer. She gave up her pleasant quarters and fled to Hans Kristoffer's home on Vágar island. "I liked the Governor & his wife," she concluded, "and we parted on very pleasant terms, but it was an unfortunate winter."

Another island home where she stayed for some time during this first long visit to the Faroes was Pastor Lorentz Peter Heilmann's parsonage, called "Onagerði" at Viðareiði, the northernmost settlement on the northernmost island of the Faroes. "I like the place and the peasants," she wrote, "and the fact that the surf is so bad that in winter no visitors can come and also that I need have no fine clothes; no winter hats, only thick stockings and mittens, sandals and kerchiefs. I put a woolen kerchief over my head & sally out in that style & I mean to wear a hood to church this winter. There is no fire in the church & it won't do to sit there in the damp. . . . There are but two shops & all the people except one shopkeeper & the schoolmaster are peasant fishermen." Here, then, were the essentials—down-to-earth people, pure air, good water. "As to society, who wants it? I don't. Everyone is courteous, there are no beggars, & the children do not bother while I'm sketching." Above all, she admonished herself, "do not look melancholy about the cold & make folks regret you are in the house."

Summer at "Onagerði," however, was busy with occasional visitors. Among those who came to Viðareiði in 1901, for example, were the priest and author, Andreas C. Evensen, and the educator Rasmus Rasmussen who were there for a short while "collecting old things. [They] have found and taken all that are in the place now." Apparently they were assembling artifacts for the Tórshavn historical museum founded in 1895, which today contains an excellent collection of exhibits illustrating Faroese daily life of the past. The excitement of their being there, however, disrupted Miss Taylor's workday and she was glad to see them leave. She greatly preferred the visitor-less peace and quiet of winter. With the Pastor frequently away on church duties and the Pastor's wife often in Denmark, Elizabeth was alone for a good part of the winter months. It was a definite change for the better after being crammed into "small nooks in noisy houses, with 'other folks' personalities crowding about my ears."

For a while Miss Taylor used the pastor's study in his absence. But she was always on the alert in case the master of the house might return. His study was her work and dining room, and in one loose scrap among her papers is a description of it "as a sight to see with large stones on the floor that serve as weights in pressing flowers; paints & paint rags; papers and sketches; flowers, botanical cases, poison bottles & a clutter of many things. It would drive an American housemother to distraction. . . . Fortunately we can see from afar when a boat comes 'around Múlin', the high promontory east of the fjord that leads to Klaksvík where visiting strangers would come from and there is almost a half hour's grace from the time a boat appears until its occupants land on the sea rocks and begin the laborious climb to the parsonage. And in that half hour much can be done." When the Pastor returned, Elizabeth would take refuge "in the seaward gable of the great attic," a "dear & friendly little room" which was dubbed the Maidens' Bower.

In one of the numerous incomplete letters in her papers, she described delightfully her 1901 Christmas at the parsonage in Viðareiði with the Pastor's two maids. The master was at Klaksvík and his wife elsewhere. So she, and Joanna, and Drikka held Yule together. "We had a tree last evening and really it was a charming little tree. I made it myself of two little spinning reels, one on top of the other. That gave me 'eight branches,' and a maul-stick made two more. All these I covered with heather and crowberry, then added smaller side branches of stocky crowberry, and decorated the tree with little paper roses and candles and some dainty little things that the English Consul & his wife sent me from Tórshavn. The tree was about three feet high and really looked wonderfully like a real one. Rossva [the Pastor's dog] and the two cats were adorned with ribbons, the shepherd Simon Peter ... was invited for the evening and we ate the true Danish supper for Christmas evening: boiled rice first and goose afterwards. The *nisse* or little brownie who is supposed to live in the loft had a dish of rice & milk to put him in the proper frame of mind for bestowing favors on the house during the coming year. And all the cows had an extra meal & the chickens also. Yesterday was 'little Jul day', today—Christmas—is 'first Jul day' when one goes to church, and no dancing is allowed; and on second and third Jul day, there will be Faroe dances at one of the houses."

Elizabeth Taylor was indeed happy at Pastor Heilmann's in Viðareiði. The first winter was also a bit more productive than the last one had been. She wrote about her experiences on Stóra Dímun, finished "Absalom's Wreath," for the *Atlantic Monthly*, and sent *Forest and Stream* letters concerning her trip to Mykines Island. And she took many notes. There was, in her opinion, "no form of writing in which one could profitably devote more time and care than in the making of notes. Notes are a writer's stock in trade." Only one problem existed, and apparently it was but a minor one: the Pastor, when he was there, was a bit too energetic for her taste. His daily practice was to "shoot at marks two feet from my window." In addition, the noise of his "wild romps with his wife & dog . . . 'make the welkin ring' (though I don't know what a welkin is)."

Wherever she traveled among the northern islands from 1900 to 1906, she found Faroese like Amtmand Baerentsen to furnish her with the information she was seeking. She and Samuel Niclassen, the schoolmaster on Mykines Island, for example, carried on what she called a "strictly ornithological flirtation. He may be seen slipping folded notes into my hand—lists of resident birds, rare ones, migratory ones, &c. We have had a rendezvous with the puffins. . . .

I have given him (at his request) the Lord's Prayer in English and the British names of the birds. He has given me the Súla Song that the men sing when they go at night to catch the gannet."

There were other families with whom she lived during those ten years on the islands: dear Hans Kristoffer who taught her much about the Faroes; the Oster family of Eiði during the war years; Joen Abrahamsen who was her host and source of information on the birdman's paradise island of Mykines; and, among others, king's peasant Jens Ole-Jacobsen on Stóra Dímun. She also visited the home of the head of the Faroe church, Provost Frederik Petersen, with whom she talked "about many things." Her friend Mads Andreas Winther, head clerk in the Judge's office, helped her with the Faroese language and was especially knowledgeable in folklore and all that pertained to Faroe life. In her papers are numerous jottings, hurriedly penciled on odd scraps of paper, recording the stories and folk beliefs that Winther and others told her. Occasional acquaintances were sources of information, too, like Rasmus Effersøe, agricultural consultant, poet, and newspaper editor. "He is very tall, handsome, a fine physique," she reported to Professor Ker in April, 1915, "which I am sorry to say is having a losing fight with tuberculosis. He has written a good little book on the Faroe livestock & agriculture & has introduced the innoculation of sheep." Effersøe died the following year.

She also met with chance acquaintances to further her knowledge of the islands. One was an elderly Tórshavn man she met in March, 1903, as he carried manure to his outfield. "We engaged in a chat about oyster catchers," she reported in one letter, "and I so approved of his views that I invited him to call." His two-and-a-half hour visit produced quite satisfactory results. "He has had tea & small cakes & two cigars & I have had such a fund of odd scraps of folklore poured into my ears." A final example of Elizabeth Taylor's receiving information from casual meetings came late in her stay. In April, 1906, before returning from England to the Faroes for the summer, she wrote to Professor Ker that when she got back she would "make a special trip to a place where I hope a little woman is still living who knows a great number of [children's] games. I discovered her stores of knowledge just as I was leaving the islands. I shall return bearing a cheap but good piece of blue serge as a stimulation to her memory & we will have a long talk."

One schoolmaster she engaged to help her occasionally had both his good and bad points. "We meet in the big kitchen, and he has a cup of tea with me and I ask him many questions. It is a wearisome piece of work—for the head. For his pride will not allow him to say he does not know the answer to a question. So he [makes one up] and I have to be on the alert to catch him."

Elizabeth Taylor was completely thorough in her investigations. An amateur herself, she nonetheless had the true scholar's inquiring mind plus the ability to report the results in delightful prose. She wanted most of all to say something that was peculiarly her own. Hers was indeed a love affair with the Faroe Islands, and her greatest wish was that others might enjoy sharing her unique experiences. As she wrote to the Professor from Yealmpton, England, early in 1906, urging him to visit the Faroes: "It really seems a pity that you who could appreciate the Faroes as few others could do, have never had a tramp over the fjelds or in a Faroe boat among the fjords. It is not right & sometime when all is changed up there, & the Faroe men are wearing bowler hats & spats, you will be sorry. It is to spare you un-availing regrets that I urge this trip upon you." Elizabeth, appar-ently, had forgotten that over the years on his frequent trips to Iceland Ker had made a number of stopovers in the Faroes. Either that, or she considered such quick visits completely inadequate. "I was there this summer for two days," the Professor had written her on December 20, 1899, "It was like coming home to get up on the moor above Trongisvágur and see the curlew and oyster catchers in their old places and also the Dímuns and Skúvoy, and the rest of the noble creations. I drew a verse of the *Tróndur Kvaedi*, more or less accidentally, from an old and partially sober boatman at Tórshavn and went to bed praising the Lord for His mercies in having kept those memories so long in the rocks of the sea." Ker urged her to write more articles like those in the *Atlantic* and offered his help with the book knowing that with what he called her "close acquain-tance with life in the Faroes" she would be able to record the old Faroese customs and beliefs in her writings and sketches. "In a few years more great changes will be made and little left of the old time life," Ker wrote. Perhaps with the Professor's continued urgings she might have finished the book.

One of Elizabeth Taylor's difficulties (a "great hindrance" she called it) was the language. It wasn't very long before she had a speaking and writing acquaintance with Danish, but at the beginning the going was rough, and the old Norse of the Faroese was even more complicated. The English books she consulted in the libraries of London and Edinburgh she found untrustworthy. They were mostly written in a patronizing and superficial way, she thought, and she complained that "every thing I want is either in Faroe or Danish. I work away at it with only the beginning of a Faerösk-Dansk little dictionary." This doubtless was the second volume of the *Faerösk Anthologie* (1891) with a glossary by Jakob Jakobsen.

Elizabeth also enjoyed small triumphs in addition to the acceptance of several more articles by the *Atlantic*. In 1904 she wrote that, after she sent most of the Faroe plants she had carefully collected to a Copenhagen botanist (C. H. Ostenfeld of the Universitets Botaniske Museum) for positive identification, he wrote her that one of the species was "new for Faroes." This, she said, "seems to be a matter for congratulation." Unlike the Mackenzie River plant and insect she discovered, this particular plant was apparently not given her name.

Another small triumph was a gift she received from Consul Villiers—especially appreciated in the light of her continuing difficulties with gardening in the Faroes. It was in the spring of 1902 that she received this unusual and welcome offering. "Mr. Villiers has imported an Icelandic pony," she reported. "So now one can have that rare luxury, *horse manure*. It is the only horse in town, and I have received the graceful kind attention of a large cracker box full, sent from His Majesty's Consulate. Do you remember that observation of Elizabeth of the German Garden—'the longer I live, the greater is my respect for nature in all its forms.' Given a place where there are no horses & no leaf mould, the matter of a proper compost requires attention & thought."

Late in 1905 Elizabeth Taylor returned to England for the winter, but on May 12, 1906, she was back in the Faroes and remained there until October 24. During that summer she had "the coldest kind of reception from Nature. Such a season of cold & storm no one could remember. Snow every month . . . cold sea fogs & northern winds week after week & violent storms. . . . I went back to my old quarters, Viðareiði, where a new little pastor—a bachelor—has come," and she accomplished "almost nothing." The replacement for Pastor Heilmann was Christian A. Faulenborg. Among her papers are no letters written that summer, except a long one from Viðareiði to Knud Andersen of the British Museum, who was an authority on birds of the Faroes. In it she described, among other things, the strange dancing of the puffins on Stóra Dímun and commented on the disregard of the laws protecting birds. "Stealing tern eggs is very common even though everyone acknowledges how useful the bird is. The schoolmasters could do much to help," she thought, "but they are equally indifferent to the protecting laws—excepting, of course, the Mykines schoolmaster."

On October 24 she went back to England, again to Yealmpton, near Plymouth, to take art lessons once more from Edward Ertz. From 1908 to 1911 Elizabeth was in the United States visiting friends and relatives, renting inexpensive quarters in out-of-the-way farmhouses, and giving illustrated talks about the Faroe Islands, their bird life and folklore to women's clubs and folklore societies in Massachusetts and Rhode Island. She called them "Parlor talks" in a 1909 letter to biologist David Starr Jordan. "Being small voiced and diffident one would think I couldn't succeed, but the few I have given . . . were very successful." These appearances were yet another effort to bolster what was still a meager income. Although she had a number of engagements along the eastern seaboard and her talks were popular enough to be handled for a short while by a New York booking firm, it is not known whether the remuneration was adequate. As a result of the talks, though, she did sell a few watercolors of Faroe scenes.

On May 9, 1913, Elizabeth Taylor returned for a fortnight to the Faroes aboard the *Tjaldur* (oyster catcher). The steamer was greeted at Tórshavn by her friend Hans Christian Thygesen whom she had first met when he was Amtmand Baerentsen's deputy. By 1913 Thygesen was the new, recently-married *Sorenskriver* who had "a charming young wife . . . & they were both as kind & good to me as they could be. I didn't think when I 'put my best licks' into teaching him conversational English eight years ago [in 1905] that he would be such a thankful person with such a good memory for a little friendly kindness." She stayed with the Judge and his wife for a little over a week and then moved on to Klaksvík. After a bout of illness there at the home of Frú Sigrid Lützen, a friend of former years and sister of Mads Andreas Winther, she resumed her planned return visit to Iceland where she spent the summer. She traveled again with guide and horse through the northern part of the country, staying at farmhouses, and "reviving old memories." It was a rewarding and happy summer, but also one "of great suffering and weakness" because she was plagued by recurring illnesses. Somehow, she always seemed to bounce back and keep going. Returning to Edinburgh for the winter, she traveled to the Faroes for the last time on May 5, 1914.

She went directly to Hans Kristoffer's home at Miðvágur. There, weak and ill, she "pottered about" in his garden all summer, as she reported to Professor Ker, except for one difficult trip to Bøur in a raging storm. Attempting to land, "the men tried to put me up on some sea rocks . . . I made a misstep & slid down into the surf and was 'yanked' up to safety by one arm, very wet & cold & scared." During September she made a visit to the village of Eiði, where she remained for four weeks with the Kruse family with whom she had first stayed for a month back in 1901.

In the meantime the first World War erupted on the continent in mid-July, 1914, and Miss Taylor was unable to leave. The Kruses offered her shelter for the duration on the northern island of Esturoy, and in late October she packed up and moved there. Her life with them in Eiði during those difficult war years is documented in the *Atlantic Monthly* article, "Five Years in a Faroe Attic," written a few years later and published in 1921. Her letters, however, give us sidelights and more personal comments which she of course could not use at the time. Through them, the delightful Kruses become even more human and colorful.

Eiði she did not particularly care for. "It is," she wrote, "a dirty disagreeable little village in the north, but the air & water are good & I'll be in a neat little cottage on the outskirts. Up in two attic rooms that I'll take care of myself." In this way her hostess Amalie (or Amalya), one of the Kruses married to Oliver Oster, would not weary of her through the long stormy winter. To fortify herself mentally, Elizabeth decided to consider life there as "a kind of Arctic Expedition."

"Mistela" as she was called by the local children, or "Nela," as the Osters nicknamed her, looked philosophically on her little duties within family life: "Dishwashing is a great restorative after a sleepless night from some awful storm; the hot water, the motion, the sense of something accomplished. Also the making of soup has a beneficial psychological effect."

She was thankful for the refuge "Malle" Oster offered her. "I used to stay here with the big Kruse family years ago," she reported to Helen Carver in 1915, "& knew them to be kind & hospitable & sincere. . . . Amalie and I are on the pleasantest of terms; when we have had 3 months together without the least shadow of a difference I think we are safe to wear through the winter. . . . All are jolly & kind & simple minded & frank & I am much attached to them,"—even though they did "sleep to truly dreadful hours."

"A Kruse knows no concealments," she concluded, "whatever is on his or her mind comes out in unmistakable terms. They have

Fishing was one of Elizabeth Taylor's favorite diversions. Here, on an Eiði lake, she is accompanied by Oli Egilstrød's father, Oliver Oster.

lively tempers, but wholesome ones, and I never knew people more appreciative of little gifts." Their lively tempers sometimes led to a great deal of colorful swearing in the Faroese language. "Even Amalie can use with vigour a variety of expressions that remind me of the old-fashioned Scottish lady who remarked that 'swearin' was a great offset to conversation.' When a whole Kruse family are discussing an exciting matter below, I laugh up in 'Kvisten' [the name for Miss Taylor's attic quarters] for there are such strange echoes of sea-life in the talk. Old Herr Kruse was a Bornholm sea captain of vigorous sea-speech & a rich vocabulary."

As in past years, Elizabeth was still fighting the problems of cultivating a garden in the Faroes. In a 1916 letter to Professor Ker she made this comment on her most recent efforts at the Oster-Kruses:

> "Last year I meant to show the Eiði people what could be done with a little garden. The result was a solemn warning to them to have nothing to do with gardens. Nature always *does* betray the heart that loves her in the Faroes."

Except for the ever-present storms, little happened in Eiði during the winter months. She philosophized, however, that it was "better to be in an out of the way place with a few simple friendly souls than to be in the Capital, Tórshavn, that has grown so fashionable that one can't wear a kerchief on the head even in the stores, nor big coarse sandals over one's boots when all is a glare of ice." In January, 1915, she described for the Professor the greatest event of the season, the pastoral visit from Provost Frederik Petersen: "In one day he had a fair amount of church, school & parish business, enough for an ordinary working day. In addition he held ordinary church service, *Altergang*, three Earth Castings, five Christenings, two weddings, 1 dance, & two wedding suppers preceded by one Christening dinner. This did not include a number of friendly calls."

In Eiði she continued to sketch out plans for her book and did some writing, mostly in the form of long, detailed letters to friends and relatives, for writing was always Elizabeth Taylor's major interest, and letter-writing was one outlet. "I take to long letters," she explained in 1915. "I get so tired of hearing and speaking no English."

Writing was certainly the thing she was best at, even though most of the time it was, for her, difficult work. Painting came second—a close second, though, because she saw its importance mainly as an adjunct to her writing. She wanted to paint and sketch well enough to record the scenes which then could serve as illustrations for her book or be used in more Faroe talks to come. The problem was that the weather and light and the good hour she wanted seldom came. "One loses much time in one's art work here because of the continued bad weather, sudden changes & varying lights."

There were so many other scenes around her, too, scenes and subjects that had what she called "a nice kind of sentiment . . . but I cannot define it. The simple courage of these peasant folks & the bigness & hardness of nature is a part of it." She wanted to paint one scene in Eiði that she was going to call "Winter Fields"—"a slope of their poor little barley patches curving over a hill side, just a tiny sliver of the fjord showing below & three or four little masts of fishing boats; a rugged line of fjords & at one side a rise of land covered with boulders and mosses." In painting or sketching, however, she found it difficult to catch "the size and grandeur of the fjelds & cliffs,"—almost too panoramic for her abilities, she thought.

Her letters contain descriptions of many more paintings she wanted to do. Whether she actually ever finished them is not known. Many are presumed burned by a later fire which destroyed her friend Blanche Dunham Hubbard's farmhouse next to Wake Robin, her Vermont cabin. For over a year-and-a-half, during the early war years, she admitted to completing only one small watercolor. But she did try, and during her first long stay on the islands, Mrs. Villiers took a portfolio of her paintings to sell to summer visitors. There is no record, though, of whether any were actually sold. "I do not think the Faroes will be profitable in the way of potboilers," she said. "The subjects are too unfamiliar and sad. Bright gay familiar subjects are what one should paint, for sale."

A scribbled note is among her papers, perhaps the beginning of an article or a reminder to be inserted somewhere. It gives a picture of the difficulties frequently encountered in Eiði and elsewhere when she would find a local boy to go along and help her on a sketching trip. And at the end of the account there is a hint of huldufólk activity—that perhaps those mischievous underground creatures of the island's folklore were really responsible for her discomfiture:

> "Sketching placidly, weather a little breezy but not more than usual. Just finished a sketch that was better than usual, a sudden cast wind fell. It closed my camp stool, folded *me* up neatly & pitched me forward [on my knees]. My hat was scraped down the length of my nose & covered my face, my water can was emptied first into my opened [paint] box & then all over my completed sketch. The paint box was deposited in the mud upside down. My large portfolio of sketches & unused fresh paper was whirled up and its contents carefully deposited in a deep ditch filled with muddy water, though there were clean grass fields close on both sides of the ditch. The devastation was complete. Nothing evil was left undone that could be done. Now I ask you whether I was a victim only of chance."

She titled her note "My Rout." Such were the trials of an artist in the Faroes!

During the years that Elizabeth Taylor lived with the Oster-Kruse family in Eiði there was a man in the family who is mentioned once in her article "Five Years in a Faroe Attic." It concerns the arrival of a British trawler and the difficulties "Niels" was having with British slang like "grub," "bac," and "tates." The Niels mentioned was Niels Kruse, who became one of the pioneer landscape painters of the Faroe Islands. John F. West in his excellent book *Faroe: The Emergence of a Nation* (1972), speaks of the lack of "tradition for artists to build upon, such as the old stories and ballads provided for the Faroese authors." Then Dr. West makes the interesting statement that "the impulse to paint was sparked off in a number of places by the example of foreign artists, mostly amateurs, who happened to visit the islands in the late nineteenth century." Elizabeth Taylor was first in Eiði visiting the Kruse family in 1901 (Niels Kruse was then thirty years old) and she returned to stay with them throughout the war years. Although she made no direct references to him in any of the existing letters written while she was living at Eiði, nevertheless a revealing comment is part of one she wrote in Danish to Malle Oster from Yealmpton on June 9, 1921: "I wish very much I could talk with Niels about paintings and hear what he has done since I left."

Not until over two years later, however, did Niels Kruse receive any recognition as a painter. That was when a fine Faroese seascape he executed in 1922 called "First Day of Autumn" was accepted by the Charlottenborg Gallery in Denmark. "I am the first Faroese painter to receive such an honor," he wrote to Elizabeth on March 15, 1924. It was this belated recognition of his abilities which was especially appreciated by Kruse because he had never received academic training, "except," he wrote, "for the good advice and valuable schooling for which I can thank Miss Taylor." True it is, then, that her sketching activities at Eiði and the discussions the two had about art definitely encouraged this pioneer artist. And Elizabeth's teachings of other artists like Mikkjal D. á Ryggi and Jógvan Waagstein is a part of Faroese history. Waagstein, a local teacher and musician, admitted that the only art lessons he ever had came from "the artist lady Miss Taylor and from Mrs. Heilmann."

On May 12, 1920, almost a year after leaving the islands for good, she wrote to Professor Ker from Sussex, England, that she still had "pangs of homesickness for the North, barren spaces and bare rocks." For a number of years she kept in touch with her friends in Eiði and with Hans Kristoffer at "Ryggi." In 1921 came the last letter from Miðvágur written by her young fishing companion of years past, Heini Joensen. It was penned on behalf of his uncle Hans Kristoffer who was ninety years old, very deaf, and almost blind. By this time Johanna Katrina was dead. Hans Kristoffer still occasionally puttered in the same garden Elizabeth Taylor had so loved, where she had spent so many hours planting trees and flowers and helping him tend. The final blow came in 1923 when her friend and mentor William Paton Ker suffered a fatal heart attack while hiking in the high Alps of Northern Italy on the Swiss border. With his sudden death, much went out of her life. It was some time before she recovered from the sudden end of what she called their "long and intimate friendship."

In August, 1919, at the age of sixty-three, "Mistela" said goodbye to her beloved Faroe Islands for the last time. Five years later this "gentle, frail little creature," as she was called by one newspaper reporter, returned to America and to Rochester, Vermont, and there she died on a wintery March day in 1932, in her primitive little two-room cabin, "Wake Robin," up North Hollow way from Rochester. She had frequently visited the Green Mountain State and in 1924, when it came to building a cabin and settling down after more than forty years of world-traveling, she chose a beautiful, wooded hilltop on the Hubbard farm, in the shadow of Cushman's Summit and the Braintree Mountains with a wide sweep of distant blue hills. "Killington is the highest of the three mountain peaks I see from my cabin," she wrote, "Killington, then Pico, then Shrewsbury in a line."

It is hard to explain just why Elizabeth Taylor most frequently turned her steps northward, but the facts are there, that in traveling her tastes were arctic, whether it be Alaska, the Mackenzie delta, Norway, Iceland, or the Faroes. Perhaps the answer lies in her love for nature and the out-of-doors at their most elemental and rugged—a personal, pioneer need and challenge that was apparently

Elizabeth Taylor working in Tent City,
her temporary summer home in Vermont.

satisfied only by colder and wilder climates, regardless of discomforts and sufferings. Throughout her life she craved most of all what she called "simple outdoor living."

In fact, to the end she was proud of her ability to withstand hardships. "I am credited by disinterested critics as being a specially hard boiled old party. One old [Vermont] farmer told me he was sure that not one woman in a hundred could be found that would live here as I do, with contentment & with no foolish fears."

Elizabeth Taylor is remembered by a few whose lives she touched, including people in the far-off Faroes. In 1950, Mr. R. K. Rasmussen, Eiði's second medical resident, sent recollections from that village: "I arrived here in June 1920, spending my first 5 weeks in the attic where she had resided 5 years. I heard her name the first day of my arrival and saw the same day her writing table, a box only—and a very little one. The table is still in the garret."

In 1978 Elizabeth Taylor was still remembered in the Faroes by scholars like John Davidsen and Professor Christian Matras who recognized her influence on the pioneer artists of the islands: Niels Kruse, Mikkjal D. á Ryggi, Flora Heilmann, Jógvan Waagstein, and others. She was also held in closer personal esteem by Oli Egilstrød, for example, who was the Oli Oster born during those five years spent in the Oster's Eiði attic. The Egilstrøds in their home above their store, treasured her "Little Bear's" chair, a few faded linen children's books, some photographs, a half-dozen well worn Christmas tree decorations, a small lusterware tea set; and one of Oli's seven children was named Elizabeth. Valborg Svaðabø (née Joensen) of Miðvágur also remembered Elizabeth Taylor and her great-uncle, "dear Hans Kristoffer." The trees in his garden have grown tall now, but the flower beds stand untended and tall grasses grow where Hans Kristoffer's primroses were once his pride and joy. Martin Joensen at the age of 83 remembered well as a small boy going fishing with his friend Guttorm Matras and Miss Taylor, when she lived in the parsonage "Onagerði" in Viðareiði. She was, in his words, "a very considerate person, who would weep at the sight of a dead bird." Mrs. Sunnuva Jacobsen of Norðragøta, then in her mid-80s, treasured letters written by Elizabeth to her crippled aunt Olivina Olsen.

Those were memories of the people who had met Elizabeth Taylor. Others who discover her in this book will find a writer and traveler who chose plain, rugged places and wrote with deep pleasure about them.

JAMES TAYLOR DUNN
Marine on St. Croix, Minnesota
June 15, 1997

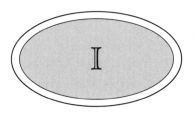

Canada and Alaska
1888–1892

Elizabeth Taylor came to know Canada well once her father became American Consul in Winnipeg in 1870. She visited him and traveled with him often over his two decades of service. When Miss Taylor wanted to test her own ability as a traveler her father contacted authorities of the Hudson's Bay Company to request permission for her to accompany one of the supply missions on the Nipigon River in 1888. The following year he arranged for a railroad pass which she used to cross Canada on her way to Sitka, Alaska. Miss Taylor spent July through September, 1889 in the Sitka area, fishing and visiting the sights. That trip turned into an unexpected adventure on her return when the steamship Ancon *struck a reef and capsized. She and her entire group of 200 tourists had to be put ashore on a nearby island where they waited five days until another steamer, the* George Elder, *could rescue them.*

Elizabeth Taylor's major Canadian trip took place in the late summer of 1892 when she was a passenger on the Hudson Bay Company's summer supply mission down the Mackenzie River to its delta. Her accounts of the Nipigon (she wrote it as "Nepigon") and Mackenzie River trips are included here, along with a set of notes she wrote on what a well-provisioned lady traveler should take along on a summer river trip in Canada.

Up the Nepigon

We started on our trip up the Nepigon one bright August afternoon. My companions were to join me at the foot of Lake Helen, above the rapids on the river, and I had a solitary walk of a mile through the woods that cover the high banks of the Nepigon at Red Rock—which is the Hudson Bay Company post on the north shore of Lake Superior, where all camping-parties prepare for the voyage up the river. Three lovely young girls in their pretty light dresses gathered on the piazza to wave me good by, and I turned away from the hospitable home, feeling like a tramp in my rough camp-dress. From time to time I looked back for another glimpse of the post, with its red roofs and white walls brilliant among the dark pines that surround it.

The air was full of the spicy odors of cedars and hemlocks, and the half-sweet, half-bitter fragrance of the poplars; not a sound was heard but the bell-like note of the "Peabody bird" or white-throated sparrow, and the occasional splash of a trout in the swift current far below, where the Nepigon foams and tumbles along to the bay, and at intervals the plaintive call of the black-throated green warbler. Above my head came his sad, languid refrain of "Hear me, Saint Theresa!" as Wilson Flagg interprets it. To my ears that afternoon it brought suggestions of doubt and misgiving. I was about to start on a trip of one hundred and twenty miles in a birch-bark canoe, with perfect strangers, with Indian guides to paddle us. We were going to a mission of the English Church on a bay in Lake Nepigon, sixty miles away, to be present at an Indian annual payment.

The head of our party was the wife of the missionary, who, with her little boy, an Indian woman, two Indian guides and myself made up the company. We embarked on the shores of Lake Helen, the lowest of the five lakes that break the course of the river on its way from Lake Nepigon forty-five miles north of Red Rock.

33

One canoe held our party, tents, blankets, personal baggage, with provisions not only for ourselves, but for the man left in charge at the mission. It was astonishing to one who had never seen a "birch-bark" loaded before to find what a quantity could be stowed away in it, and when that was done, and it seemed quite impossible for it to hold anything more and float, one after another of our party climbed in, and the guide motioned for me to come down to the shore. I looked over the lake we were to cross, where the waves were running high with a strong north wind, and climbed down the bank and into the canoe with the calmness of despair. Before we camped that night my opinion of a birch-bark had undergone a great change. At first it seemed as if we should certainly be swamped, but as each wave swept by, and the canoe lightly rose and fell with only the crest of a wave curling in once in awhile, the fear passed by, and a delightful feeling of exhilaration took its place.

As we neared the upper end of the lake the water grew calmer, and the turn into the river was very beautiful. Here and there on the banks were the tents of the families of the Indian guides, and we were greeted by a chorus from the Indian dogs that stood on the shore in long rows, with noses uplifted in the air, howling dismally.

It was after sundown that night when we made our camp at the foot of the "Long Portage" above Camp Alexander; upon the brow of the hill, the dark woods around us, and the rapids below thundering by with a deep roar, we partook of a banquet fit for gods and men: bacon fried with onions, and eaten from a tin plate with an uncertain steel fork.

The next morning by seven o'clock we were toiling over the portage of two and a half miles. On this day we experienced the trials that, sooner or later, try the patience of the camper. Heat, fog, a slow drizzle, black flies, musquitoes and punkies by the thousand; everything wet and disagreeable, the portage rough and stony. It was just as well to have this experience at first, for after that, whenever anything went wrong, we had only to recall that morning on the long portage, and everything seemed to brighten.

By noon we were on our way up the river, passing through Lakes Jessie and Maria, and stopping only to make a short portage of two hundred and fifty yards at Split Rock, where the river is divided by a great tower of rock several hundred feet high, around which the water foams incessantly.

The sun was just setting when we drew near the rocky island on which we were to camp that night. There, in the rapids, was a canoe with two gentlemen fly-fishing, and as we stopped to exchange greetings, we had the delight of seeing four magnificent trout landed, one fine fish by one angler, and the others at a cast by his companion.

We hoped to reach the shores of Lake Nepigon next day, but evening found us at the southern end of the mile portage that separated us from it. The day had been delightful, for our route lay through some of the finest views on the river, over two lakes and the two miles of the beautiful Pine Portage, past numberless rapids and islands, and between frowning cliffs of black trap rock, that rise in one place to a height of six hundred feet. It was while crossing one of the small portages that I saw my first "Whisky Jack." All along the way I had been looking for him—I had heard so much of his self-confident ways and impertinent curiosity, and was anxious to make his acquaintance. As I was sitting at the upper end of the portage, waiting for the guides, a long bluish slate-colored bird flitted lightly down to within a few yards of my resting-place. He paid no attention whatever to me, but began arranging his plumage with a preoccupied air, as if his thoughts were far away. He made quite an elaborate toilet, shaking up the loose, fluffy masses of feathers, stretching his wings and pluming himself carefully. I moved a little from time to time to attract his attention, and he occasionally glanced at me with a rather bored air, as if my presence was undesirable, but showed not the slightest sign of fear. After some time, he left his perch, and uttering a low call, sailed gracefully away.

Among some of the Indian tribes he is known as the "Wischa-shon," and that was changed by the white men into Whisky John, and so to Whisky Jack. The Ojibwas, I believe, call him "Guin-qui-shi."

I am inclined to think that Whisky Jack has been maligned, and to agree with our guide, with whom I talked about it. He said: "The Whisky Jack is not an impertinent bird; all the gentlemen that come up call him so, but they don't understand him. They camp in his woods and make a big noise and disturb him, and why should he care for them? This is *his* country, where he has always lived—he is at home, and why need he be shy? He does not like new-comers, and perhaps he shows it, and then they call him impertinent."

I was told before leaving Red Rock, by a gentleman who had been up the river, that I should not find more than a dozen kinds of birds, but by diligent search on the portages, a list of thirty-eight was made; and many more, I am sure, could have been found earlier in the season, when they are in song.

The bird one hears oftener than any other is the "Dah-je-ba," or white-throated sparrow, the "Rossignol" of the Eastern Provinces. A guide from the Sault Ste. Marie called him the "Onak." His wild, sweet note sounded on every portage, though it was with the greatest difficulty that I caught sight of him

We often beheld the black-capped chickadee talking cheerfully to himself as he flitted up and down between the boughs. I had met him last in the far-away marsh islands of Point Seakonnet, in Rhode Island, and his voice sounded like that of an old friend. The Indian name for him, "Ge-je-ge-je-ga-na-she," when said quickly, is a much better imitation of his usual call than our chickadee. Longfellow gives the name of "Opeechee" to the robin which we found only near Red Rock, but all the North-shore Ojibwas that I asked about it called him the "Kwushqua."

The owl seemed to be the "Ko-ko-ko-o" everywhere; the white-headed eagle, the "Me-ge-ze"; and the loon, the "Maung," or "brave-hearted." To one familiar with the quiet, dignified, gentlemanly ways of the cedar-bird, his Indian name of "O-gi-ma-bi-ni-shi" will seem a good one—"the bird that is king."

One morning I had the good fortune to see two rare birds, the Philadelphia vireo and the solitary vireo. I was sitting on a rock, resting, after a hard climb for some ferns, when I noticed these birds at some distance among the underbrush that surrounded me. I tried a device that had proved successful many times before—began whistling with a low, crooning sound, sitting perfectly quiet, and allowing the insects to attack me undisturbed; and soon the birds began to circle about me, coming closer and closer, until I had a satisfactory view of them. The red-eyed and the yellow-throated vireos were met with on the river, and the American red-start, black and white creeper, willow-warbler, tree and song sparrows, wood-pewee, grass-finch, and several kinds of wood-peckers.

The novice in camping is the recipient of much advice from experienced friends. Let me suggest that the would-be camper cultivate an interest in birds. If anything can make one forget the ravages of black flies and musquitoes, the sight of a flock of pintail grouse or rare warbler will have that effect, and there are few sights more charming than a ruff-grouse seen as you peer through the dusky hemlocks, standing erect and graceful, with her bright eyes fixed on you, ready to start at the first sign of danger.

The bird of the Nepigon, however, is the kingfisher. On the lake itself the loon, or the great herring-gull, takes its place; but at every turn, while on the river, we saw him perched on some limb overhanging the water, and launching himself into the air with his cheerful rattle as we passed. "O-gush-ke-muh-ne-see"—the Indian name for him is very appropriate—"cut up to the point," in allusions to his style of wearing his top-knot.

The mile portage that brings one to the shores of Lake Nepigon, along the western route—that taken by the Hudson Bay Company packers—is over great rocks, most of the way, covered with a mingled growth of blueberries, red raspberries, the running or swamp raspberry, *Spiranthes* or ladies-tresses, white pyrolas and the *Potentilla tridentata* or three-fingered cinque-foil, in great profusion, the leaves of the latter already turning scarlet, and making a beautiful contrast with the large patches of the gray reindeer moss.

There is not a great variety in the flora of the Nepigon. I found only forty-five varieties, but most of these grew in great abundance. At one portage the path was lined with a continuous growth of the *Clintonia borealis*, and the dwarf cornel still gleamed white in its bed of moss, though it was the middle of August. As for the twin-flower, the *Linnaea borealis*, how it must fill these woods with fragrance in its time of blooming! The delicate trailing vines completely covered the ground in some places, and here and there I could see the swinging pink and white bells making their presence known by the perfume that the wind brought to me.

I found the round-leaved white orchid, with the northern green orchid growing near by, and the ladies-tresses were very common.

On the shores of Lake Nepigon I saw the grass of Parnassus; the flowers were large, and—a new feature to me—beautifully veined with lilac.

The flower of the Nepigon that ranks first, as the kingfisher does among the birds, is the great willow-herb, the *Epilobium angusti-folium*. The portages are gay with its spikes of pink blossom; it grows to the very water's edge and trails down the swift current, and at sunset the rosy clouds seem reflected alike on land and water.

Growing on the overhanging rocks in secluded nooks above the rapids, I often found the graceful northern fern, the *Aspidium fra-grans*, and traced it by the delightful spicy perfume. It grew luxuri-antly, sending up many long, delicate fronds out of a tuft of the last year's chaffy growth. The common polypody, or rock-fern, generally accompanied it, while at the base of the rocks, in the damp, mossy earth, the Labrador-tea grew in thick clumps.

The next day was spent on Lake Nepigon, and in making a mile portage over a long peninsula. We were storm-bound for some time on an island by a sudden, violent thunder-storm, and it was sunset when we set out again for the mission, seven miles away. The storm-clouds were still in sight, heaped in great masses towards the west, and were aflame with the brilliant sunset colors; we passed many is-lands covered with a beautiful growth of evergreens, and as the night drew on island and shore were mingled together in the dusk, the stars came out with a brilliancy I had seldom seen equaled, and in the north the wavering lights flashed now and then from horizon to zenith. With these wild surroundings, it seemed quite appropriate that Joseph should sing an Ojibwa war-song as he paddled, begin-ning with a high, plaintive note, rising and falling with a wild, crooning sound, and sinking finally with a refrain of "A-hai-ya! A-hai-ya!" to a deep chest-note almost inaudible.

But the aurora and the war-song died away, the night grew cold, and we shivered in our heavy shawls and strained our ears for some sound from the mission. It was long after ten o'clock when we heard at last the far-off howls of the Indian dogs, and knew that we were nearing our journey's end. We climbed stiffly out of the canoe, and up the steep hill to the house, and I folded my Hudson Bay Company blanket about me and lay down to sleep heavily after our hard day's journey.

The mission consisted of a well-built, roomy log-house for the missionary and his family, a little chapel erected under direction by the Indians themselves, and a few small cabins. The next morning I wandered out to the chapel where a grave-yard, with its twenty graves, over-looked Lake Nepigon, its waters stretching farther than the eye could see. One grave was especially noticeable; it was that of a young Indian, who seemed to have been a great favorite, who died in the woods while cariboo-hunting. In chopping wood one day, the ax glanced and severed the artery of his leg. His companions tried in vain to stop the bleeding, taking turns in applying great pressure and even sewing up the wound, in the hope of staying the hemorrhage. For several days they thought to save him, but again and again the wound broke out anew, and in despair the poor fellow begged them not to try again, but to let him die. His body was brought in to the mission, forty miles distant from the camp, on a toboggan, and buried in this little grave-yard. At the foot, on a wooden board, was carefully pinned a large gray satin bow, much draggled and weather-stained, while the wooden cross at the head bore pieces of tissue-paper cut out in many devices, and some Christmas cards. On one of them, chosen evidently for the colors, and not the sentiment, was printed:

> "I send you this, with my best wishes, hoping that your coming
> year will be a happy one."

The five days we passed at the mission were very pleasant ones. The Indian Agent and a Government surveyor arrived next day, coming from Nepigon House, a Hudson Bay Company post fifty miles north of us, on the lake. We had forgotten to bring kerosene-oil with us from Red Rock, and I had only a piece of candle; we expected to find plenty of oil at the mission, but when we reached there, the last had just been used. The supply of matches had failed, and the man in charge had been burning a lamp day and night for five weeks to keep fire. We hoped that the Indian Agent would have lights with him. The sound of a gun off on the lake, after dark, told us that they were approaching, and our first question was: "Have you any candles?" The surveyor had one, and needed most of that for his evening observations, so after that, during our stay, we went to bed by daylight, and saved our two little candle-ends for the last evening, when the payment was to take place.

We were very busy while at the mission, the men with the survey, the guides being pressed into service, while our guide Joseph, a little Indian boy and I went trolling up a beautiful river about a mile away to get fish for our large family, an occupation rendered doubly necessary after the stealing of our bacon and ham by the Indian dogs about the houses.

The fourth night we had a dance given in our honor in the kitchen of the mission. The "Ogina," or Indian Agent, the missionary's wife and I sat in chairs at one end; on a long bench, and in rows on the floor, were the dancers, about twenty in number, while the Indian women, children and a few dogs were clustered in a little group in one corner on the floor. The three musicians sat in another corner with the tom-tom and the queer little sticks they beat it with. A table stood in the middle of the floor, and on it was a large frying-pan, tilted up a little, and containing half-cooked pork rinds, out of which trailed a bit of cotton cloth, lighted at one end. After we had taken our places, the dance began without further ceremony; the musicians beat upon the tom-tom with perfect time, singing a monotonous song which began high and ended in a deep growl, then started anew; and this was kept up as long as the dancers kept the floor.

We had the "Warrior's Dance," the "Triumphant Song," the "Mohawk's Dance," and the "Rabbit Dance," or "Wah-booso-she-mow-in." The figures were very simple. In one dance the performers stood in a long row, and bent the knees, dipping the body without moving the heels from the ground. They sang with the tom-tom players, keeping time to the music with the motion of their bodies. I advise those who think this dance easy to try it for a few minutes, being careful not to stir the heels from their position on the floor. In another dance they went about in rows, throwing their bodies into every imaginable position, till it seemed as if the joints would certainly be dislocated. In the "Warrior's Dance" they filed around the table, one close behind the other, bending the arms and throwing themselves from one foot to the other, singing at the same time, and occasionally going through the motion of snatching up a gun, aiming and firing, giving a wild war-whoop, catching an imaginary foe by the hair and making a horribly suggestive motion of the scalping-knife. Round and round they went, the tom-toms beating faster and faster, the men quickening their pace, the singing increasing in volume and shrillness as the women and children took up the song. The war-whoops rang out, the house fairly shook with the heavy thud of moccasined feet and the leaps of the dancers, and the pork-rind light smoked and flared, and added the smell of burning fat to the air that was already quite heavy enough with the fumes of a dozen pipes. It was very interesting at first, but after three hours we were quite willing to withdraw and let the dancers take possession of the cook-stove and make unlimited quantities of strong tea, which, with bread, was our contribution to the feast.

The next night the Indians received their annual payment of four dollars apiece for every man, woman and child, in one of the neat little Indian cabins. It was conducted with great seriousness. The Agent, two Counselors, our guide Joseph, who acted as interpreter, and I had chairs, while the others sat on the bench and on the floor. The room was prettily draped with two flags, and our last two precious bits of candle in bottles graced the table, lighted one after the other. There was much business to attend to—complaints to be heard, the payment made, advice given, etc.—and it was almost midnight when we stepped into our canoe to return to the house, while the Indians stood on the bank with lighted pieces of birch-bark to enable us to avoid the submerged rocks in the lake.

We were up and busy, preparing for our homeward journey, at five o'clock next morning, and by seven were on our way across the southern part of Lake Nepigon, bound for the head of the river, twenty miles away. We stopped for dinner on an island, and then hurried on. Aside from the anglers that visit these shores, few people in the States know of the existence of this beautiful lake. Yet, as far back as 1679, Daniel Greysolon du Luth explored the country around here, and founded a trading-post on the north-eastern corner of the lake to divert the trade of the Indians from the English that had already begun to traffic with them on the shores of Hudson Bay.

The guides were already waiting with the canoe, and with fly-rod in hand I climbed in, and we started for the base of the falls, or as near it as we dared go. It certainly was hardly the place for one's first attempt at fly-fishing, with the rapids surging about us, tossing the canoe in all directions, the foaming waves occasionally curling in, and the spray dashing over us. One wanted to hold on tight and shut one's eyes, not to calmly throw the fly in all that confusion. But the tales I had heard of big trout at that point sustained me. I grew accustomed to the turmoil, and the possibility of a five-pounder was wonderfully calming. He was not caught that morning, but a smaller fish did rise, and was received with the heart-felt gratitude that one only feels on catching one's first trout. He was a fighter, and the little experience I had had in taking black bass with light tackle and bait-rod was of great use. He did not break water like a bass after the first jump, but charged on the canoe, and down the rapids, ran to and fro, and jerked vigorously at the line. After a hard struggle he began to tire, and with aching arms and wrists I reeled him slowly in, with only a few short rushes on his part. But when he was near the canoe, the reel suddenly refused to work, the fish rose steadily towards us, the line was becoming slack, and in despair I sprang to my feet, though the tossing of the canoe in the rapids made it anything but an easy matter. Standing on tiptoe and stretching up my arm as far as I could, and bending the rod back as much as possible, the line was kept taut without an inch to spare; and as the fish was drawing nearer, Joseph, with a dextrous swoop of the net, landed him in the canoe. And after all that struggle he weighed only two and a half pounds. In a short time I had taken another, weighing three pounds, that did not fight half as hard as the first. There was a great difference between them. The first was a long, silvery fish, with light fins and tail, while the other had deep-red, white bordered fins, red flesh, and most brilliant colors and spots.

We staid only a day at Virgin Falls, and then left for Camp Victoria, a two-hours run down the river. It is beautifully situated on a rocky point of land, the rapids in front of it, a dense growth of evergreens behind. From its fine situation and good fishing, it is a favorite camping-place for anglers. The canoes are carried to the head of the great rapids, and the fishermen have a short walk through the woods from the camp to reach them. Here some of the largest fish in the river are caught, the canoes being held in position by the paddles of the guides, in the smaller rapids above, while the fisherman casts all about him. Almost every one had a chance for a big trout, but they frequently tear out in the strong rush of the current.

The morning we left I hooked *my* big fish, but was not equal to the occasion. He did not rise from underneath the fly, but jumped for it more than two feet while near the canoe, completely clearing the water and giving me a chance to see him distinctly—a six pounder, Joseph said, and these guides are good judges of the weight of fish. I saw his broad side and great red tail and fins, and it was too much for my equanimity. I "struck" too feebly. It needed more than the "slight turn of the wrist" to put the large hook through his mouth, and though the reel sang as he turned downward with the fly, I knew that I should lose him. He remained on perhaps two minutes, until he had become thoroughly alarmed, and then, with his first determined rush down the rapids, he tore away. I shall never forget the reproachful look that Joseph turned upon me as the fly floated free on the water. It was not a time for words. Indeed, I felt that I was under a cloud until I had run the Victoria Rapids, below those on the fishing-ground.

The guides were to take down the canoe that morning, to load it for the homeward trip, and soon after I lost my fish we started for the camp. They stopped at the head of the portage, for me to land, and I was about to step out of the canoe, when Joseph said: "You would not like to go down the rapids with us?" "Is it dangerous, Joseph?" I asked. He hesitated a moment, and then replied: "The gentlemen do not often run these rapids; sometimes they go down near the shore." Then, after a moment, "We will be very careful, if you feel that you would like to go down with us." I thought a moment, looked at the rapids running white below us; then, turning to the waiting guides, "I'll go down, Joseph." He gave a nod of approval, said a few words in Indian to the under-guide, and pushed off from shore to the middle of the stream. I settled myself in the bottom of the canoe, grasped the thwarts firmly, and wondered if I was very foolish. I had a curious sensation as the fierce current seized the canoe and I felt there was no going back. The canoe reared on

pitching our tent at the lower landing, where from the door we could see the rapids below us shining in the moonlight, which was so bright that we ate our late supper by the light. It had been a hard day, and soon after supper we were glad to roll ourselves up in our blankets, for our last night on the river. Nip, the Indian dog, barked loudly about the tent, and we feared some Indians might be prowling around but we slept soundly in spite of that and the cold high wind which shook the tent above our heads. Next morning we were up early, for we had a long journey before us—the "Long Portage" to make—and the wind, which was strong, was against us.

Running down the rapids and crossing Island Portage, we rowed laboriously over Lake Maria, the large waves and fierce wind making our progress very slow. When almost across, we saw the dark clouds gathering quickly behind us. We hesitated about going on, but as we talked about it the angry sky warned us that there was but one wise course to pursue. Hastily we rowed towards land, we reached shore just as the storm burst. We tumbled out of the canoe in all directions; fishing-tackle, tents, blankets, frying-pans and kettles were thrown here and there, and in two minutes we were under the canoe, all mixed up with our baggage, and helpless with laughter and excitement. The wind blew a gale, the water was lashed to foam, and the rain fell in torrents; but in ten minutes the worst was over, and before long the guides were building a fire, cooking the fish caught on the way down, and we ate a hurried dinner, trying to dry ourselves at the fire at the same time.

As the storm subsided the wind changed, and as we re-embarked we found that a favoring breeze increased the prospect that we might reach Red Rock that night. We had very little for supper and nothing for breakfast, and with our Nepigon appetites, it was important to get as quickly as possible to the Hudson Bay Company post, with its supplies.

We made the "Long Portage" that afternoon, and the guides worked hard; but the sun was low in the sky when we left the lower end for the final unbroken run of twelve miles down to Red Rock. Soon the scattered tents of the Indians camping by the river near Lake Helen came into sight, and as we passed quickly by, the guides exchanged greetings with the groups on the bank, receiving from all the assurance that they were wanted badly at the post—that two clergymen had been waiting impatiently several days for them.

The rosy clouds were reflected in the river, the pine-trees stood in dark relief against the sky, the white-fish were leaping on every side, and the voices of the Indian women sounded plaintively across the water as they called to one-another, and as we turned into Lake Helen, across the water came the klingle-klangle of the cow-bells at the mission. We were nearing home, it is true, but it was hard to say good-by to our wild life, our beds of hemlock-boughs and the fragrant, spicy air. It was dark when we landed at the foot of the lake, and left the missionary's wife and her little boy at their Summer home, and then the guides and I started for the mile run down the rapids to the post. The moon shone bright and cold on the high cliffs as we were carried swiftly down the dark braided current of the river, and in a few minutes we had landed. I had climbed the hill, given one lingering look at the shining river and dark forest beyond, and knocked on the door of the Hudson Bay Company agent.

Published in *Frank Leslie's Popular Monthly*, September, 1889, 309–316.

Up the Mackenzie River to the Polar Sea

A Lady's Journey in Arctic America

The last day of May in '92 a small steamboat left a post of the Hudson Bay Fur Company on the far Athabasca. Her route lay northward, and her mission was to carry for the first stage of the journey the precious mail and supplies sent once a year to the Fur posts of the Far North. From Montreal, 2,300 miles south-east, most of the bales and boxes had been forwarded. But a long journey still lay before them. On one steamboat after another, by open boats rowed by Indians, they would go down the Athabasca and Slave rivers (for these rivers flow northward, unreasonable as it may seem), across the Athabasca and the Great Slave Lakes, and down the mighty flood of the Mackenzie to its delta at the Polar Sea, a journey from this point of forty-five days' duration and 2,300 miles in length. Truly this is a land of magnificent distances and difficulties.

I had been so fortunate as to obtain permission of the Governor of the Company to "go in" with the expedition. After a journey from Paris of twenty days, I reached "The Landing" on the Athabasca, and was much relieved to find I was to have some travelling companions; the wise and good Bishop of the Mackenzie returning to his distant mission after a visit to England, and two young men from the east, who were to start missions for the Great Slave Lake Indians and the Delta Eskimos. These three clergymen, myself, a score or so of Indians, our respective camp equipments, the mail and freight made up "the outfit" of our little steamboat.

When at last we left the post not a sign of human life did we see for the next ten days. The hills rose in bold headlands, clothed from the water's edge to their summits in virgin forests of spruce and pine. The air was cold and sweet with the bursting leaf buds of the balsam poplar. Occasionally a beaver would be seen swimming across a bay or a heron flapping slowly from a point of land. And once a sudden turn in the river revealed two black bears shambling hastily away among the trees.

At last one evening we heard a hoarse roar in the distance, and knew that we were nearing the Grand Rapids, and that the first stage of our journey was over. For here the steamboat was to unload us all, bag and baggage, and hurry back to the post, and with seven "sturgeon head boats" and fifty Indians we were to run the rapids eighty-six miles to where the second boat was awaiting us.

All this unloading and reloading was a matter of time. For one week we camped on an island in the rapids, and meantime the missionaries and I learnt how to make camp bread, clean knives in the sand, wash dishes with moss, and build up fragrant elastic beds with twigs of hemlock and of spruce. Our Indians were a rough wild set of men, and I felt a little troubled in having my tent pitched so near them, but the Bishop assured me that I was as safe as at home, for a twofold reason: I was in the Company's charge, and the Indians could get no liquor. "If they were white men I would not advise it," he added. One can trust the advice of a Bishop of twenty-five years' experience with Indians, and after that I had no fears, even though later, at the Rapids of the Drowned, 2,500 Indians were in the neighbourhood.

Before this presence of the steamboat had been a reminder of civilisation. But when she left us in the wilderness then I felt indeed like an old-time voyageur. The pieces, as the bales and boxes are called, are stowed in the bottom of the boat, eight tons' weight to each boat; the Indians take their places, the steersman by the long sweep in the stern, and away we go down the rapids. The most skilful guide leads the way, the other boats follow in line, imitating exactly every turn and twist and plunge of their leader. On his courage and skill depends the fate of all. When he begins to falter and doubt himself he will be relegated to a rear place, much as the engine driver of a flying express, when he loses his "nerve," is changed to a goods or omnibus train.

For these rapids of the Athabasca are "strong rapids," and should a boat be swamped the crew has small chance of escaping from the boiling whirlpools and jagged rocks. In order to have a boat under control its speed must exceed that of the current. It is an exciting moment when the "white water" is neared. All are alert, and at a signal each man throws his whole weight on his great oar, rising to his feet, and giving a wild shout with each stroke. And with spray dashing, and the great boats plunging and tossing, we charge into the foaming water. It is so exciting and so beautiful that one forgets to be afraid, and then "Arrête!" "Chuskwa!" comes the signal from the steersman, the oars are shipped as we glide into smoother water, and the men, lying at full length on the bales, smoke peacefully while the swift current bears us down the stream. But the steersman keeps his place always at the sweep, and as the next bad place is neared, rouses with his warning note the resting men.

On the old days the voyageur crews were up and on the river by 3 a.m. On the Athabasca at five o'clock a ringing sonorous call would rouse our sleeping camp, "Ho, lève! lève! lève!" and then would come the sleepy stirring of the men, and the fragrance of poplar and birch as the camp fires were lighted. We were on our way before seven, put ashore for dinner at twelve, again at four (the Indian loves his tea next to his tobacco), and about eight to make camp for the night. When one has once felt the charm of this wild life (many never do), all other pleasures seem to cheapen in comparison. It is unreasonable, I confess. One is scorched by the hot sun, drenched in storms, bitten by mosquitoes, gnats and deer flies, lives on bacon and camp bread, sleeps on the ground, and is perfectly happy withal.

One afternoon we killed our first "moose" or elk. As we were floating down a quiet stretch of rapids, I heard a low, excited exclamation from the Indian: "Moose—wah!" and looking ahead saw a great ungainly creature walking in the shallows and watching anxiously the woods on shore. A moose's ears are quicker than his eyes. The hills had echoed the sound of our oars, making him think that the danger lay landward. Suddenly he turned and plunging into the current, struck out for the opposite shore. Our boat was ahead, but we had no guns on board. We must reach the shore first and turn him back. It was a close chase. Our Indians strained every nerve, but the moose was only a few yards from land when the boat reached the shallows. "Vite! vite!" cried the steersman, "Kwa-sko-tik!" (Jump!) shouted the Indians up the stream, and jumping into the water, our men floundered to shore, reaching it just before the moose, and with a despairing look the poor animal turned back towards midstream. By that time the others had come up, and five guns opened fire. There must have been some bad cases of "buck ague" among those hunters, or the erratic rowing of the excited crews may have been to blame. For certainly forty or fifty shots were fired, each futile shot calling out howls of execration from the Indians. At last one bullet took effect—the great head fell forward on the water, a few convulsive struggles, and the carcass floated quietly down stream. In two minutes we reached the moose, tied it to the stern, and with one accord all the boats turned to shore. Fires were lighted, the moose skinned and cut up, and an hour later we were dining on broiled moose steaks.

The next day we reached Fort MacMurray, changed to another steamer, and a week later arrived at a point midway down the Slave river, where thirty-two miles of dangerous rapids barred all navigation. We had crossed Lake Athabasca on our way. A lake 250 miles in length, and most beautiful in a sad northern fashion, with its rugged shores of red and grey granite, its many spruce-covered islands, and little bays with shining pink sands. At Slave River portage, everything had to be transferred in rough carts across country to a point below the rapids where the third and last steamboat was to meet us. We had brought a dozen oxen with us from Fort MacMurray, where there is some good grassland, and for twelve days and nights these poor beasts struggled with their loads through the mudholes and over the rocks that form the "portage." Meantime the Bishop, missionaries, and I crossed and made camp above the Rapids of the Drowned. From this point the *Wrigley*, a tiny steamer, but staunchly built to weather the storms of Great Slave Lake and the Mackenzie, would carry us down to the Delta, 1,200 miles farther north.

At last came the day when everything was on board. The *Wrigley* had no cabin, and for a dining-room only a mere box of a place, with no window. Six people when seated, quite filled the room. Here one missionary slept at night on top of the table and one below it. My little room was simply furnished with a sack of hay, as was the case on the preceding boats. Every yard of the deck was piled high with bales and boxes, and the Indians slept wherever they could find a sheltered nook. They seemed to need little sleep, however; they preferred to gamble, to sing, and to play the tom-tom at all hours of the night.

Heavily laden as we were, it seemed a fool-hardy thing to cross the Great Slave Lake in this little craft. The lake is 300 miles in length, has an area of 10,400 square miles, and can show storm waves that would do credit to the ocean. Its southern shores are rather low, but on the north they rise in sombre imposing cliffs of perpendicular rock, crowned by stunted firs and aspens, and here the water is deep, clear, and has a wonderful blue-green color.

It was the sixth of July when we left the shelter of the Slave River and started across the lake. But all around us were great ice-fields that threatened with a rising wind to "nip" the little *Wrigley*. The thermometer stood above freezing point, on the bleak shores the alders and willows were just bursting into leaf, and here and there a patch of green showed in the sheltered places. That day for the first time I saw "sun dogs" in July; those false suns not uncommon on bitterly cold winter mornings in Manitoba and Ontario.

All that night we steamed cautiously northward over the lake. I sat wrapped in blankets on the cargo, watching the strange and beautiful effects of violet mists above the ice-fields, for we had reached a land which has at least a two-months day. Towards morning I turned in to my bunk, and when I awoke we had left the lake behind us, and were safe in the great Mackenzie, which is at that point three or four miles in width.

Great Slave Lake was discovered by Samuel Hearne in 1771. In 1789 Alexander Mackenzie crossed the lake, discovered the Mackenzie, and followed it to the sea. Sir John Franklin and Sir John Richardson took the same course in their famous land expedition. Life in the far north has changed little since Franklin saw the isolated fur posts of the Mackenzie Basin. The fur traders and a few missionaries are the only white people. The "Forts," as they are called, lie about three hundred miles apart, and between them there is not a house to be seen. Two mails a year are sent in by the Company (one going with dogs and sledges over the winter's snow). A "Fort" may mean three cabins, or a large group of roomy log houses and a mission. The advent of the *Wrigley* is the great event of the year. Even if he is starving, no Indian will leave the river to hunt when the time draws near for its arrival. As we drop anchor before a post we see them standing in close ranks on the steep shores, silent and apparently indifferent, while their bands of dogs howl dismally in chorus. Life is hard in the far north and food scarcer every year. This one small boat can bring in only limited supplies, and the Company's people must rely in great measure on the resources of the country—fish, reindeer, and moose meat, and the wild fowl shot on their annual migrations. If these fail, many Indians will starve and the white people suffer great privations.

For magnificent scenery the far north must yield the palm to the Selkirk range of British Columbia, or the Rockies of Alberta. But this majestic river, sweeping always to the north, the lakes of Athabasca, Great Slave, and Great Bear, the Arctic Rockies, the midnight sun, the wonderful atmospheric effects, all combine to make the journey one of peculiar interest. That it is one of much exposure and some hardships can be readily imagined.

For several degrees of latitude the Mackenzie passes between

The steamship Wrigley *(photographed circa 1881) was one of the vessels on which Elizabeth Taylor went down the Mackenzie River to its delta in 1892.*

ranges of the Rocky Mountains, or the "Rockies," as they are familiarly called. They first come in sight near Fort Providence, in the Horn Mountains, 3,000 feet above the river's level, then are lost to sight again in latitude 62° 15'. Here are the Nahánés, and most beautiful they are seen at midnight with the sunset glow on their bleak summits, their valleys filled with purple clouds. There are no glaciers in the Rockies north of latitude 54°. The intense cold and the dry air prevent a large snow fall, and the sunny summer nights rapidly melt the winter's snow. The peaks were almost bare when I passed in July. Occasionally a detached mass of rock rises sheer from the water's edge, as *La Roche Carcajou*, 1,000 feet, *La Roche qui Trempe à l'Eau*, 1,500 feet, and *Bear Rock*, 1,400 feet, at the junction of Great Bear Lake with the Mackenzie. Near the Arctic Circle are the Ramparts where the Mackenzie narrows to a width of only 500 yards, and whirls with great velocity between vertical cliffs, about 200 feet high, of creamy white limestone. In some places the cliffs seem to bend over the water, and are worn into strange shapes, like castle turrets and stately columns.

Once released from the Ramparts the river widens rapidly, and as we cross the Arctic Circle the banks are low and covered with stunted firs, and the mountain range has trended out of sight to the westward, to be seen no more until we reach the Delta, where it sinks to the Polar Sea.

The wind blew keenly from the Arctic ice floes, bringing with it a smell of the sea. For a distance of twelve miles we made our way among the islands of the Delta (the Mackenzie at this point is eight miles wide) and entered a river on the west. Peel's River Fort, the most northern post in British America, is situated eighteen miles up this river, and here the Eskimos gather once a year from their homes on the Bay, to meet the *Wrigley* and do their annual trading. There was great excitement on the shore. As we came into sight the Eskimos in their *kayacks*, the hunting canoes, and *omiacks*, or family boats, put off to meet us, and soon the little *Wrigley* was swarming with them. The Delta natives, though of pure blood, differ much from other Eskimos. They are of large size and stature and fierce and warlike by nature. Every woman I saw was taller than myself, and three chiefs were fully six feet tall in their sealskin shoes. They all wore beautiful dresses of reindeer and seal skins. Everything was of pure native workmanship, the only signs of civilisation being a few beads on their tobacco pouches and in the walrus ivory fishhooks.

Two days we spent at Peel's River post. No one thought of going to bed. Trading and letter writing, Eskimo dances given in our honour, the loading of furs, kept everyone busy, and I wished to collect plants and sketch. Few of the Eskimos had ever seen a white woman, and they evidently found me very strange and amusing. But they all treated me with the greatest courtesy, urging me to come into their skin tents, and presenting me with arrows and fishhooks of walrus ivory (of course expecting gifts in return). I would gladly have seen them in their homes on the Bay, but the Delta channels have never been fully explored, and the *Wrigley* never ventures quite to the open sea. Two nights later, we were on our southern way, and this time we made only brief stays at the posts to gather in the furs. Once only we deviated from our incoming route, and that was to visit Fort Rae on the northern coast of Great Slave Lake. So, with changes from boat to portage and to boat again we came slowly southward. But this time there was no exciting race down the Athabasca rapids.

In July of 1892 Elizabeth Taylor photographed these Eskimos gathered at Peel's River to greet the arrival of the steamship Wrigley.

57

We "tracked" up instead, with eight Indians in harness for each boat. The men made twelve miles a day, toiling painfully along the shore, over rocks and often waist-high in water, while I sat curled up comfortably on the bales of furs. We were eight days on the Athabasca tracking in this fashion.

From the landing I took horses for Edmonton, on the North Saskatchewan River, one hundred miles to the south, and from that point, four and a half days' journey to the main and branch lines of the Canadian Pacific Railway brought me to Montreal.

Published in *Travel*, April 1899, 559–564.

Articles Found Useful
on my Mackenzie River Trip

In camp. My pieces of mackintosh have been in almost constant use. In pleasant weather, I would spread one down in front on my tent in the daytime to keep the dust and leaves from flying in, and to keep my dress from any dust or grass there might be there, or to make a shelter from sun or wind, tied to the tent and to a stick driven in the ground. In road travel, I used them to keep off dust and rain. On ship board the first night they were invaluable to catch leaking water on the upper berth; on deck I used them to sit on either in wet weather or where the cinders fell and made the deck dirty, and to cover luggage, unprotected on the deck.

My camp dress [leaf brown checked skirt, mantle with detachable hood, blouse, full knickerbockers, gaiters and cuffs] has been just the thing, light comfortable, and has passed through great circumstances, and still looks respectable. I really must be covered with spots and grease, but the skirt at first glance looks clean, and the blouse has only a general tolerable shabbiness. My hat is still good as regards form and color, this English felt though expensive, paid. The dirt seems to take a general tone, and the color is almost unchanged. The silk handkerchief is all faded and looked badly in a few days of hard wear. Something else should be devised, brown preferably.

As to gloves, my stout Paris dog skin ones though good, rather pretty, and serviceable, are not thick enough for mosquitoes. Not all bite through, but enough to make one uncomfortable. But I cannot think of anything that would be better, unless it is the very heavy moose skin gloves that one sees in this country. I presume these are to be found in towns, or something resembling them. In coming another time, I should like these same Paris gloves, and a thicker pair for walks in places where the mosquitoes are very bad.

My large head net has not been a complete success. It is too large, slips about in all directions, and flaps too much. In quality and color,

I think it is about as good as anything I have seen, certainly much better than those used by the men and bought at the company's stores.

I should take knives in going this way again. They are always acceptable, even if one has one already. They are useful to cut up tobacco with the Indians. Silk handkerchiefs I should take, too, larger ones than most that I brought.

As to shoes, my light horseskin shoes bought in London have been so comfortable that I have worn them all the time. My heavy horseskin shoes have been worn only once. To be sure, for muskeg tramps and such expeditions, the former shoes are too light, but by supplementing them with overshoes, I have done very well. Moccasins are good for a change, and I fancy will be comfortable in the sturgeon-head boats, but the decks are dirty here, and the men spit everywhere, and I cannot bear to wear them on board.

Black cashmere stockings, comfortable on all occasions.

Should have taken a great supply of blotting paper, old newspapers, stiff supporters for the plants, to put in between the leaves.

"My large head net has not been a complete success.
It is too large, slips about in all directions, and flaps too much."
Sketched by Elizabeth Taylor on her Mackenzie River trip in 1892.

More and harder lead pencils, perhaps charcoal, plenty of fixitif, plenty of small shot, some large fine pointed needles like darning needles for arranging the plumage of small birds.

Sketch books successful and convenient, though I often miss putting down things that would have gone into a smaller hand book.

Food: It depends on what kind of a trip one is going to take. In almost any case, bacon. We had the Star Bacon, of Armour (I think), put up in canvas bags, very good, flour of course. We liked the Hudson's Bay tea put up in half pound and pound packages, lump sugar, pepper and salt, perhaps mustard. A bottle of sauce, if possible, a few tins of brawn, not corned beef, some biscuits of some kind, soda are good, hard tack also, but very hard. Tinned goods, first tomatoes, and of fruits—peaches, and pears. Corn is good, but not so refreshing as tomatoes, which can be eaten hot or cold, raw or cooked. Once I mixed them with the brawn, and with biscuit, and eked out a meal. Marmalade to be taken, first orange, but anything tasted good, damson plums, jams, anything sweet one craves. Chocolate in $\frac{1}{2}$ lb. packages very nice, to eat a little as dessert when one has nothing else, and to eat with biscuits when the meals are delayed, or in the night.

Another time I should take as many prunes as possible, good raw or cooked, very refreshing. I gave half of mine away. Wish I could have had ten times the quantity. Cocoa, Van Houten's, convenient, for use and for little gifts on the way, when one does not want to take tea just before turning in, the cocoa is very nice. Condensed coffee good and convenient and condensed milk is liked very much. Wish we had more. The canned oysters tasted good, once, and the Chollets vegetables I should take again, and the potted turkey. I liked the Strasbourg meats, but not more so than the other less expensive kinds. Johnson's fluid beef to be taken. The Canadian cheese in glass jars was good, but did not keep well, turned blue too soon.

About beds. I think I would hardly take a rubber bed again unless I was in a place where I must have my luggage in the smallest possible compass. One is always liable to accident from pin or needle prick. So far I have failed to stop the leak. Then the exertion, not great in itself, but quite a task when one is tired at night. Then I must say the bed does feel a little squirmy. On such a place as the Nipigon, I should trust to the hemlock boughs, nothing is pleasanter and more comfortable when carefully arranged. Only I should take a extra pillow slip or so of good size, to be filled with grass or ferns, or hay while travelling.

Medicines: quinine, pain killer, powders, vaseline, cramp medicine, chlorate of potash, brandy and whiskey, something for colds, almond oil, carbolic soap, camphor, alcohol for lamps, syringe, oiled silk, flannel, ammonia or aromated spirits of ammonia, cholera medicine, rhubarb, mild liver pills.

Other supplies: frying pan, copper kettle, stew pan, wash hand pan, tin quart cup for water, 2 granite ware plates (one dinner plate, one soup plate), granite or hard white wear cup and saucer, knife, fork, and spoon, cooking fork and large spoon, 2 dishcloths, bag for carrying these things, alcohol lamp, salt cellar and pepper; glass, wide mouthed bottle for holding fruit or vegetables taken from the can, something for meat, tight, for protection against flies.

Elizabeth Taylor Papers, Minnesota Historical Society.

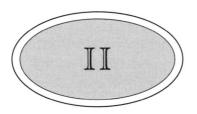

Europe for the First Time
1890

In the late spring of 1890 Elizabeth Taylor made her first trip to Europe. She landed in England, visited cathedrals and other London sights, and the Isle of Wight, before crossing by ship to Bergen, Norway. There, she also toured alone before meeting a group in Stavanger. This group of "Hoosiers," as she called them, were on a Summer Outing led by Dr. David Starr Jordan. Then President of Indiana University, Jordan arranged trips that aimed to see "the real life of the people," as he wrote in his autobiography The Days of a Man, *(1921). Jordan's tour groups stayed in third-class hotels and often walked rather than paying for carriages. They walked down to Italy from the Swiss Alps, for example, and usually this was "merely tedious," not dangerous as it was when Elizabeth Taylor and the Hoosiers crossed the St. Théodule Pass that July. Miss Taylor's account, never published, is found in letters to friends; in this case, from a letter written to Helen Carver.*

My Alpine Tramp

At six o'clock the next morning we left Jomein for our tramp over the [St. Théodule] pass. The sky was threatening, but we were tired of waiting, and decided not to delay for better weather. We walked quickly the four mile stretch up to the snow level. The clouds swept down from the great expanse of the glacier above us, as we climbed the steep grassy knolls, and shut out from our sight the valley below; only once in a while they would part, and we would have glimpses of such lovely views—a stretch of green valley—a group of chalets or a choir of cows browsing down in some sheltered nook, the tinkle of their bells and the calling of the little herdsmen coming up faintly to our ears, then the mists would drift across, and we would toil on again.

The snow began to fall when we were a mile away from the glacier, but we thought it would be only an ordinary storm, and did not think of turning back. We had walked only a little way, however, over the glacier when a blizzard struck us, and such a blizzard! You remember that one in New York, in '88, when we had such a struggle to get to school, only three blocks away? Well this was as bad or worse than that one, and there we were at almost 11,000 feet above the sea, and two miles still from the little refuge hut on the summit. The snow was heavy on the trail and we sank down at every step. The fierce gusts took away my breath. I was blinded by the sharp cutting sleet, and my lungs felt like a squeezed sponge so I had to fight for every breath. We could see only a few feet from us, and the others were soon lost to view, and the guide and I seemed alone in the world. I fell many times from sheer exhaustion, and would lie there in the snow until I could get my breath again, and I could hear the kind old guide, Césare Carrel, murmuring "Ah, bien fatigué. Bien fatigué!" He would have tried to carry me, but I wasn't going to be carried on my first real Alpine tramp as long as I could help it.

It really was a dreadful struggle and I know now how those people feel who die in the blizzards out West. After the first pain is over, it seems the most delightful thing in the world just to curl up in a drift and sleep, even if death will be the end of it. But just at the moment when I had done all I could, we heard a shout from the gray cloud in front of us and knew that we had reached the refuge hut! I couldn't see anything then, but Carrel helped me up to it, and I felt the boards of the floor under my feet and then I collapsed in a little heap and in ten minutes had been rubbed and "brought to" and stowed away in a big bed with five other unfortunate damsels. When I opened my eyes it was to see a queer little room, filled with our panting, breathless party. There was a stove, a rough table with benches around it, and this big bed, low ceiling, rough board walls and that was all. Just opposite was another stone cabin, where the kitchen was, and where the guides, and the man in charge, slept.

Well, we stayed there two days. I hope I'm properly thankful for the "experience" but I don't care to think about those two days very much. You see there were fifteen of us, not counting our guides and porters, and everything was wet and muddy, and the floors were cold. The little low room was stifling and close, so we had to open the door every few minutes for fresh air, and let in a cloud of steam and snow. We hadn't enough benches for all, so some of us were packed like sardines on the bed and ate our dinner there.

About four o'clock the first day, happening to look out of our little window, we saw five strange looking figures coming up the slope to our hut, tied together with ropes, the last one on his hands and knees. They stumbled into the room and leaned up against the wall and feebly panted, "Be Jove, ye know!" They were covered with snow from head to foot, icicles hanging from hats and whiskers, and their faces swollen and with the skin off. They were three Englishmen and their guides; they had come from the Riffelberg and had been eight hours in the storm.

So that made eighteen of us in that little place. There was the room where we all stayed, and on each side two tiny rooms just big enough for two beds, but these opened out only to the storm and had no communication with the central room. Towards night the head of our party [Dr. Jordan] went to see our sleeping quarters, and came back to report cheerfully that "they'd be all right," as the snow was being shovelled out from under the beds. When bedtime came we were bundled up and the guides carried us all to our rooms—men and all. The men went "pick-a-back," but us girls were carried like a sack of flour. One heavy girl was blown over with the guide into a big drift, but on the whole it was great fun.

I must say we thought we had had about enough of it by the evening of the second day. It is no easy matter to keep quite serene and good tempered with so many people crowded in together and such noise and confusion. We could see nothing but a wild whirl of snow until the third day, the provisions were running short, and during the last night the storm was worse than ever. We were wakened often by the dull thud on the stone walls of the hut as the fierce gusts struck them. But towards morning, a welcome calm came, and at six o'clock when we scraped the hoar frost from the window and looked out, the clouds were gone, the sun shining and the great range of mountains that we had never seen showed sharp and clear all about us.

Then there was such a bustle! People flying about tying on masks made of handkerchiefs, pinning up skirts, and preparing an impromptu Alpine outfit. For you see we were to have a tramp of 12 miles over the second glacier down to Zermatt and none of us had made proper preparations, not expecting a great storm. I liked the appearance of the Professor of the Dead Languages as well as any. He wore a mask made of a towel, with holes cut in it for his mouth, nose and eyes, an old felt hat tied over his ears, and above all a big blue veil with rampant ends; a pair of old woolen socks, bought of the cook, flapped on his hands, and his trousers were tied down with white rags. The guides always have gray veils and wear green goggles in crossing the pass, for the glare of the summer sun on the snow is very trying to the eyes and brings on inflammation and snow blindness if they are not properly protected.

By eight o'clock we were being roped together in batches of five and six, with a porter or guide at each end. The first day it was not necessary, but the second glacier has many crevasses which change often, and it is not safe to cross without this precaution. When we used to read about the Swiss glaciers, we did not quite understand about this roping process. It seems that the tourists and their guides stand in Indian file, while a guide ties them together with a long, strong rope, with about twelve feet between them. They keep this distance from one another in walking, so that the rope is kept almost taut. Then if anyone falls into a crevass, which may have been bridged over and hidden by the newly fallen snow, he is kept from going far by the weight of the others, who brace themselves, still in line and hold him up till he can scramble out on a firm footing.

There was a great depth of snow on the trail, but the Englishmen, who were experienced mountain climbers, went first, and "made the steps," and we followed, and I found that a stalwart six footer does not make steps that are suited to a small person. The stronger members of our party were at the head of our division, and those who had given out the first day, brought up the rear to have the advantage of the broken trail. I'll confess that I was next to the last in the procession, but that had its advantages too, for Carrel, my guide of the first day, was tied just behind me, and was a great help. Whenever I would slip into a hole or break through the old crust which lay beneath the new snow, I'd feel a steady pull behind me, and would be pulled up like a codfish on a line, and set on my feet again. The little crevasses were filled with the tightly packed snow, and we crossed the glacier without trouble.

It was a wonderful tramp. The air was like crystal, the sky overhead seemed an indigo color, every peak and crag sharp and distinct, and wonderful shadows on the snow. Not a sign of life but the wavering trail over the glacier. We might have come to Switzerland a hundred times and yet have failed to see the sight we saw that morning. The Jungfrau showed seventy miles away, and all around us was ranged that magnificent circle of the "High Alps," the Gorner Grat, the Breithorn, the Dent Blanche, Monte Rosa, the Little Cervin, and the far off mountains of the Bernese Oberland.

And above all towered the great Matterhorn, rearing its great curved peak 8,000 feet about the glaciers at the foot. It made me shudder to look up at the stupendous mass of rock, too steep from snow to rise on it, and think that people dared to venture there. The head of our party had made the ascent of the Matterhorn some years before, and we knew its dangers. From the summit, and from others of the High Alps, frothing white streamers stretching off to the south showed that the gale was still blowing up there and carrying the loose snow with it. Before us, sweeping over the mountain side lay the great glacier in ripples and curves, and below that a stretch of shifting mists, soft blues and violets and changing purples, rosy vapors and lines of dove color: as we looked they waved and rose and fell and took on a hundred lovely shapes. What did it mean? Why were the mists there? And then they told me that I was looking down on the valley of Zermatt where the storm was still raging, and that far below us, shut out from our sight by the clouds, lay the little village of Zermatt where we were going. And to think that we were there in that glorious sunlight, and that the storm clouds that seemed so dark and gloomy to the poor people in the village were things of wonderful beauty seen from above, by the light of the sun. It seemed to me there was a good sermon in that.

But we could not stay long even with such a sight before our eyes. The snow was melting fast, and the walking grew more difficult every minute. After we had crossed the glacier the snow turned to slush and then to little streams and waterfalls rushing down the steep trail. We found that the drifts extended far down into the valley; the wheat stacks were covered with snow and the pale pink Alpine lilies were bending under the weight of it, and when we passed under the fir trees the boughs shook down upon us the frothing masses. At one point we made miniature avalanches of ourselves. We left the trail for the steep grassy hillside and at every step the snow slipping over the smooth turf, carried us down as if we had on seven league boots. Some of us lost our balance and tumbled and rolled down the hillside but we couldn't get hurt in the soft snow. We made a strange looking procession as we tramped into Zermatt, wet and covered with mud, in our queer, impromptu Alpine outfit. We were mountaineers from the "High Alps," and our proper feeling of pride reconciled us to our appearance as we marched by the dainty young lady tourists we met, picking their way gingerly over the muddy places.

I had always wondered why small boys enjoyed walking through mud puddles, and now was my chance to find out. I could never wear my shoes again, all cut as they were by the glacier ice, so I splashed right through the biggest and deepest of the puddles, to the horror of some old ladies, and, do you know, Helen, it's great fun. There is a pleasing squishiness about a big puddle, and a little excitement in seeing how deep one is going to go.

We wondered a little at the interest shown in us. People looked after us as we passed, and whispered, "Those are the people!" and when Carrel and I marched up to the piazza of the great Hotel Zermatthof, filled with tourists, bows and smiles were bestowed on us in a congratulatory way which puzzled me until I found out that those at the hotel had been much troubled about us. It was known that we had started from Jomein two days before and there had been the worst storm known in the Alps in twenty-one years.

So that was the end of my one long Alpine tramp. To be sure we had several delightful walks in the Bernese Oberland, a fortnight before, but only near the Matterhorn had we found the real spirit of the Alps, as we had always imagined it. In spite of our precautions, we had three cases of snow-blindness in our party, and several painful swollen faces and lame knees and ankles. So it was rather a battered, depressed set of tourists that filed into the station at St. Nicholas the next day, to take the train for Geneva. "What have those people been about?" I heard a fashionable lady traveller say to her husband. "Oh, they tried to cross a pass near the Matterhorn, and were caught in that storm," he answered. "Dear me, why will people be so foolish!" she explained impatiently. But we, remembering the glorious sight after the storm, smiled quietly to ourselves, and thought we had had the best of it.

Elizabeth Taylor Papers, Minnesota Historical Society.

Norway
1893

Elizabeth Taylor first visited Norway in 1890 before her summer outing with an Indiana University tour group led by Dr. David Starr Jordan. She published nothing about that first trip, but wrote to friends about a wild ride near Stalheim when the cariole in which she rode tipped over and she, her belongings, horse, and postboy all fell out.

In the summer of 1893 she did return, making back-to-back treks through the Hardanger Vidda and Saeterdal valley. Her paean to a northern berry relates to both her Norwegian and Canadian travels. One treasured purchase probably made on her second Norwegian trip was a Hardanger rug which she kept for the rest of her life and which is now in the collections of the Minnesota Historical Society.

Over Hardanger Vidda

THE UPLAND SUMMER PASTURES OF NORWAY

I had planned, for more reasons than one, to cross the Vidda, the great upland summer pastures of Norway, through the pass of Voringfos; but one was a good one: for close by the great waterfall of Voringfos stood Ole Garen's little hotel, where one could, until the fates were propitious, stay in comfort, and make excursions, and botanize, and sketch, and catch mountain trout. It is not at all times one can cross the Vidda.

When I made this resolve, I was still in Ullensvang, which is, perhaps, the most charming spot in Southwestern Norway. Orchards of plums, cherries, and apples grow on the fertile hillsides, protected by the mountains from the chilling sea breezes, and on the slopes are the grass meadows bright with bluebells, yellow vetches, pink catchfly and spotted orchids.

The houses of the peasants are roofed with sod, and in that balmy, moist air a lovely growth of flowers soon springs up. Botanizing on the house tops was one of my diversions. One roof was covered with lightly tossing golden and white daisies; another was a charming mosaic of color made by sheep sorrel, bluebells, little ferns, and forget-me-nots, while many were purple from hundreds of tri-colored heart's-ease.

These little pansies, the "Johnnie-jump-ups" of our old-fashioned gardens; the "Stedmor-blomster," or "stepmother flower" of the Norwegians, grew luxuriantly along the country roads and in the meadows. Often, when seated on some grassy slope above the Fjord, I would see long, purple bands of these pansies looking like sky reflecting brooks, which appeared to flow over the crest of the hill and mingle with the steel-blue waters below.

The crop of these steep hillsides is not large enough to feed the cattle all the year, and in the spring the farmers wait impatiently for the time when the cows can be sent to their Vidda pasturage. One large patch of snow on a mountain across the Fjord at Ullensvang serves as a guide; when it has dwindled to a certain size, they know that on the Vidda the grasses are long enough, and the cattle may leave the valley. The past winter has been severe, and the snows lingered late.

At length, one afternoon, I saw several large barges crossing the Fjord, towed by smaller boats, in which a number of young girls were rowing. The cows were on their way to the Vidda at last, and surely it was time, for already the crimson foxgloves, those true midsummer flowers, were opening their heavy racemes. The barges stopped a short distance from land, and I wondered how the cows were to get to the shore; but they evidently knew what was expected of them; one by one they plunged boldly over the boat's edge into the water and waded to the land. Once on the bank, they went off at a brisk trot, and the group disappeared up the road, tossing horns, tails and red bodices, half-hidden in a whirl of dust.

On her first visit to Norway in 1890 Elizabeth Taylor wrote to friends about a wild ride near Stalheim when the cariole, shown here, tipped over.

But I was not to follow yet. For a week thereafter storm-clouds swept over from the Vidda, shutting us in from the outside world.

We could hear the uproar of the little brooks, swollen to thrice their usual size, while the mighty Voringfos Falls fairly thundered in its leap to the valley, five hundred feet below, making the windows shiver and the house tremble—sometimes a sudden current of air would part the clouds, and we could snatch a fleeting glimpse down the rocky gorge, and see the foaming river, and the precipitous cliffs, seamed with scores of the tiny streams, which appear only in times of storm.

Our inn, Fosslé, was almost deserted. Now and then a hardy Norseman, bound on a fishing trip, would take refuge with us, or an English tourist climb up from the valley to see the great waterfall through the clouds of mist and spray which filled the chasm. But we fared well in our imprisonment. Reindeer steaks and mountain trout we had daily, and on the walls of the wide entry hung beautiful robes, gloves, and Lapp boots, all made of reindeer skins.

These signs of Arctic life showed that we were on the borders of the great mountain plateau, the Hardanger Vidda. In that latitude, an elevation above the sea of 3,000 to 5,000 feet is sufficient to bring one into quite another world from that known to the average tourist in the sheltered Fjords. One finds on these barren heights a true Arctic country, like that which encircles the earth by the shores of the Polar Sea. Reindeer, white foxes, wolverine and lemmings are seen alike on the Vidda and in the barren lands of Northern Canada, and many of the same species of small, bright Alpine plants grow both in Siberia and on this Norwegian plateau.

The Vidda plays an important part in the lives of the farmers in the valleys—many of them own or rent land on its borders, and send up their cattle to graze there during the short summer months. Beyond the cattle range, flocks of sheep and herds of semi-domesticated reindeer find pasturage, while the remoter districts remain almost unknown, and afford refuge for bands of wild reindeer.

I meant to traverse the Vidda throughout its greatest length—a difficult five-days' journey. I was warned against the obstacles of the trip, the streams to be forded, the exposure to storms, and the danger of falling ill on the way. But with a thoroughly reliable guide, one may undertake difficult journeys, and I had in mind one of the best of guides—Ole E. Legreid, of Vik.

At last the day of deliverance came, and then we prepared for our Vidda excursion. "We" meant Ole, Freya, and myself. Ole looked as if he had stepped out of one of Tidemand's paintings of old Norwegian life, and I never grew accustomed to his taking his place in this workaday world. He was tall, and strongly built, with clear, hazel eyes that had a direct, simple, boy-like look, and his frank smile showed a wonderful set of flawless teeth—a splendid specimen of a Norseman. Well versed in the lore of Vidda travel, fertile in expedient, thoughtful, faithful, and an intelligent, pleasant companion, a woman might venture with him to take the Vidda journey without too many misgivings.

Then there was Freya; she had so much character and ability, and such a personality of her own, that I often forgot, in speaking of the adventures of "we three," to mention that she was a pretty, buff-colored pony of true Norse blood. Round, fat and sure-footed was Freya, with large, dark eyes and ears, tail, and mane of a dusky brown. One great brown lock fell over her face almost to her nose, but the rest was clipped, and stood erect in a heavy brush, making her look, with her full neck and short body, like one of the chariot horses of some old Greek bas-relief.

Freya, like all Norwegian ponies, ignored "whoas," or pulling on the lines, unless accompanied by the sound "p-r-r-r-r-r-t!" This I had practiced on a former visit to Norway, in public and in private, and so far had not succeeded in making any noise which the ponies recognized as a command to halt. This disqualification of mine had at first troubled me, but I soon found that it would have made no difference. A moment's inspection had convinced Freya that I was a "tenderfoot" in all matters relating to Vidda travel. Therefore, she thought herself justified in ignoring all my wishes, and judging what was the best for both of us. Several times, my pride being hurt by this decision of hers, I made a feeble effort to assert my dignity and authority, when Freya would pause, turn her head and look me in the eye with an expression which said clearly—"Come, now, who knows most about this kind of thing—you or I?" and really, after that, there was nothing to be said.

Then there was a pack-horse, a very good one in his way, but hardly "one of us." I chose a Norwegian saddle for Freya, just like the top of a child's high chair. In this wide, roomy seat, one sits sideways on the horse's back, with both feet resting on a small shelf of wood, which serves as a stirrup.

It was a perfect day when Freya and I left Fosslé. The sun shone warm and clear, and a spicy, sweet smell arose from the rain-soaked moss and heather. During the first part of the day the trail was too difficult for riding. Freya led the way willingly enough; the pack-horse followed under Ole's guidance, and I brought up the rear, not being accustomed to the rough way.

After two hours of wearisome plodding through marshes and over rocks of the steep declivities, we reached higher barren ground, and, as we climbed to the northward, we saw splendid views of the distant glacier, the Hardanger Jokul.

About one o'clock we reached a saeter, or mountain dairy, placed in a sheltered nook between the crags, where the grass grew fine and

With Guide and packhorse

"I chose a Norwegian saddle for Freya, just like the top of a child's high chair. In this wide, roomy seat, one sits sideways on the horse's back, with both feet resting on a small shelf of wood, which serves as a stirrup." Sketch by Elizabeth Taylor, 1893.

green. The only other saeter I had ever seen was on the Dovrefjeld, in another part of Norway, which was a good-sized four-roomed cabin, with white sanded floors strewn with juniper twigs, and everything as neat as possible.

With this delectable day in mind, the Vidda saeter was a great disappointment. It was a rough little affair of turf and stones, with mud floor, no furniture but a bunk in one corner, and a small bench; no light but that which came in from the open chimney-place, where a large kettle of cheese was simmering. A sleepy-eyed girl rose from the bed as we entered, and heated some milk for us over a fire of dwarf birch twigs. A small room opened out of the one we were in, and there the milk and cheese were kept, and on the back side of the bunk, among the rough peasant coverlids, we saw the great cakes of "gammel ost," or old cheese, placed there to ripen during the summer months—not an attractive sight to one fond of gammel ost.

The life of these saeter girls is not an easy one. They remain upon the Vidda for about three months, living alone in these wretched shelters of turf and stone. There is butter and cheese to be made, the cows to be milked, the saeter work done, and dwarf birch and juniper cut and dried for fuel, and brought from a long distance. We drank our milk with much enjoyment, smoky and flavored with birch leaves though it was, and soon after started on our way again.

We climbed up and down the barren hills, forded streams, and passed over the rocky uplands where the snow lay in the hollows, and where the only vegetation was the crisp reindeer moss, and beds of bright-eyed Alpine pinks and gentians. Then, as the sun sank low, we entered the shallow valley of the Bjor. Here are a number of saeters some distance apart, built of lichen-covered rocks, and roofed with green sod, harmonizing so perfectly with the surrounding turf and boulders that it was with difficulty that one could detect them. Sometimes it was the open door which made a dark accent and attracted the eye, or the blue smoke that curled slowly from the mossy chimney in the still air of the valley.

At last, not far away, we saw Ole's saeter and the refuge hut. As we approached, some ponies were seen feeding not far away, and Ole said: "There are people in the refuge hut, may be three or four huntsmen." I thought some long thoughts as I looked at the tiny one-roomed hut, and reflected that we had no other quarters for the night. But one must expect rude quarters in Vidda travel, and I explained to the occupants that I had "roughed-it" in America, and would not mind, if they didn't. So we had supper together in the most amicable fashion, and I heard tales of big trout and fine fishing to be had on some lakes near the center of the plateau.

After supper, I went over to the saeter where Ole's two daughters, Britta and Karen, and his little boy, Hans, lived during the summer months. Britta was calling home the cows. At the door of the saeter she stood, with head raised and throat bare, sending her fresh young voice ringing far across the wild rocky slopes of the Vidda.

It was no peaceful pasture-land that stretched around the saeter. The snow-flecked hills looked dark and forbidding, outlined against the level golden bars of the west. Violet mists were creeping up their rugged sides, and a cold breath of air stole up the valley, bearing with it a wild northern odor of peat and moss and dwarf birch. The great spaces and the silence oppressed me, and Britta's coaxing voice was a welcome sound as she again took up the refrain, summoning from their rocky feeding grounds Golden Rose, Roseleaf, Mountain Rose and the other cows, all of the rose family. Chilled with the evening air, I went back to the refuge hut, where Ole had made a fire of birch twigs on the high, raised hearthstone.

Then I unpacked my traps at the hut, and with a large shawl and "thumbtacks," screened off one bunk from public view, and, within its shelter, crawled into my sleeping bag of reindeer skins. Ole, as "chaperon," slept on the floor by the fireside, and soon a peaceful silence fell upon the rough hut.

We were all up early on the following morning—the hunters bound for the Voringfos, on their homeward journey. I wanted to catch some trout, and Ole was to hunt up a herd of 1,000 semi-domesticated reindeer, known to be grazing somewhere in the neighborhood, and bring it down for me to see.

During a long journey to Arctic America, the year before, I had become much interested in the subject of reindeer, not only our two native species, the Barren Ground and the Woodland reindeer, but the domesticated variety of Siberia and Lapland. I had heard of Dr. Sheldon Jackson's plan to introduce the Siberian deer into Alaska for the benefit of the starving Eskimos, and the doctor had asked me to take some measurements of the Norwegian animals, to see how they compared in size with those from Siberia.

Within the last twelve or fifteen years the domesticated reindeer have been brought from Lapland to the high mountain lands of Southern Norway. Their owners do not depend upon the herds for entire support, as do the Lapps and Finns, but still they make a good profit by the sale of the skins, horns and meat. The deer are never milked, but are tended like sheep on the distant Fjelds, the herd being owned by four or five farmers, who live in the lower country and take turns in sending a man to watch them. They require less care than sheep, and afford a larger profit, as the latter must be fed during the long Norwegian winters, while the deer live out all the year without shelter, scraping away the snow which covers the moss and lichens.

It was late in the afternoon when I heard Hans cry out "Rans-dyerne!" (the reindeer) pointing towards one of the hills back of the hut. There I saw a great crawling mass of brown and gray objects, looking as if a slowing moving avalanche of Vidda rocks was descending upon us. As it approached, I could see the tossing horns, and hear a confused mingling of sound, cries of the herdsmen, the grunting of the tired fawns, which sounded like that made by a pig when he meditatively digs his way down some country lane and the peculiar crackling of the large, elastic hoofs, which open when the foot is placed upon the ground, and close when it is raised. I was delighted to see the fawns take refreshment as the herd came to rest near me. Down they plumped, like so many lambs, on their knees, their funny white tails wagging supreme satisfaction at the rate of five hundred wags to the minute.

Hans, who had a bag of salt, began to sing a quaint old Norsk tune, with which the herdsmen call the deer together, and at once they came crowding about him, with their long necks outstretched, their eyes protruding, and with many backward starts of alarm. I succeeded in coaxing two shabby old does up to take salt from my hand, but most of the deer were very timid, not being accustomed to the sight of a woman's dress.

We left the Bjor hut early next morning, with a high, cold wind blowing, and the clouds hanging low. Freya was reluctant to leave the sheltered saeter lands. She disapproved of my trip from beginning to end. It was a new experience for her. She understood (and despised!) the manner of the tourist, whom she was perpetually carrying from the excursion steamers to see the Voringfos. She comprehended, also, her fortnightly visit to the saeter, to carry provisions and bring back butter and cheese to the valley, but what this small person meant by leaving the beaten tracks, and going off into the wild Vidda, was a problem too deep for her sagacity. Being a pony of principle, she did her duty without serious objection; but being also a feminine pony, she showed her impatience in a score of airy affectations.

We crossed the Bjor early in the afternoon, and arrived at a small "fiskebod," or fisherman's hovel, on a barren height above one of the numerous Vidda lakes. There we found an old man, living a solitary life, seeing no one for weeks, fishing in the lakes for the great Alpine trout, and salting them for winter use. The rough shelter was welcome enough, for I was chilled with our long ride, and a storm was sweeping down upon us.

The old man seemed glad to see us. He brought out a five-pound trout, caught that morning in the lake, and boiled it for our lunch. Then with a bit of newspaper for a plate, and a "tol knife" serving as both knife and fork, I curled up on a stone before the open fireplace and made a good meal. The old man listened eagerly to Ole's report of news from the Fjord, and the men talked steadily on in the singsong cadence of the Norse tongue, while the wind howled furiously around the fiskebod, and blew down the chimney in gusts, scattering the ashes on the hearth.

We had to reach Sandhang, the next refuge hut, that night, and the rain was already splashing down in great drops as we said goodby to the old man. A pitiless icy blast drove the rain full in our faces, and I could not walk fast enough to keep warm, for the wind almost carried me off my feet. There was nothing to do but huddle into as small a heap as possible, and, with bowed head and closed mouth, bear it as well as one could, leaving Freya to take care of me. She, all her airs and graces gone, toiled on patiently and faithfully through the long afternoon.

As I looked out now and then from under the shelter of my ca-puchin, I saw always the same sight — gray, angry clouds, gray hills, over which the gray mists were sweeping, and long stretches of gray Alpine lakes, the surface of the water gleaming with flashes of foam.

How welcome Ole's cheerful voice was breaking in upon a half-stupor from cold and fatigue, telling me that Sandhang was in sight! I looked up, and saw on the shores of Normandslaagen, in a waste of rocks and moss, a small cabin of boards, and a fiskebod where a fisherman, Sylvest Koamme, lived during the summer months.

We spent the night at Sandhang, and the next morning left even this slight link with the outside world, and started on, over the high-est land of the plateau, a country desolate beyond expression, but charming in color.

"Monotonous, dreary and uninteresting," I had heard the Vidda called; but as I surveyed the beauty of its changing color, I thought of the line: "God leaves no spot of earth unglorified."

Our stopping place for that night was at the shooting camp of a party of young Scotchmen. Our only alternative was the wretched hovel of a Lapp reindeer herder some distance further on, and I de-cided, though with some misgiving, to ask for shelter at the camp.

Our journey the next day was to be the hardest of all; ten and a half hours' travel to the first gaard on the southern borders of the Vidda—that of Lars Bernanuten. We rose early at the shooting camp and said good-by to our kind hosts, and started with the Lapp as a guide. A strange little creature, he was, dressed in true Lapp cos-tume, and carrying on his back a great pouch of reindeer skin, and an old-fashioned gun in a reindeer skin case. Long tufts of faded hair showed from under his cap of hair seal, and skin, eyes and dress were the same neutral tint, like the dried moss of the Vidda. As I looked at this gnome-like little figure skimming lightly over the ground ahead of me, and then at the wild surroundings, I felt as if I were part of an old Norse fairy tale.

That day we passed over the barrenest region on the Vidda. As far as the eye could reach, rocks, nothing but rocks everywhere—almost all traces of vegetation had disappeared. Only a dark green mould and occasional tufts of the reindeer leaf growing in the little hollows. Immense boulders were outlined against the sky, looking like the relics of some old Druid worship. A bitter wind swept from the snow fields of the Hankili mountains far off to the northwest. We ate our lunch sitting under the shelter of some overhanging crags, and after the ponies had rested for an hour or so, started on our way again. There was no trail—right over the hills we went, and through the marshes, shortening the distance in every possible way to enable us to reach the difficult descent to Bernanuten before the twilight came.

At last, just at dusk, we reached the crest of a high hill, and, looking down over the rocky ledges, saw far below us the sodded roofs of the Gaard of Bernanuten. We could hear the call of the saeter girls, and in the still clear air arose the voices of the farmer and his wife, who sat outside the gaard door churning, and wondering at the visitors who were descending upon them. In the fast failing light, we had a difficult scramble down the hill. The man took the horses one by one, while Ole helped me to slip down the steep rocks and over the deep miry holes between.

When we reached the bottom, covered with mud and quite tired out, we had a pleasant welcome from Lars Bernanuten and his wife. They opened the door of a small, two-roomed log cabin, a short distance from the farm-house, and soon sent a good fire crackling up the three-cornered chimney. Flatbrod, milk, and dried mutton, tough and tasteless, were all they could give us to eat. The day had been a hard one, and it was pleasant to see a bed once more.

The Bernanuten place was only a "grass farm," too cold for even potatoes to grow. Hay-making was in progress, and the air was filled with a fragrance like that of sweet clover. Rough and bleak though it was, the farm seemed pleasant enough after the barren Vidda.

All next day we traveled steadily downwards, passing the timber limit, and seeing once more the dusky pine forests and fertile meadows. Just before dark, Ole pointed to the valley below, and there I could distinguish, between the masses of foliage, a curving white line. It was a post road, something I had not seen for more than five weeks.

An hour after, we arrived at a farm-house, where Ole borrowed a stolkjaerre, or country cart. We loaded our traps behind, took off Freya's saddle, and put her in harness, and were soon fairly flying along the smooth road towards a farmhouse, where we expected to pass the night.

It was quite dark by this time, and the rain poured down steadily, but the white road could be followed easily.

By seven o'clock, we had left the farm-house, and were spinning down the road again—an exhilarating drive in the fragrant, pine-scented air. There was a little inn further on, where we knew we could have a dinner, a real dinner, once more; and our journey ended in a cozy, clean inn.

Published in *Outing*, April, 1900, 664–670.

Remote Norway

A Woman's Trip
Through the Upper Saeterdal

Several years ago, an elderly Norwegian gentleman, who knew his native country well, said to me: "You ought to visit the Upper Saeterdal. You will find there the most primitive and interesting people in all Norway. You will be safe enough, the country people are all kind and honest, but you will have some experiences!"—nodding his head with a grim chuckle.

During the last few years, travel in the unbeaten tracks has been made possible for women by the exertions of the Christiansand Tourist Company. At certain points along the mountain trails a room in the gaards is set aside for the use of any chance traveler, containing a comparatively clean bed, a table, chair and a few dishes. There are fixed charges arranged by the company, and the names given of some reliable men in the neighborhood who can serve as guides.

The sun was high in the heavens when Ole, my guide, Freya, my pony, and I started from the Thelemarken post road for the first stage of the journey, a nine hours' stretch over the mountain range. Our goal was to be the gaard at the head of the Saeterdal Valley which extends from the Laagefjeld on the north to Christiansand by the sea—a distance of about one hundred and eighty-five miles.

Five hours of hard climbing over rock and morass brought us to the summit of the mountain ridge which divides the Thelemarken range from the Saeterdal. After that we went on more rapidly through a wild country that filled my guide Ole with admiration for its advantages as a range for sheep and cattle. Air like crystal; springs of pure, sweet water gushing out from the hillside; dwarf birch and juniper for fuel, and clear, deep lakes filled with trout. "Just the place for saeters" (mountain dairies), Ole said, "if there was only a market within a reasonable distance."

Not until dusk did we reach the gaard. The first glimpse I had of the great living room, black with smoke and dirt, recalled to mind what my Norwegian friend had said about the Saeterdal folk, but I was too tired to care much about my surroundings. Ole and I had supper of crackers and sardines brought with us, and then I went to bed in a little room partitioned off from the rest of the house, where at least the hay on the bed was clean and the farm animals could not enter.

Next morning we were up and on our way at half past five o'clock, one of the farm men going with us as a guide, for Ole had never been in the Saeterdal. In fact, I had intended that Ole should leave me at this point and return to his home in Eidfjord with my pony, Freya, and the pack-horse. Ole had been my faithful guide during a week's hard travel from Vik, in Eidfjord, over the Hardanger Vidda; and after depending on him so long I dreaded going on alone in this remote valley where no English was spoken, so I persuaded him to accompany me for just one day more before turning back on his long homeward journey.

That morning, in crossing a ridge of barren hills, we saw a large number of semi-domesticated reindeer with their Lapp herders. Stopping to rest at one of their lodges we found the people in great trouble, one of their men having died suddenly on the fjeld while watching the deer. We sat down around the fire, which was built on the ground while the Lapps poured out their grief to Ole. In the dim light it was hard to believe that we were not in the tepee of some Northern Indian. The framework was conical in shape, and made of slender saplings, which were covered by sods and strips of bark, a hole being left at the apex for the passage of smoke. Small poplar branches were placed on the ground for a carpet, and hanging above were sides of venison drying in the smoke. There was no furniture, reindeer skins serving as couches in the daytime and beds at night.

After resting an hour or so with the lodge, we went on and reached the next gaard in the early afternoon. We found here a typical Saeterdal farm beautifully situated among the hills above a lake, farmhouses, staburs, or storehouses, barns and the smokehouse forming quite a little settlement. The peasants greeted us pleasantly, though they were very curious about me, as I was the first American who had come to the upper valley.

One woman, noticing that I was examining with interest a finely carved stabur, took me by the hand and carried me off to see the interior. In the lower room cheese, fladbrod, barley, and dried venison and mutton were stored, while the room above, to which we climbed up a ladder, was used for the family treasures. Hanging from beams overhead were the whitest, fleeciest sheepskins, men's jackets, ornamented with silver buttons, petticoats, white and red striped woolen sheets and blankets, taper or heavy bed rugs with bright stripes, gay sashes, and the dainty little blankets used to wrap the babies in at baptism, and handed down from one generation to another.

I saw, too, some harness made of reindeer sinew which was a marvel of lightness and strength. This is often made by the women, the sinew being first chewed thoroughly until it is quite soft and then rolled on the lap, or, better still, the cheek, to work it into long strands, which are then braided.

It was interesting to see how independent these isolated farms are of the outside world. The furniture, dishes, spoons, churns and other articles of domestic use are made on the farm which provides also wool for the homespun garments, fuel, and fodder for the live stock. The lakes which abound in the valley furnish fish, and the sale of cattle, butter, or timber enables them to procure the few necessary articles of foreign production, such as coffee, sugar, cotton cloth, and iron ware.

This gaard was not a station of the Tourist Company. Having heard the day before that no ponies were to be had at the next station, we had turned from the main trail, hoping to find horses here. As I knew nothing of the people the thought of being here alone filled me with misgivings. Ole assured me, however, that the people seemed kind and honest, and that I need have no fears. But I was exhausted with the experiences of the preceding week; insufficient food, exposure, and a severe feverish cold caught on the Vidda had taken away my "nerve," and with a heavy, anxious heart I saw Ole making his preparations for departure. Putting my arms about Freya's neck, I looked into her soft dark eyes, saying, "Farvel, mein Freya, farvel!" but Freya freed herself gently and stepped off toward a tempting bit of grass, unmoved, indifferent to the last. I said good-by to my faithful Ole, and as they disappeared over the crest of the hill and I saw the last wave of Freya's long tail and the dainty tread of her dusky hoofs, a great wave of loneliness swept over me. I sat down disconsolately on a stone in the barnyard and struggled with a wish to run after Ole and retrace my way ignominiously over the Vidda rather than go down the Saeterdal alone.

Soon after Ole and Freya left me, I saw the grandmother of the gaard hurrying across the yard with my dinner. I followed promptly, for during the last eleven hours I had eaten only a few crackers. But as I did so, a dreadful smell was wafted to me, coming from the dish the old woman was carrying. My heart sank, for I felt there was to be no dinner for me. It proved to be "raske fiske," an article of food uneatable from the Anglo-Saxon point of view.

It is made by putting away fish in slightly salted water to spoil for several weeks, after which it is considered a great delicacy, though why the Norwegian who eats of it does not die is a mystery. So I had fladbrod and milk substituted for "raske fiske," and thought of the fleshpots of Egypt with bitterness of spirit.

The farm people soon scattered to the hay-fields, leaving the grandmother and myself the only ones on the place. The main living-room was delightfully picturesque. The ceiling, with its great beams, was black with smoke, the walls of hewn logs were painted a green blue, softened and faded by age, the furniture of quaint patterns was colored olive green and dull reds, beautifully carved racks held the carved wooden spoons and ladles, and the dishes and troughs, which were also painted in greens and reds.

One side of the room was occupied by two wide beds, built into the wall, and an armoire which divided them. The beds were filled with hay and sheepskins, black with dirt and grease.

From the beams above hung sides of dried mutton and venison with strings of onions.

Across one corner of the room was an immense fireplace, where a great black kettle of goat's cheese was simmering. This part of the room was lighted only by the fire, the flame showing the long, grizzled hair and deep sunken eyes of the old woman as she bent over the cauldron, crooning and smoking a long, black pipe. Her tattered, filthy garments were fairly dropping from her gaunt frame; and in the fitful light she looked like some old witch, as she muttered and stirred and watched me through her long, gray hair.

Looking about me, I wondered whether I could brave the squalor of my surroundings and stay for a few days to make some studies of this picturesque interior. But everywhere the sickening smells of fermenting cheese and spoiled fish assailed me, and the dirt and confusion and the vermin which infest these houses made me lose courage, so I decided to go on my way in the morning, hoping to find cleaner quarters at the next gaard.

That night I slept in a small loghouse a short distance from the farmhouse. My room opened out of a large one where the milk and cheese were stored. Row on row of gaily painted milk bowls filled the shelves, and here were vats of cheese, kegs of butter and churns, these last carved and painted like the furniture. Fortunately, I had my own blankets, and could discard the bedding and sleep on the hay that filled the bed.

It was dusk when I went to my room to sleep, and I noticed that in my absence of an hour a mysterious trap-door had been opened to an attic above and a ladder placed there. The thought occurred to me that it was a good place for a villain to have secreted himself to come down and murder me as I slept, but I dismissed this as a foolish fancy and went to bed in a fairly serene frame of mind, and my overfatigue must be responsible for the troubled night that followed. I was haunted by feverish dreams of trapdoors, ladders and midnight attacks, and started up over and over again in a panic, exclaiming, "Oh, the ladder! the ladder!"

At last the weary night was over. I was conscious, in a troubled doze, that through the window glimmered a faint rosy light. It was five o'clock, a beautiful, calm morning, and already the two farmmen were waiting to go with me to the next gaard, arrayed in their best clothes, their jackets with silver buttons, red sashes, their broad-brimmed felt hats with silver ornaments on them, and trousers fastened at the knee with bright leggin straps.

I rode a large clumsy farm-horse, which stumbled and slid about on the rough trail in a fashion very trying after Freya's sure, light footsteps. Our nine hours' ride was broken by rests for the horses at farmhouses along the way, where I was displayed with great pride by my guides as if I had been a traveling bear. I sat meekly on a stone while the horses were grazing, and the peasants came from all directions and made a semicircle on the ground in front of me. The first and most important piece of information given by my guide was that I was an "Amerikanske dame." Here he was interrupted by a chorus of exclamations of surprise—"Nay! nay! nay! nay! nay!" said very fast, with shakes of the head and uplifted hands. The next was that I had traveled over the Vidda (more exclamations), and then followed in detail all the facts that a careful questioning had previously extracted—my family history, experiences in the past and plans for the future. This lecture ended, the audience ventured on a catechism of its own. Promptly came the question—always the first— "Aer de gift?" (Are you married?); then "Hoor gammel aer de?" (How old are you?) Often they exclaimed, "But you are brave! To travel alone! We would like to go to America, but we are afraid." At one little joke related by the guides they never failed to laugh heartily; that was that the Amerikanske dame was not afraid to cross

*"I was displayed with great pride by my guides as if I had been
a traveling bear. I sat meekly on a stone . . . and the peasants came
from all directions and made a semicircle on the ground . . ."*
Sketch by Elizabeth Taylor, 1893.

the Vidda or go through the Saeterdal alone, nor did she fear Indianer (Indians), but she *was* afraid of Saeterdal cows! They usually crowded up around me before I left, feeling my dress, turning over and laughing at my hands, examining the buttons on my boots. Then my guides always called their attention to a hunting bag brought from Arctic America. This never failed to excite great enthusiasm, and no detail was overlooked, the embroidery of porcupine quills and the closely woven meshes of reindeer skin being much admired.

I seemed to be an object of horrible fascination for a two-year-old baby, who, his face distorted with fear, kept peering around at me from various points of shelter. He wore one brief and scanty garment, fastened at the neck by an immense silver brooch of antique pattern and fine workmanship. Indeed everyone—men, women and children—had beautiful silver ornaments, chains looped across the breast, buckles, and "knapper," or large double buttons fastening shirt collar and sleeves.

Farther up the Saeterdal the costume had been more or less influenced by the neighboring district of Thelemarken, but this day the true Saeterdal dress was seen in all its perfection. It was on a young man about twenty years of age, large and stout, with a smooth, solemn face. His head was shaven close but for one long lock which fell over his forehead, and his costume was eight-tenths trousers and two-tenths shirt-collar, with a huge pair of wooden sabots in addition, which seemed to moor him firmly to the ground. The trousers were very baggy and roomy above, but fitted closely around the ankles, while leathern seams ran down the legs in front instead of at the sides. They were further adorned behind by a large black patch of shiny leather, which extended from a little below the shoulders to the middle of the thighs. The front part of the trousers, which came quite up to the neck, was beautifully embroidered in bright wools, and had double rows of silver buttons. I had been told that the young men of the Saeterdal, at the present time, are inclined to conform more to modern dress, and lower the trousers to somewhere near the waist line. But conservative principles were stamped on every line of this youth's stolid, solemn face, and his trousers were a trifle nearer his ears than even his grandfather's.

Perhaps he had never seen a woman in any dress but that of the Saeterdal, for he seemed to find me quite as interesting as I did him, and, probably, quite as absurd. We sat and looked at each other until we blushed with embarrassment, but we couldn't refrain. I hope I did not look amused, but he must have seen (and no doubt felt flattered) that he possessed much interest for me.

Old men and small boys wore the same kind of costume. The women's dress was almost as odd, the shortness of the skirts being in inverse ratio to the height of the men's trousers. Two skirts were worn, the lower one being several inches longer than the upper, and both were stiffened around the hem so that the fold stood out widely. The costume is admirably adapted to the heavy farm and house work done by the women, and is comfortable and hygienic. But it seems strange to see a great-grandmother going about in the abbreviated skirts of a six-year-old child, her poor old legs exposed to wind and weather, while our grandmothers are draped in voluminous folds.

The next station, though not at all clean, as we understand the term, was habitable for a short stay, and the people were kind and attentive. This place is at the head of a wagon-road, and I found that about fifteen travelers had visited the station during the summer. I remained here several days, enjoying a much-needed rest before continuing my journey down the valley. The food I had was very simple, the farm affording only milk, coffee, a few eggs and the fladbrod, which is the peasant's staff of life. The Norwegians bake the fladbrod two or three times a year, generally in June and September. The Saeterdal folk make it of ground barley, potato flour, salt and water, baking it on a griddle in cakes about thirty inches in diameter and the sixteenth of an inch thick. Great piles of it are stocked in the stabur or other houses, and one finds it tucked away on shelves and in bureau drawers like old newspapers in untidy households. Eating fladbrod was for me a slow and painful process, as it broke up in sharp splinters and hurt the mouth, and a large quantity is necessary to satisfy hunger. It seemed a thing to toy with delicately at five o'clock tea, or with after-dinner coffee—not to serve as the staple article of diet. My inability to master a sufficient amount troubled my kind hostess, and at every meal she deposited about three square feet in front of me, saying in Norwegian, with emphasis, "Be so good as to finish that!"

In summer the fare of the peasants is usually fladbrod, cheese and gruel. The cows go to the mountain pastures in June and remain until the latter part of September, and between those months one finds little milk at the farms distant from the tourist routes. In the winter their food is more varied, milk, and salted and fresh meat being added to the bill of fare.

During my stay at this farm the cattle returned from the fjelds for the winter. That morning the great barns had been swept and cleaned, the mangers filled with new fragrant hay and the troughs with water. Little pens were put up in the fields where the harvest had not been gathered.

As the day wore on, one felt expectancy in the air. The old folks gathered at the door-steps and watched the far-off mountain slopes; the old sheep-dog, too feeble for duty on the heights, became restless, pacing to and fro between the house and the barns, with his ears pricked up for distant sounds, while the one stay-at-home cow, picketed out on the slope near by, tugged at her rope and lowed plaintively. The grandmother saw them first, and clapping her hands called us to look. first came a flock of goats with bells tinkling as they trotted briskly down the steep path and vanished into a neighbor's barn; then, a few minutes later, came the sheep, black and white, ambling up to the space in front of the barn where the boys stood ready to pen them in. Then we saw the cows, showing red and white among the leafy bushes on the hillside, each little band turning from the common trail to its home; and last, the ponies, laden with kettles and milking-cans, bedding and clothes from the mountain saeters, and the girls, each bearing on her shoulders a burden of butter and cheese.

One clear, cold morning I left the station to drive to Viken, the next station. All the men were busy with the hay, but my hostess said her married daughter would be my driver. After seeing the soiled and tattered clothes worn by the peasants on the farm, I was surprised at the gay little creature who presented herself at the hour of starting. A bright flowered kerchief was bound around her head like a turban, and she wore a snowy blouse with high embroidered collar, a short scarlet bodice trimmed with silver braid, short black skirt with red and green bands on the hem, black wool stockings of elaborate pattern, homemade leather shoes, the points curving upward like a Chinese shoe, mitts worked with red and green wools, and ornaments of silver were on the bodice at neck and sleeves. With all this sparkle and gaiety she suggested a bright butterfly, and I, in my brown travel-stained clothes seemed in comparison a very shabby moth.

The road to Viken, though new, was a good one, and as we were whisked along in the peasant cart, traveling appeared very easy after the rough mountain trails I had traversed with Freya.

Our course followed the beautiful Otteraa, a river which recalled the Nepigon, north of Lake Superior, with its rapids, cascades, and deep, eddying pools. The thick forests were a lesson to us, who allow our woodland districts to be destroyed without a thought of the future. Here was a valley settled since Viking times, and yet the great evergreens stood in close ranks, protected by the people with care and intelligence. Young trees are fostered, old ones cut judiciously, all parts being used, and precautions are taken against forest fires. Under the dusky branches I could see beds of Arctic cranberries in an abundance sufficient to furnish sauce for all the Thanksgiving turkeys in America.

The Saeterdal is a narrow valley; at a glance one sees the bare fjelds on either hand rising in precipitous cliffs from the fertile farmlands that fill the space between. There are no real villages, but at intervals of a few hours' travel one sees a little white church, a farmhouse which is also a post-office and general store, and the Proestgaard or parsonage. The farmhouses stand a little more closely in the neighborhood of the church, but soon file away along the river course at good distances from one another. We had now reached a comparatively well-settled country. From this point down to Christiansand there are good post-roads, and every station on the southern way shows increasing comforts and cleanliness.

At Viken I remained a fortnight. Everywhere I met with the greatest kindness and courtesy from the peasants. In taking walks about the valley I often saw them working in the fields or riding along the roads. No preliminaries seemed necessary to a brisk conversation. They would leave their work; or stop their ponies and begin the inevitable questioning. Who was I? Where did I come from? and not only "was I married?" but "was I promised?" As I knew, by this time, a little Norwegian, our talk went on well for a while, but when they ventured on new fields of interrogation I could not understand them and was then allowed to depart.

One day I crossed the river and explored some interesting old gaards perched high up on the hillside. There were a stabur and a house there, which must have been several hundred years old. The only light entered through a square hole in the roof, and here escaped the smoke from a large central fireplace, raised on flat stones, upon the mud floor of the general living room. The bed was built around the immense curving logs, which formed the walls, and bed, doors, settees and door-posts bore traces of half-effaced carvings, where dragons twisted and turned. As usual, in the Saeterdal houses, the dirt was dreadful. Vermin abounded there, and I had a moment of doubt whether to flee or remain to make a sketch of this really charming interior—charming that is, in its picturesqueness. I compromised, finally, on a hasty twenty minutes sketch, and seated myself to draw the fireplace, while the children gathered around to watch me as I worked.

There was a most amusing baby in the room, fully three years old, and talking well, but still drawing nourishment from the maternal font.

Before I left Viken I attended service at the parish church. The peasants collected long before the time for service, visiting the graves in the churchyard and placing flowers on them, or sitting in little groups on the turf where they could have a quiet gossip over the events of the week. As the bell tolled the last strokes they entered the church, the men going to the right and the women to the left. The women's side was a blaze of vivid color, for all, from three-year-old baby girls to the grandmothers, wore scarlet home-made shawls about the shoulders.

After the sermon there was a little talk to some of the children, who came forward and stood in two rows facing each other, just outside the chancel rails. The priest spoke to them in a low, pleasant tone, sometimes asking a question and placing a hand kindly on a child's shoulder as he bent to hear the faltering reply.

It was a pretty subject for a picture: the priest, with his black flowing robes and the white Van Dyck ruff, which made a picturesque setting for his fine serious face; the gay little maidens in their bright turbans, snowy sleeves and embroidered dresses, and the boys looking like grandfathers in miniature with their round flaxen heads half hidden by their ambitious collars.

The Saeterdal peasants are a fine hardy race; kind, honest, and intelligent. Probably their way of living is no worse than that in other isolated districts before the age of roads and the growth of towns.

A railway will soon be built through the valley, and the disagreeable features of travel will disappear as well as the simplicity of the people and the delightful picturesqueness of the old houses.

Drunkenness seems to be the worst failing of the peasants. It is more prevalent than in the west and north of Norway. During a cattle fair, which was held while I was at Viken, the place was filled with intoxicated men, and I could see from my window the poor little ponies galloping recklessly down the road, being lashed by their owners, who could hardly keep their places in the peasants' carts. I remained in my room that afternoon and evening, not daring to venture out. Fortunately my door had that rarity in the Saeterdal—a good lock. As the evening went on, one of the girls knocked at my door and pushed in hurriedly some fladbrod and milk, saying that she had not been able to come before, as the farmyard was full of men "angry drunk." But this was the only time I had any unpleasant experience in the Saeterdal.

Looking back on my journey through the valley I can recall only kindness and courtesy even from the roughest peasants. I would have been content for many reasons to remain much longer, but the poor fare was becoming very tiresome, the weather was frosty and stormy, and the flocks and herds, having all returned from the fields, made my walks abroad anything but "paths of peace." Bristling horns met me at every turn, and the cows and goats, happily-conspicuous by their absence in the summer, proved quite as curious about the "Amerikanske dame" as their owners.

Perhaps the crowning touch to my growing homesickness was

given the morning I came down to my solitary breakfast and found the biggest billy goat—the patriarch of the flock—on the breakfast-table, where wild confusion reigned. With one hoof in the sugar-bowl and his long beard covered with butter, he raised his head and bestowed on me a dignified reproving glance as I shrieked and fled for assistance. This was getting very much too familiar.

The letters, for which I was waiting, arriving that day, the next found me on my way to Christiansand, traveling in the peasant carts, and on two little steamboats which ply upon the lakes along the course of the Otteraa. Three pleasant days were passed in this way, and at noon of the fourth day I caught a glimpse of blue among the trees, a breath of cool, salt air came stealing up the valley, a cluster of masts showed above the red-tiled roofs of a town—I had reached Christiansand, and the end of one of the most interesting rambles I had had, even in remote Norway where all is so interesting to a way-farer from a country in which there is remoteness, true, but little that is ancient or unknown.

Published in *Outing*, July 1899, 367–374.

A Northern Berry

I write to sound the praises of a berry; one that grows the world around in northern countries, but which with us is almost unknown. It is called the cloud-berry in the highlands of Scotland and Wales, in Norway the *multebaer*, and in arctic America the yellow-berry. Wherever found and under whatever name, it is admirable.

I saw it first several years ago in Norway, when traveling along the half-beaten track where solid Norwegian comforts could be obtained, and yet where the contaminating influence of the English and American tourist had not made itself felt. Under such propitious circumstances, the fortunate wayfarer may meet the multebaer accompanied by rich and foamy cream, which is brought to the table in a bedroom pitcher of a noble size. With the advent of the English tourist, the size of the cream-jug and the quality of its contents will deteriorate, and one must not hope to enjoy the multebaer in its best estate where the Anglo-Saxon tongue is heard.

A *multemyr*, or moor where the multebaer grows, is a thing of beauty from the time when the white blossoms open, in June, until the frost turns the myr to a mosaic of reds and yellows. The five-petaled flower, three quarters of an inch in diameter, looks, with its yellow centre, like a single white rose. The stem runs along the ground, lifting its blossoms and crinkled dark green leaves above the silvery reindeer moss and alpine plants which surround it. Here are the waxy bells of the arctic cranberry, the pink and white twin flowers of the Linnaea, starry saxifrage, marsh marigolds and violets, purple butterwort, and the white orchids spotted with pink called by the Norwegians "our Lady's hand." On the hillocks and higher rocky ledges about the marsh grow tangles of juniper, heather, dwarf birch, and the soft gray tufts of the arctic willow.

Later, when the opening heather is sending a crimson flush over the swells of land, the myr is at its brightest. The solid round fruit, resembling a large raspberry, turns a vivid scarlet, while the sepals, curving backwards, are a clear gold color. The leaves, too, by this time, are variegated with buff and maroon, and the brilliant berries of the cornel mingle with alpine gentians of an intense blue.

When the berry is quite ripe it is a pale salmon-yellow, cool, refreshing, and with a peculiar honey-like flavor quite its own. The botany says, "It cloys when eaten in large quantities," but my experience has been that it could never be furnished in an abundance sufficient to produce such a result.

To really appreciate the berry you should gather it yourself, if possible on some barren elevated plateau above tree limit on a fjeld of western Norway. There the air is a delight to breathe, so clean and cool and tonic it is on those wind and storm swept heights, so laden with that aromatic northern fragrance of peat and juniper and heather. In the distance, snow-covered peaks lift themselves above the treeless table-land, and from the precipices come the voices of many streams, blending in a harmony which swells and dies away with the blowing of the winds.

My first gathering of the multebaer was one of those happy experiences which come oftenest when unsought. In fact, Gunhilde and I had gone a-fishing for fjeld trout. Gunhilde had no points of resemblance in common with the goddess of northern mythology. She was only a little maiden of eight years, with shy blue eyes and tightly braided flaxen tails. But she was full of kindly, gentle impulses, had the gift of serene silence, and an unwavering love for her barren hills and for trout-fishing.

My light tackle was four thousand miles away, but I did not disdain, therefore, to catch trout by more primitive methods. Gunhilde dug worms in the good old-fashioned way, tying them up in one of her small stockings; then she brought out two young saplings which were to serve as rods, and we started for the fishing-grounds, three miles away.

I will not stop to describe our sport that morning; suffice it to say that Gunhilde and I jerked by main force so many mountain trout from that little stream that we felt fairly entitled to pause, on our way home, at a multemyr, and refresh ourselves largely.

Not only does the multebaer grow in comparatively sheltered

marshes, but I have found it while passing over the highest ridges of the Hardanger Vidda, a desolate waste where all traces of vegetation had apparently disappeared.

Ole my guide, Freya my pony, and I had had a long, fatiguing day. We had forded swift streams, eaten at noon our *fladbrod* and cheese in a sheltered hollow, and were hurrying to reach a refuge hut still far away, when the sun was low in the sky. For hours the only sight of life had been the whir of the *rypen*, or arctic grouse, as they sprang from our feet as we passed, the twittering of the grassfinch's young brood, and the plaintive cry of gray gulls that swept by us as we skirted some rocky lake shores. All day the clouds had hung low, sometimes inclosing us in a chilling gray mist so dense that Ole's figure, only steps ahead, loomed vaguely in distorted giant form; then a sudden current of air would toss the mist to right and left, making a clear passage through which we could see a far-off snowy ridge or stretch of glacier. Once, Ole, with a field glass had discerned and pointed out to me a herd of wild reindeer feeding on a distant ledge.

Great masses of granite were strewn over the barren ground, where the only trace of vegetation was a few gray lichens. But while passing by a giant boulder which looked like some sort of Druid worship, I saw a glimmer of scarlet and gold. Slipping down from Freya's back, I went to investigate. There was the multebaer growing in a little circle where the rock gave it shelter from the keen winds that blew from the ice-fields. The plant was lower and the leaves were smaller, but the berry was just as large, as juicy, as finely flavored, as on the lower levels. Under the lee of each rock I found a small handful of fruit; how refreshing the cool, juicy berries were to our throats, parched with fatigue! We could not have left them un-gathered, though we had still far to go, and the setting sun warned us not to linger.

✦❦✦

In pleasant contrast to my rough Vidda experience was the next appearance of the multebaer. It was in the Latin Quarter of Paris; not the truly Bohemian neighborhood near the Pantheon, but the "Annex" beyond the Luxembourg gardens, where the English and

100

American students congregate. I had gone out one evening with two artist friends to call on a Norwegian lady, an old resident of Paris. We found her in a cosy little sitting-room, surrounded by trophies of travel and home souvenirs. Our talk ranged widely from land to land, for we were all born wanderers, and eager to exchange suggestions for future jaunts. Before we parted, our hostess, after heating water in a quaint little *bouillotte* among the embers, produced a bottle of *multesaft*, or syrup made of multebaer juice and sugar, poured a little into some high glasses, added just a dash of Cognac, filled the glasses with boiling water, and brought out a box of Holland gingercakes formed like all manner of men and beasts. Then, with a "Vaer saa god" from our hostess, we gathered around the tiny table, bright with its curious Norwegian glass and silver. And when we had finished, we three guests stood in a row before the dear old lady, holding up our petticoats on either side, in true peasant fashion, bobbed a little curtsy, and said in chorus, "Tak for maden" (Thanks for the food); and she, inclining her snowy head, murmured sweetly, "Velbekommen" (May it agree with you).

In America, the multebaer, called there the yellow berry or cloudberry, is found on the White Mountains at tree limit, in some parts of Maine, Nova Scotia, and Newfoundland, on the summits of the Canadian Rockies, and throughout the most northern portions of the continent. It is common on the mossy plains near the Polar Sea, but bears fruit only in favorable seasons.

While taking a long voyage to the delta of the Mackenzie River, in company with the Northern Brigade of the Hudson Bay Company, I saw the cloud-berry on the shores of Great Slave Lake and at several places along the Mackenzie River. At the most northern point, Peel River post, near the Arctic Sea, I found the half-ripe berry on July 15. The natives sometimes preserve the fruit with syrup made from the sap of the canoe birch tree. This lacks the fine maple flavor, and requires a much larger quantity of sap to form the syrup, but it serves well enough as a substitute for sugar. Even in that country, where life is hard, where the struggle for a bare existence never ceases, there is a summer, a short period when all vegetation seems to spring forward at a bound, when ten days of the unsetting sun is enough to bring leaves from the bud to full perfection. As the snow melts away, the low-growing flowers will be seen already in bloom, and one courageous anemone—the pasque flower—unfolds its fur-covered petals as early on the distant Mackenzie as on the prairies of Minnesota and Dakota.

One night, when still within the arctic circle, we stopped for wood at a place where the steep high banks were crowned by a stunted but dense growth of spruce and white birch. It was mid-night, but behind the distant foot-hills of the Rockies the sun's beams glanced towards the zenith, and the great spaces above were all aflame with rose-color.

Going on shore, I climbed over the boulders, among which grew the yellow arnica's showy flowers, Siberian asters, and brilliant blue Mackenzie lupine. The hillside was covered with thickets of rose-bushes and the silver-berry, or *sac-à-commis* of the early voyageurs. Making my way through these, I reached the summit, and entered the freer dusky spaces beneath the trees. Here was a soft twilight, where large gray moths flittered to and fro, and where the only sound was the threadlike plaintive note of some anxious little wood-bird, as, unseen by me, he peered down through the thick branches. Far below I could see the great river shining between the tree-trunks, and hear faintly the voices of the Indians as they ran from the shore to the boat with their burdens of wood.

Moss everywhere! burying the prostrate trees, covering the rugged boulders, filling up hollows, and softening all outlines like a heavy fall of snow. A beautiful carpet, soft as feathers to the touch, formed of miniature fir-trees, palms, and delicate fern patterns. There was the silvery reindeer moss interwoven with sage-green filaments crowned with tiny scarlet salvers, the snowy cetraria, the haircap moss, blood-red peat moss, and dainty gray lichens resting lightly on the mosses, and bearing a strange resemblance to the dusky moths that hovered above them. My feet sank deep in the soft mosses and felt the elastic bound of mosses still below, and the breaking and crackling of dry branches of trees long since buried from sight and preserved from decay.

At some former time, Indians had been there for canoe birch, leaving behind them sections of the slender tree-trunks and frag-ments of bark. The latter had curled in fantastic shapes, some forming baskets, others scrolls and cornucopias, and in these had grown miniature gardens. Trailing mosses drooped over the sides; here swayed the fragrant bells of the Linnaea; here were pale green and yellow pyrolas, and the deep pink blossoms of the arctic dew-berry sending out a strong fragrance of bitter almonds. And all around what a wonderful growth of flowers for a forest nook north of the arctic circle! The lady's-smock grew fair and tall, and near it rosy clusters of valerian. At the foot of the larger plants were beds of low-growing green and white orchids, the waxy moneses, pink and white vetches, arctic anemones, coral-root, broom-rape, and the starlike blossoms of the northern bedstraw. The flowers of spring, summer, and autumn seemed to unite here, the Labrador tea still retaining some spicy white clusters, though the fireweed was opening its crimson blossoms, and the bear-berry was weighed down with its spikes and scarlet berries. And here, growing in the moister places, I discovered my old friend the multebaer. I bent down and gathered some trailing sprays, finding them of more luxuriant growth than those of higher altitudes on Norwegian fjelds, though this place was much father north. Here the great Mackenzie, flowing from the south, brings softer winds, and extends the limits of the forests which give shelter to these delicate flowers.

The hidden wood-bird no longer sounded his note of alarm, and from a thicket swelled the song of a hermit thrush greeting the sun as it rose after its brief hour of eclipse beyond the mountain range. But as I listened there came the summons to the boat, the old voyageur cry, "Ah ho! Ah ho! Il faut partir!" I gave one farewell look at this arctic garden, seen for the first time by a white woman's eyes, climbed down through the roses and silver-berries, and a few minutes later our little boat was on its southern way, stemming bravely the mighty flood of the Mackenzie.

Published in *Atlantic Monthly*, September 1895, 427–430.

Iceland

1895

The summer of 1895 found Elizabeth Taylor in Iceland. She visited an eider-duck farm, looked at lava fields, and collected plants for museums during her ten week stay. Three published articles resulted from that trip; two are reprinted here. Iceland offered the simple lifestyle, the birds and flowers of the north that so appealed to Miss Taylor, but it had already become a tourist destination which tempered her enthusiasm. In 1913 she traveled to Iceland once more, before returning to the Faroe Islands, where her primary interest really lay.

Eider-Duck Farms in Iceland

It was near Reykjavik, the capital of Iceland, that I first made the acquaintance of eider-ducks. Fru Zoëga, my kind hostess at the little inn, arranged for me a trip to one of the eider-duck farms on an island in the harbour, and sent her pretty daughter, Valla, to keep me company. The day was fine, and far in the distance we could see the snow-capped ranges that line the rugged coast. Our steamer, the *Laura*, lay anchored in the fjord, and boats were briskly plying to and fro, unloading the cargo she had brought from Denmark and Scotland. After a stormy six days' voyage from Edinburgh, we had arrived the night before in company with a Danish man-of-war and a French despatch-boat sent to look after the interests of the Breton codfish fleet. Three steamers at once was quite an event for the quiet little town, but not a single salute was fired from shore or on board, and those tourists on the *Laura* who wished to shoot sea-birds were sternly suppressed. Eider-ducks, it seems, are birds of importance in Iceland, and as they dislike noise, the firing of guns within a mile of their nests is forbidden, and every means is taken to induce them to frequent the farm lands along the shore.

A half-hour's brisk row brought us to Engey, one of the eider-farm islands. Valla led the way, and we went first to the farmhouse to ask permission to visit the nesting grounds. In front of the turf-roofed little buildings, on the stony ground, a quantity of down was drying—fluffy masses of brownish grey, looking as if the first puff of wind would blow them out to sea. But Valla told me that the down was so interwoven with blades of dry grass that an ordinary wind would not stir it.

The farmer's wife readily gave her consent, adding that we should find her daughter Gudrun collecting down from the deserted nests. Following a rough trail we soon reached the low pastures near the sea. By the action of frost and damp the surface had been upheaved into hillocks about eighteen inches high, and between these the ducks were nesting. I was toiling over the uneven ground, when suddenly a large greyish-brown duck burst like a bomb from almost under my feet, and I balanced to and fro on my hillock, fearing to advance a step lest I crushed the eggs. Looking carefully about me I soon found them; seven great eggs, as large as those of a goose, peeping out from the down which swelled up around them in a thick roll. A little further on, I was surrounded by excited, perturbed mothers, some still brooding, and others with ducklings hardly out of the shell. The mottled and low-toned plumage so harmonized with the grey rocks and dead grasses around me that I could hardly distinguish the ducks at a distance of a few paces.

Just then I saw Gudrun coming with her apron packed full of down. Gudrun was on terms of pleasant intimacy with her ducks, and they stayed tranquilly on their eggs at her approach, and even allowed her to stroke their heads and see if the eggs were hatching. Of Valla, too, they seemed to have little fear, though she was a stranger to them.

"Why is it, Gudrun," I asked, "that the ducks are so afraid of me?"

Gudrun smiled shyly, and replied: "I think, Fröken, that they do not like your hat!"

That was the trouble! Accustomed as they were to the simple kerchief, or the small black "hufa" worn by Icelandic women, with its heavy silk tassel hanging down on one side, they had taken umbrage at my straw travelling hat with its "perky" ribbon bows. However, the ducks were not unreasonable. When they saw that Valla and Gudrun talked amicably with me, they waived their objections to my headgear, and finally permitted me to caress their sleek heads and wings.

Only one drake did I see on the nesting-grounds. He was a splendid fellow, weighing fully seven pounds, and quite different in plumage from his soberly-dressed spouse. His back, sides of his head and neck, and upper part of the breast were white, the latter tinged with a little brownish-yellow; the bill was yellow, changing to dull green at the tip; the crown, forehead, wings and lower part of the body were a rich velvety black, and on the sides of the head was a streak of light green. The drakes, it seems, help the ducks to make the nests, and then, when incubation has fairly begun, they go off in little bands of four or five, and lead a care-free existence out at sea. You can see them rising and falling on the great swells, just beyond the breakers, their soft "ah-oo! ah-oo!" sounding like the cooing of wood pigeons.

All the accounts I have read about eider-ducks say that nests are robbed of their down twice, the duck supplying it each time from her own body; the third time the drake gives his white down, and this is allowed to remain. But I was told by farmers in Iceland that now they never take the down until the little ones are hatched. It has been found that the birds thrive better and increase faster when they are allowed to live as Nature meant them to do. So now the poor mothers are no longer obliged to strip themselves of all their down to refurnish their despoiled nests. Sometimes, if the quantity is very great, a little may be taken, but enough must be left to cover the eggs when the duck leaves the nest for food.

Eider-ducks are found along the sea coast of Arctic America and Siberia, Greenland, Norway, Sweden, Lapland, Iceland, the Faroe Islands, Spitzbergen and Nova Zembla. On some of the northern coasts of Great Britain also they are still found in small numbers, but the down is of inferior quality in these more southern districts. Lieutenant Greeley saw them as far north as eighty-three degrees. They are true ocean birds, living during the winter out at sea, and diving for their food, which consists of small fish, shell-fish and crabs. In April they begin to gather in little groups near the shores. Often one bird will visit the nesting-grounds, and if his report is favourable, his companions soon return to their old haunts, and nest-building begins. Both ducks and drakes work together, laying a foundation of seaweed or coarse grasses, and upon this the bed of down is arranged, and heaped up around the margin. About May 20 the ducks begin to lay, six or seven eggs being the usual clutch, although ten are sometimes seen. A few of these are taken by the farmer for his own use, but the sale of eggs is forbidden. Often two ducks will lay side by side in one nest, each furnishing her own quota of down, and doing her part in hatching and rearing of the double family.

Eider-ducks, though often very tame, can hardly be classed with domestic birds. They live in a wild state in every part of Iceland where they can find suitable breeding-places. Often a prosperous "varpet," as the nesting-grounds are called, can be formed by the farmers whose land possesses the proper attractions. A small island that slopes to the sea is the best place, but a cape, or a neck of land, is often chosen. If the land has many hillocks there is no need of making artificial nests, otherwise the turf must be cut in blocks and set on end to form small oblong compartments. These are often roofed over with pieces of turf or wood. Sometimes the nests are made of stones, but in this case, as the stones are old, the bottom must be well covered with plenty of crumbled turf or coarse grass. Eider-ducks have their fancies about the situation of their nest, some preferring one that overlooks the neighbourhood and others choosing a sheltered nook in a hollow. Everything must be in readiness before it is time for the birds to come from the sea. The ducks seem to like to have some life or movement on the neighbouring farm lands, as they probably feel more secure from their natural enemies, foxes and ravens; but on the varpet itself all must be peace and serenity.

If the new varpet must be visited, it is best to go when the weather is fine and sea at high tide. The approach should be made always from the same direction, and the farmer should not look about him too curiously or the birds will become troubled and suspicious. Any object that shines or has colour and certain sounds are very attractive to the birds. So the would-be owner of a varpet often sets up at intervals small sticks to which coloured rags are tied, or he puts, on pieces of wire, mussel-shells, which rattle in the wind. A little bell rung by the wind also seems to please them, and the crowing of cocks.

Another way of inducing the wild birds to build is to employ "lukke-fugl," or decoy ducks of rubber or plaster. Some are placed on the slopes of land in a sitting position, and others are moored in the water by strings long enough to allow them to move to and fro as if swimming.

The growth of a varpet is necessarily slow at first, but once fairly established it yields a good profit. Engey, the island that I visited, and Videy, not far away, produce about three hundred pounds annually, and great quantities are taken in Isafjord in Northern Iceland. A writer upon Iceland, in speaking of a visit to one of the Isafjord farms, wrote: "On the coast was a wall built of large stones, just above high-water level, about three feet high and of considerable thickness at the bottom. On both sides of it alternate stones had been left out so as to form a series of square compartments for the ducks to make their nests in. Almost every compartment was occupied, and as we walked along the shore a long line of ducks flew out, one after another. The house was a marvel; the earthern walls that surround it and the window embrasures were occupied with ducks. On the turf slopes of the rook we could see ducks, and a duck sat on the scraper."

About ten thousand pounds of eider-down are collected annually in Iceland, seven thousand being exported to foreign countries. Formerly the peasants used to receive over twenty-one shillings a pound, but the price has now fallen to half that amount. The peasants seldom receive money, and are obliged to barter their down for merchandise furnished by the Danish merchants at the little settlements on the fjords.

An old Icelandic proverb illustrates the strange elasticity of the down: "What is it that is higher when the head is off?" "An eider-down pillow," is the answer. A pound of down can be compressed into a ball the size of a pint bowl, but, once released, it swells and mounts like something alive until it would fill a bushel basket. A pound and a half is enough to fill an ordinary bed-puff. These very comfortable articles are found in the guest-room of every Icelandic farm, however poor and small it may be. After a long, hard day in the saddle the traveller longs for warmth and shelter. But these little guest-rooms have never had a fire in them, and built as they are on the ground-floor there is in them a dreadful chill. Once tucked away in bed, however, and well covered with the down-puff, a delightful sense of comfort follows, and tired bones lose their pains and stiffness.

The last days of my ten weeks' visit in Iceland were spent in Laxamyri, one of the finest farms in Iceland. Many sheep grazed on the neighbouring hills; the river teemed with river-trout, sea-trout and salmon; the sea furnished codfish and seals, and large numbers of eider-ducks rested on the little islands where the river broadened to the sea. On one side of the comfortable modern farmhouse picturesque old outhouses formed a kind of square. In one the farm tools and the salmon nets and cages are kept; one served as sleeping quarters for the farm labourers, and another for the supply peat, and in another was an open fireplace with a high raised hearth of stone. Here, during the winter, the eider-down is cleansed. It is first placed in a large open cauldron over a hot fire in order to have the dried grasses and other refuse burned away. A flat plate of iron fits in the bottom, raising the down from the too intense heat of the fire. As it is stirred and turned quickly the foreign matter is destroyed before the down suffers. But this process only partially cleanses it. The dust, ashes and harder bits of grass stalks must now be removed. This is done by rubbing the down over stout thongs of sealskins, which are stretched from side to side on an oblong wooden frame about three feet long. The worker, sitting a short distance from the wall, tilts one end of the frame against it while the other rests in her lap. Then, taking a bunch of down in each hand, she scrubs it up and down across the thongs with an alternate motion. After this the down is looked over carefully, and every remaining bit of grass or dirt is removed by hand.

Many other species besides the eider-duck nest around the streams and lakes of the interior. When I left Iceland, mallards and pintails, grebes, harlequins, and scaup-ducks were prepared to migrate to warmer southern quarters. But the eider had no fears of the Polar winter. From the steamer we could see them well out at sea, tossing serenely on the waves. They were the last sight of Icelandic life that met our eyes as the shining glaciers of the Vatna Jokull, our last view of the island, sank slowly below the northern horizon.

Published in *Good Words*, October, 1897, 688–692.

Mythological Relics in Iceland

In the 10th century, when the old gods of Iceland made way for Christianity, they left behind them among the birds and flowers traces of their former reign in the island. To-day you will find the name-children of Balder, Thor and Frejya growing side by side with those of Our Lady and St. Peter. Here are "Odin's eyes," as the pretty blue speedwell is called; the violets of Tir (god of war) and "Frejya grass," or the spotted orchis (*Orchis maculata*), which in Norway is called "Mary's hand." This plant had several names which are also given to three other orchids. They all have the reputation of being efficacious as love charms, and are placed under the pillow to be 'dreamed on,' as our young girls dream on wedding cake. On sheltered, grassy roofs a large species of camomile is frequently seen. This is the Balders-brow, and its circle of shining white petals is a fit reminder of the White God, Balder the Beautiful. Several plants derive their names from the Virgin. The silvery gray Lady's Mantle or Mary's Mantle, as it is called in England, is the "Mariustakkr," in Iceland, and the "Marukaabe" in Norway. The buckbean, with its heavily fringed snowy petals is "Mary's-hair," and the gentians are called "Mariuvondr." The alpine daisy is "Jacob's-fifill," the white dryas "Petrssoley," and the large catchfly (*Saline maritima*) "Petrs-budda," or Peter's purse.

Many of the common names are merely translations of the Latin terms, while others, descended from the old Norse vernacular, are to be found, with little variation, in Norway, Iceland, Denmark, and in some instances, Scotland. A large proportion of Icelandic names are given for some peculiarity of flower and leaf. The Alpine Lady's Mantle is often called "Ljons-fotr" (Lion's-Foot), the Marsh marigold, "Hof-bladka" (hoof-leaf), and the herb-willow "Kotungs-lauf" (cow's-tongue leaf). The wild forget-me-not is "Katter-auga" (cat's eyes), and the Alpine lychnis has the pretty name of "Lios-beri" (light-bearer). The dainty rose-colored flowers which crown the slender bare stem, and the flat whirl of radical leaves suggest a candle and a little candlestick. All the buttercups, and a number of other flowers which in form resemble them, have the name of "Soley," with some descriptive prefix; the "Myra (marsh) Soley" being the Grass of Parnassus, the "Vatu-Soley" the water buttercup, the "Bla-(blue) Soley" the larger wild geranium or crane's bill, etc. With us the wild geranium is a pale magenta pink, but in Iceland, at Reyk-jahlid, it had a deep rich purple hue.

Iceland is said to possess more wonders than any other country of the same size. But, though grateful for flowers, geysers and volcanoes, it is the kindness of the simple peasants which has the first place in my memories.

Published in *Popular Science News*, April, 1898, 83.

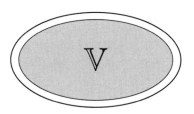

Scotland
Mid-1890's

Although Elizabeth Taylor only published one article about Scottish life, she spent much time in the area. Steamers such as the Tjaldur *sailed from Leith (Edinburgh) bound for the Faroe Islands and Iceland. The flowers and fish reminded her of what she saw near the Polar Sea, so she felt at home in Scotland. Thus, she resided occasionally in Edinburgh and vacationed at the home of her friend Florence Grieve in the Cheviot Hills.*

A Highland Ben

"Let the sandalwood perfume the seas,
Give the roses to Rhodes and to Crete,
We are more than content, if you please,
With the smell of bog-myrtle and peat."
                                A. LANG

Tales of Scottish life have made us familiar with "buts" and "bens"
but to few tourists is a closer acquaintance granted. It has fallen to
my lot to have special privileges; to spend seven weeks in a "ben-
end," owned by one of Lochiel's shepherds.

The inhabitants of our cottage are unequally distributed. The
"but-end" and the loft are occupied by the shepherd, Mr. MacNab
and his wife, four sons and daughters, a borrowed grandchild, three
cats and six collie dogs. But in my "ben" I dwell in solitary state. My
plaid is draped at the window for a curtain, a toilet table is impro-
vised from a chair, the bed is clean, and I have a bright, open fire of
peats. In fact, all the essentials of healthful living are here, and the air
is just as pure, as fragrant with bog-myrtle and heather as if I were
paying five dollars a day in a fashionable Highland hotel.

The supreme characteristic of "ben" life is repose. There is no
other house in our glen. No "tourist-bodies," or "glaiket Englishers,"
invade our precincts. During my walks abroad I encounter nothing
more formidable than a black-faced ewe. She pauses, snorts at me,
and then goes plunging down through the bracken, tearing off great
pieces that hang in wreaths about her shaggy neck, making her look
as if adorned for some ancient sacrificial procession. More rarely I
hear a furtive rustle under the birches among the heather, and find a
dainty little roebuck watching me with wide, startled eyes, horns
high, ready for flight; but realizing that the danger is not imminent,
since the intruder is only a gun-less woman.

At the foot of the glen, two miles away, is the post road. This is, for me, effectually barred by a Highland bull, with sharp, wide-spreading horns, and fierce eyes shining out of a shock of yellow hair. He parades up and down the road and keeps me well up the glen. In vain I recall a reassuring tale of three English sportsmen who, while shooting, met a Highland bull. Seized with a panic, they threw away their guns and fled, when a small maiden of six years emerged from the door of a shieling and, a twig in hand, drove way the animal, saying, reproachfully: "Ye bad beastie, to frighten the gentry-folk!"

Only once have I ventured from our glen into the tourist world. Then, perched on a hamper of bread in a grocer's cart, I made a pilgrimage to Glenfinnan, laughing to scorn my horned enemy as I passed him on the road. At Glenfinnan a monument marks the spot where Prince Charles awaited the gathering of the clans and unfurled the standard on the nineteenth of August, 1745. One turns, perforce, a Jacobite while in this romantic land of the Camerons. The whole neighborhood is full of reminiscences of the Young Chevalier–his landing at Moidart, his visits to country houses, his wretched life as a fugitive after the battle of Culloden. Near here Charles waited for Lochiel's answer to his summons, and an anxious time it must have been. As Sir Walter Scott says in his "Tales of a Grandfather," "Lochiel's decision was the signal for the commencement of the rebellion"; for it was generally understood at the time that there was not a chief in the Highlands who would have risen had Lochiel maintained his pacific purpose. Later, when at last the Prince had triumphed over the more prudent resolve of Lochiel, it was past this glen that the Chief of the Camerons marched at the head of his seven hundred followers.

The Lochiel of to-day upholds well the family name, but times have changed since that memorable "45." These wild mountains and glens of the Camerons are given up to deer and sheep. Portions of the shooting lands are rented, at high prices, to English noblemen, and bring in far more profit than the flocks in these days of keen competition with Australia and America.

This is emphatically the country of the black-faced sheep. Throughout the Highlands this ancient and native race is found to the exclusion of other species. The black-faces seem to thrive on high, rough land covered with heather, bracken and a scanty growth of grass. No hay is stored for them, and during the snows of winter they must work hard for a living. Agile, pretty creatures they are, with long, shaggy, white wool, black or mottled faces and large bright eyes. Even the ewes and lambs have horns, which give them a belligerent aspect. A great extent of this wild land is required to support a flock of sheep. I heard of an English farmer who asked a Scotch shepherd how many sheep were allowed to the acre. "Ah! mon," was the reply, "that's nae the way we count in the hielands; it's how mony acres to a sheep."

The flocks of Lochiel number about thirty thousand sheep, and twenty-five shepherds have the care of them. In our hirsel between three and four thousand feed during the year; but of this number over five hundred remain only a few weeks, preparatory to their sale in the autumn markets. These are lambs that are sent here from the neighboring hirsels to be "speaned," or weaned. They have just arrived, poor things, and the glen is vocal with their lamentations. A pretty sight they made coming up the glen, their black faces looking like so many polka dots against the mass of white fleeces, the anxious tired collies circling around them, barking hoarsely, while Mr. Mac-Nab and Aleck brought up the rear, shouting directions to the dogs. The lambs are big, fat fellows, as round as balls, but keeping their baby faces and baby voices. An old ewe led them, and it was pitiful to see them, tired as they were, trailing painfully after her wherever she went on the feeding grounds. Poor lammies! she is the only thing representing maternity that is left to them.

For these large flocks, each shepherd must keep several good, working collies. The Black-faces, however, need far less care than the border sheep. In the open feeding grounds of the southern counties the shepherds and dogs take a general survey of the hirsel twice a day. Here, especially where the flock is composed of "wedders" (wethers) once a week is considered sufficient during the summer time, and the dogs have little to do except at shearing time and "gatherings." They must, however, keep a watchful eye for trespassers on the neighboring grasslands which are reserved for the cows' hay.

I have heard an old shepherd declare that "collies ken most as much as folks." Their intelligence leads them, sometimes, into mischief—such as egg stealing. If our collies hear a hen cackling who has hidden her nest among the heather, they quietly note the place and, later, go there and eat the egg. Again, if a dog hears the crows cawing and hovering above the distant hills, he makes a mental note of the exact location, hoping to find a dead sheep. He knows that to touch a dead sheep is prohibited, so he waits until he thinks himself unobserved and then slinks off to the hills. Sheep eating is prohibited for three reasons: the skin, if much torn prevents the shepherd from ascertaining to which hirsel the animal belongs; damaged skins cannot be sold, and the shepherd is deprived of the meat for his own use. If the sheep has died recently, and has fallen a victim to "braxy" (a certain disease which runs a rapid course) the meat is salted and pickled for the shepherd's family. Disagreeable tho the idea seems of eating such meat, it does no harm if properly prepared, and it forms an important part of the shepherd's fare.

Occasionally a collie becomes a sheep killer. Convicted of only a single offence, sure retribution follows: he is shot at once. Long experience has proved that a reform cannot be effected, and the murderer will lead other collies into evil ways. As a rule the collies love their work and are trained easily; but sometimes a young dog with all the advantages of "good family" and instruction, is utterly useless as a sheep dog. We have one here, a handsome fellow, who was elected to lead a life of ease. He refuses, graciously but firmly, to do a stroke of work; he will not "run," will not obey the slightest command; in short, he is incorrigible, and is to be shot before winter. As I am told this, he looks earnestly from one face to another, apprehension clouding his fine eyes; for he knows well his sins of omission. It is interesting to see the contract between this sybarite and the puppy of the household, a beautiful black-and-white collie, eight months old. He is fairly bubbling over with enthusiasm, anxious to learn, impatient of the restraint which forbids him to be trained before he is a year old, while he still "lacks judgment." And he certainly has not arrived at months of discretion. He is affectionate, impulsive, and always in disgrace; he bothers the staid older dogs, and gets bitten; he tumbles about underfoot, and gets kicked; and life must be, to him, one long disillusion. The "ben" is forbidden ground; but sometimes, if the door stands open, I see the collie crouching in the doorway. Then he pretends to be asleep, or turns his head aside with a fine air of indifference, and all the time he is worming himself nearer and nearer until he reaches my knee, and, laying on it his charming head, rolls up his eyes in a most irresistible fashion. But discipline must be maintained. As Mrs. McNab says, "It winna do to be always clappin' (patting) up the collies; they will no be respectin' you, and will no work so fine."

Certainly our collies have little "clappin'," or indulgence. Once a day only they are fed, on boiled potatoes and milk, with a handful of oatmeal thrown in. Each dog has his own saucepan or kettle, and never thinks of touching his neighbor's food. In a patient row they stand, with dripping chops and wishful eyes, watching Mrs. McNab as she prepares their meal. Now and then the puppy gives a smothered whine; but he is silenced by a growl from one of the older dogs; for they feel that the puppy's training in "manners" devolves upon them.

The dogs' food, meager tho it is, taxes seriously the shepherd's slender resources. His wages are seldom more than ninety dollars a year. In addition, he has free use of a cottage and a small piece of land, six and a half bolls of oatmeal (equivalent to 640 pounds) a year, and an extra allowance of meal if the annual sheep-dipping, with its congregation of shepherds, is held on his hirsel. The Factor allows them to keep chickens, a cow, a pig, and a few sheep that are classed as "pets," and permitted to graze with the main herd. Peats are to be had in abundance, potatoes and a few vegetables are raised on the garden plot, and a little grass land near the house furnishes hay for the cow. The "braxy" mutton is a great resource, and trout fishing, in some neighboring burn, is allowed on some hirsels. The skin of dead sheep and lambs are perquisites of the shepherds, and traveling tinkers give a trifle for them in money or barter.

A shepherd's wages are fixed by custom throughout the country, and a proprietor cannot raise them at will; but he can, if generously inclined, aid his herds materially by allowing a little more latitude in the keeping of "pet" sheep and an additional cow or pig.

The first years of married life are very hard for a shepherd's wife. The babies are often numerous, no servant is kept, the care of the home live stock devolves upon her, with the making of cheese and butter. But as the children grow up and "flit" from home, life becomes easier for the mother; one of the girls remains at home to help with the housework, while the others go into service; the boys secure places as gillies, grooms and gamekeepers, or go to the cities as clerks or traveling agents. Often a son assists his father and in time succeeds to the whole charge of the hirsel. In the neighboring glens several children may be settled into little cottages of their own, and there is much visiting in times of leisure.

One finds a true Highland welcome when away from the tourist route. Food is prepared at once for the visitor, without regard to time of day or the family's meals. I noticed that whenever I hear a new voice in the "but-end," the singing of the teakettle and the rattling of teacups follow promptly, and the whole family sit down to "a cup of kindness" with the new arrival.

But of course there are periods of grave anxiety in a shepherd's life—winter storms, sickness among the sheep, losses at lambing and from foxes.

As a rule, the hill shepherds are intelligent, respectable men, fond of reading, fairly well posted on the questions of the day, sober and temperate, except an occasional "tasting" at clipping or dipping times. Their lives are spent in the pure, bracing air of these beautiful Highland glens, and they are spared the thousand-and-one petty cares and distractions of city life.

Our glen, in its main features, resembles the scores of other glens that diverge from the lochs north of the Caledonian Canal. Rising high on either side are rugged mountains of metamorphic rocks, their bare upper slopes glistening like diamonds in the sun. Bright-hued mosses and lichen creep up to meet the upper ridges, and below grow the fields of purple heather. Then come scattered remnants of the old Scotch fir forests, their red trunks and twisted branches rearing above the light green birches. And then comes our burn, which has an unwritable, unpronounceable, Gaelic name, full of fs, gs, and hs.

Our burn's great charm is its variety; there are golden shallows, little waterfalls, swift rapids, dark gorges and deep black pools surrounded by precipitous rocks. Rowan trees, with their bright scarlet berries, line the banks, together with a luxuriant growth of heather and bracken. In pleasant weather the burn is a modest little stream; but when it is in "spate," when "the waters cam doon," it turns to a roaring, raging torrent. Its dark, foam-streaked waters surge so high that the drooping rowan branches are tossed up and down in the flood, the bright berries flashing in the foam.

If our burn were on a tourist route in England there would be rustic seats and tea houses by its side, with tea and buttered muffins at ninepence; or hot water furnished to a party at sixpence. As it is, the clegs (horseflies) and I have it all to ourselves. Many hours I have spent by our burn. We are far away from the "fleshers," eggs become wearisome as a steady diet, and I find it necessary to go a-fishing for food. The burn trout will not take the artificial fly, and I am reduced to bait fishing. I sally forth, armed with six hooks, on which are arranged six worms. When these are gone, with groans loud and deep, I manage to put on two or three more worms, after a fashion. This fishing is toilsome work; midges and clegs assail me in swarms, and, what with slapping at them, putting on worms and taking off fish, I return home with my countenance in a gruesome state, weary with toiling up and down steep banks and through bogs, vowing that I will fish no more. A useless vow! The kelpie that haunts the Black Pool has laid me under a spell, and the next day finds me suffering at the burn again. I catch small brown "trouties," but beautiful sea trout are often taken when the burn is in spate. Sea trout are fastidious creatures, prefer their worms fresh and wiggly, live in pools difficult of access and "take" best during storms. How I have toiled for sea trout, getting drenched and tired, bringing home only brown trouties, and ashamed to meet on my return the scornful eyes of the youngest boy of our household—an accomplished sea trouter. Only one sea trout had I caught, and that was due to the kindness of Mrs. MacNab; she went with me one stormy day to a dangerous pool and baited my hook for me. Sitting on the brink of the high, slippery rocks, I fished the deep pool below, Mrs. MacNab bracing herself behind, clutching my skirts and wailing: "Oh! for ony's sake, tak' keer! It's a sair place, whatefer!" But I caught my sea trout, with Mrs. MacNab's fresh, wiggly worm; he was a beauty, and I think my kind hostess was even more pleased than I was.

The prevailing color of the Highland glens is red—the tints and hues of red. We have, in America, far more variety in color and species during the late summer months. I miss the glory of our golden-rod, the purples, blues and whites of our asters, closed and fringed gentians, and the yellow of our wild sunflowers. But for acres of wonderful, rich color, I have seen nothing to compare with the heather of these remote glens. The tourist along the well-beaten tracks knows little of it. At last I realized what is meant by "heather mixture." Among the trees, where the old unburned heather grows waist high, the pink and purple hues shine out against a dark background of ashy gray twigs, twisty brown stems and deep bronze greens. It is a royal sight—these masses of rich, glowing color, in the shadows of the fragrant birches and stately Scotch firs. But for unbroken fields of bloom you must visit the sunny, open hillsides where the heather has been cut two years before to improve the pasture. It is about six inches high, the stems pale green in color, and the racimes crowded full of blossoms. This is the *Calluna vulgaris*, the common "ling" of Norway, Iceland, and the Faroe Islands, the species that gives the splendid color to the Scottish mountains from the middle of July until the latter part of September. Two other species grow with it, in less abundance; one is the *Erica tetralix*, with pale pink blossoms and blue green foliage, and the other *Erica cinerea*, with long spikes of deep crimson or purple flowers.

Already the color of the hills is fading, and I must soon leave the shelter of the glen. Mrs. MacNab, neglecting her butter making, has gone in search of the rare white heather which brings good luck to its possessor. Provided with a besom of this magic flower, I shall leave my peaceful "ben" and venture reluctantly into the world of tourist bodies.

Published in *The Independent* (Boston), December 24, 1896, 1757–1758.

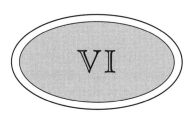

The Faroe Islands
1895–1919

Travelers have often visited the Faroe Islands for a few hours en route to Iceland as Elizabeth Taylor did in 1895. On her return trip to the Faroes after visiting the eider-ducks in Iceland, she decided to remain a while longer in Tórshavn, the capital city, and catch a later steamer back to Scotland. Something about the Faroe Islands intrigued Miss Taylor and the chance meeting on shipboard with Professor William Paton Ker gave her the inspiration to focus on the Faroe Islands.

In 1900, armed with a contract for a series of articles for Forest and Stream *magazine (four of the five articles are reprinted in this Part VI), Elizabeth Taylor returned for a five year stay. Summer was the traditional time for tourists to visit the Faroe Islands, although even in the most clement season storms and surf could make inter-island travel next to impossible. Elizabeth Taylor refers often to changed plans and disappointments due to weather; especially the four days which became a sixteen-day ordeal of puffins with their skins on when she visited Stóra Dímun island.*

Miss Taylor spent a summer in the Faroe Islands in 1906, returning to Scotland that October, and made a second summer visit in 1913. In May of 1914 she planned another long summer sojourn, but the first World War intervened and she was forced to remain on the Islands until 1919 when peace had finally come.

As James Taylor Dunn describes in his "Introduction," Elizabeth Taylor stayed at the homes of many Faroese families who became dear friends: Hans Kristoffer, the Heilmanns, and the Kruses. While at first she was only a summer visitor, learning, sketching, and recording Faroese life, Miss Taylor shortly became an observer-participant, taking part in weddings, baptisms, and hosting parties. It should be noted that when Miss Taylor wrote these articles she used Danish place names, but, for the convenience of readers, these names have been changed to their Faroese equivalents.

FÆRÖERNE.

Danske Mil.

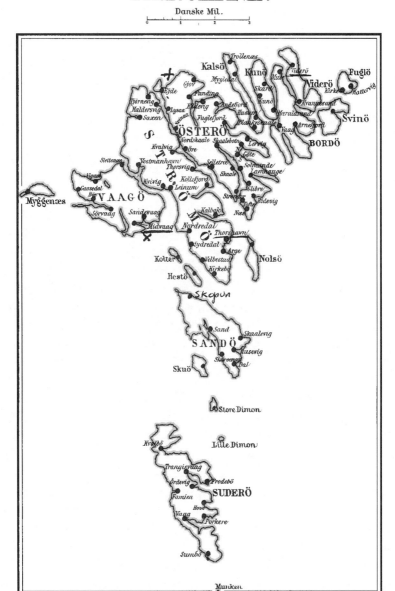

This is Elizabeth Taylor's own map of the Faroe Islands. It gives city names in Danish and is annotated with places she most often stayed: Midvaag (Miðvágur), Thorshavn (Tórshavn), Ejde (Eiði), and Viderö (Viðareiði).

To the Bird Islands

"Some high rocks arising out of the Wild Sea; high hills of hard
Stone, strangely divided from each other by deep and rapid
Streams of Water. . . . It cannot well be expressed with a pen how
fierce the Sea is, nor to what a height it raiseth itself."

LUCAS DEBES, 1670

When we left Scotland for the Faroe Islands we sailed into a
nor'easter, a three days' storm, which was still blowing in fitful gusts
when the islands came in sight. On the left we could see dimly
through the driving mists black crags with surf dashing high, long
sweeps of barren fjelds, the bold promontories of Suðuroy, Sandoy,
Skúvoy, Vágar, the two Dímuns, and Streymoy—seven out of the
twenty-two islands which form the Faroe group. Then came Nólsoy
on the right, giving shelter from the northeast winds, and we cast
anchor in the open fjord (it could hardly be called a harbor) before
Tórshavn.

I knew and loved of old this little capital of 1,200 souls, but it was
looking its worst that morning, and I felt sorry for Montagu Villiers,
the new English consul and his family as they saw for the first time
their future home. Snow and sleet were whirling down from the
fjelds, and the only really green places were the sodded house roofs
where the grass turns first in the spring, owing to the warmth below.
Then came the pale green of the home patches or "infields" and then
the wild "outfields," gray and seared as in mid-winter. As I looked
over the water I saw Louis Bergh the head schoolmaster of all the
Faroes waving his hand from a high-prowed Faroe boat, and shouting "Velkommen!" and soon I was with old friends in his comfortable cottage.

One must expect changes in a metropolis after almost five years
time, and I notice with regret that the city fathers have blasted some
reefs and boulders out of the principal lane, have trimmed the grass,

and a few cottages and fish houses have been erected. But the ducks still sleep peacefully in the middle of the lanes (there are no horses in Tórshavn) and the hens hop from roof to roof, scratching among the long grasses. The city lamps have been unhooked and sent to the Blikkenslagers for repairs, there to remain until darkness returns with autumn nights. We are in latitude sixty-two degrees forty minutes, and all night long I can hear the titlarks trilling and the curlews skirling in the outfields.

Small as it is, Tórshavn is by far the largest settlement in the Faroes. Here live governor, judge, sheriff, head schoolmaster, and head doctor. Here in the summer is the local parliament; British and Danish gunboats visit these waters to look after troublesome trawlers, and many tourists come on shore when the Iceland-bound steamers pause here for a few hours. Iceland is fast becoming popular for summer outings, but the Faroes, fortunately, are not yet considered "worthwhile," the tourists judging of their attractions by the surroundings of Tórshavn, which are comparatively monotonous.

Since my last visit a tiny steamer, the *Smyril*, has begun to ply among the islands. Its goings and comings are most erratic; its time table distracting, but for many excursions it is safer and cheaper than the usual mode of Faroe traveling—eight men and a boat. After three weeks in Tórshavn, I left one stormy morning for Miðvágur,

The harbor at Tórshavn. Photographed circa 1900 by Elizabeth Taylor.

on Vágar, one of the western islands. The schoolmaster borrowed two large Normal school pupils and a codfish boat; the codfish were taken out and I was put in, and we started for the little *Smyril,* which was plunging out in the fjord. Only desperation made it possible for me to swing myself out of our tossing boat and up the loosely swinging ladder. There is no wharf or quay in all the islands. I reflected that there are twenty-two in number—seventeen inhabited—and my ambition to see them all oozed rapidly away.

It was too stormy to remain on deck, but from time to time I put my head above the stairs. There was little to be seen; only flying scud, vague giant shapes looming up in the mist with cloud wreaths streaming from their rocky summits, all bleak and desolate, no sign of human life but at one place, where a long strip of green hillside and a tiny stone church marked the site of Kirkjubøur. So we went on for three hours; then suddenly we felt happier down below, and found we had turned into Miðvágur harbor, and already boats were putting out from shore for passengers and freight.

The head schoolmaster had previously sent a letter of introduction to a certain kóngsbondi or King's peasant, known among his friends as Hans Kristoffer. But no one came forward when I landed to greet me, though one-half the population surveyed me from doorways and behind stone walls and around corners. So I asked to see a shopkeeper who I knew spoke excellent English, and he arriving, promptly dragged forth Hans Kristoffer from a group of men nearby. He had been watching me all the time, knew who it was and had been expecting me for a week. These are Faroe manners, and do not denote unfriendliness. The stranger is expected to make all advances. Herr Hans Kristoffer now intimated that I was welcome to his house, and we started off at once, he paddling along lightly and silently in his Faroe moccasins.

My host is a type of the best class of Faroe peasant. His family has held crown lands (paying a small annual rent) for many generations. The house is a story and a half cottage, grass-sodded and painted with tar. At the "but" end, as it would be called in Scotland, are the living rooms, an outer kitchen with earth floor, where the cooking is done and where cats, dogs, and chickens wander in and out; then a general family room, where they sit, eat, and spin; small bedrooms open out of this and others are in the loft above. In the "ben" end is a guest sitting room, rarely used, and a tiny guest bedroom. The floor is bare, with unpainted boards, there is a sofa, table, cupboard, chairs, a queer old stove bearing the date 1724 and decorated in raised iron work with crowns, garlands, warriors, and portraits of Frederick II and his Queen. This is built into the wall and the fuel is put in by a door out in the entry. There are many photographs of family and friends, a lithograph of Martin Luther and two from Rembrandt's etchings, bright flowers in the windows, and Nottingham curtains. In the bedroom is a narrow, short box bed, with feathers to lie upon and a large feather puff above.

In these two rooms a foreign guest is expected to live. It is a mark of especial friendliness if he is invited to the "but". Here kind Frú Hans waits upon the guest, serving sweet soup for dinner, probably frikkadellir of fresh pounded codfish and whipped cream and sago. One must not expect to fare so well in all Faroe hamlets. The good eating here is due to a combination of generous hospitality and a knowledge of Danish cookery, acquired from several wives of Danish pastors.

A Faroe village is not a model of hygiene. There is a superfluity of cods' heads, whales' vertebrae, and birds' wings; there are piles of manure and garbage, and pools of stagnant water close to the houses, and unpleasant strips of last year's whale meat hanging from the eaves. One is glad to hurry through, breathing as little as possible, to the sweet grass and sea-scented air beyond. But here Hans Kristoffer's guest room looks out on the prettiest little garden in the Faroes, and here he fights frost in summer and gales at all times of the year.

Aside from the few small trees which have been planted in gardens, there is not one in all the Faroes; not even a bush breaks the outline of the hills. The climate must have changed since the exiled Vikings first came to the Faroes in the tenth century, for many fragments of birch and juniper, of good size, are found in peat bogs. The great changes of temperature and the fierce gales, and not the severity of the cold in winter, destroy the trees. Fortunately, the supply of peat is abundant and good, and the cutting and drying of it is the all-important work of the early summer months.

A Faroe peasant must of necessity be an all-around man—a farmer in a small way, a peat worker, fisherman, sailor, oarsman, mountain climber, a shepherd occasionally, a carpenter, and odd jobber. In all these ways combined he ekes out a simple living, sometimes doing little for days at a time, then working steadily all day and far into the night, the weather determining his activity. The uncertainty of his work and his isolation from the outside world has made the Faroe man the least punctual of mortals and this trait the foreign traveler finds at times most trying. But no one can be quicker, braver, more resolute than he in time of danger.

Think what it means to be a "flink fjeldmand"—a clever cliff man, going down with the line after seafowl, suspended in midair, crawling along ledges hundreds of feet above the sea, ledges that crumble, with rocks above that fall. I heard here of a father and son who went to the northern cliffs of Vágar for guillemots' eggs. They descended to a narrow ledge just wide enough for a man to stand, except in one place, where it jutted out, forming a shelf about five feet wide. As the men gathered eggs they piled them up there, until a large quantity had been collected. Just then some small stones, always a signal of danger, began to fall from the cliffs above. The father succeeded in climbing up a little way to a point where he could command a view of the fjelds. Suddenly he called out sharply, "Throw yourself on the eggs!" Like a flash the boy flung himself forward, and an instant later a great boulder crashed down, breaking away in its fall the ledge on which he had been standing.

This island, Vágar, does not rank among the best of bird islands. There are some fine cliffs for auks and guillemots, but as a rule the highest rocks face northward, an unfavorable exposure for bird colonies. Mykines, the most western of the Faroe group, has especial advantages from its isolation and its precipitous coast. One can go there only in a kind of weather requiring such a combination of smiling circumstances and promise of future blessings that visitors to Mykines are few and far between. One makes no important engagements for the future when one goes to Mykines.

Since beginning this letter, I have left Miðvágur and am now at Bøur, the nearest hamlet to Mykines, on the western coast of Vágar. The morning I started was so beautiful that it was hard to find a guide and bearers for my luggage. We have few warm, dry, sunny days in Faroes, and when one does come every man, woman, and child is seized with preternatural activity, and falls to work cod fishing, bird catching, peat cutting and piling, weeding, washing the new wool, dyeing, spinning yarn, churning, washing the family pattens, clothes, and milk pans in the brook, all in addition to the usual farm and housework. The No. 3 babies are tending the No. 1 babies, while the No. 2 babies are marching up and down in the sun, dragging by a string their "horses"—a small whale's vertebra.

Under such busy circumstances it is customary for the would-be traveler to go to the "Skydsskaffer," an official whose business it is to secure guides or oarsmen. In the Faroes every man is required to serve in this way in lieu of military service in Denmark. There is no fixed tariff of wages, and the men serve in turn. No one officially summoned by the Skydsskaffer can refuse to go under penalty of a fine. But why ask the Skydsskaffer to drag a stout young man whose labor is of value from his work in the peat fields when a Faroe grandfather thinks nothing of taking forty pounds on his back, supported by a broad woolen band around the forehead, and trotting off with it across the fjelds? So these matters are often arranged privately, and those who can best be spared go with the traveler. In this case, Hans Kristoffer succeeded in securing an old man and two boys, and we started for Bøur.

It was not a difficult journey—one mile by land to Sørvágur Lake or vatn, two by boat to the northern end, two over the hills to Sørvágur village and two by fjord to Bøur. The trail was what is called here "a good way"—that is, it was not over high hills or watery marshes. Such trifles as stones, boggy spots, and hillocks are not considered worthy of mention.

We passed quickly through Sørvágur village and made no calls. A scourge of typhus, brought in a ship from Iceland, had ravaged the little place and there had been many deaths. The few people we saw looked wan and haggard. But the stagnant pools and piles of refuse near the houses still remained. I waited on a grassy hillside while a boat was brought from the other side of the fjord. It stranded, being low tide, some distance from the shore. But the grandfather was not at all put out. He took off his moccasins, rolled up his knee breeches, waded ashore, picked me up without a word and marched with me through the waves, carried all my traps to the boat, and soon we were on our way to Bøur.

I had pictured Bøur as quite a village, and find only half a dozen houses huddled together between the fjord and the fjeld. There is nothing to do but watch the beautiful view and the eider ducks and talk with the men of Bøur about the chances of my going to Mykines. That island is only nine miles out, but the seas are big, the currents exceptionally strong, and there are sudden surprises of fog, surf, and squalls. There is but one place where the island can be reached, and that is possible only under certain conditions. When the tide is favorable, sea calm, no surf, barometer high and rising, air clear, and a tendency to light northeast breezes, that is true "Mykines six-man weather." It had been gently intimated to me that when eight men are thought necessary, such a coward as I had better stay "to hum." I am sure I do not wish to go in "eight-man weather." "One small boy weather," if there was such a thing, would suit me best. So here I wait at Bøur, seeing across the sea the misty cliff walls of my "desired haven."

Published in *Forest and Stream. The Journal of Rod and Gun,* March 2, 1901, 162–163.

To Mykines in Six-Man Weather

I might have waited at Bøur for several weeks for the right kind of weather in which to go to Mykines, but fortune smiled upon me. After only two days of Western storm and fog, the wind changed to the northeast; the men of Bøur took counsel together, looked at the glass, consulted the almanac, watched the surf line on the other islands, and decided it was "Mykines six-man weather," and I could go with the turn of the tide.

Never, not even in Venice during my first ride in a gondola, have I felt so much like a personage as when I started in a large eight-oared boat with six sturdy men, half the adult population of Bøur. All were clad in golden brown, homespun coats and mixed brown and gray knee breeches. These have a row of brass buttons on the outer leg seam, but are always left unbuttoned, and display a bright, striped pair of garters and long, soft, brown stockings. On the feet are moccasins of sheep skin, bound around the ankles with thongs of knitted white wool; on their heads the Faroe "Higoa," or long, soft cap, of hand-woven cloth, dark blue with red stripes, or stripes of black and blue. This has a soft, gathered crown which droops over the ear or rests on the brow. The men had that calm, far-seeing look in their blue eyes that one sees often in sailors and prairie dwellers, and full, fair beards. After the manner of Faroe folk, all talked together and all the time.

I noted with satisfaction their powerful sweep at the long oars, and the perfect time they kept. But the big waves soon reduced me to a humble frame of mind, and I clutched tight hold of the gunwale, and would gladly have exchanged my state for a flat-bottomed boat on a pond. Once under the cliffs of an island, there was a conflict of wind and time called a "roost" in the Shetland dialect, a battering kind of squall beat down upon us from the summit, and the men called out to me that I was not to be afraid, and that it would soon be over. Then out into the open sea we passed with beautiful views of the mountains and precipices of Vágar, their bare rocks glowing in the afternoon sun. The first Mykinesers we met were hundreds of puffins floating on the waves and watching us with the utmost unconcern; then, as we reached them, in a twinkling, up flashed their little red feet, and not a puffin was to be seen.

It was not long before we reached the eastern promontory of Mykines, but we had to go to the extreme western end, and in all that way there was not one place where a shipwrecked man could land and climb the cliffs. A cruel-looking coast it was, of brown, red, and ash-gray trap rock, from 150 to 1,300 feet in height, capped and wreathed with cloud mists. Thousands of auks, gulls and guillemots, puffins, kittiwakes, and cormorants flashed back and forth, looking in the far distance like motes in a sunbeam.

At last we reached the western end of the island, and made apparently for the face of the cliff; but it opened to a wide rift, with jagged ledges on either side, over which the surf was surging and falling back with an ugly, sucking sound. A line of green water lay between, and in we went on that line. There was no surf that day, and the wind was northeast, so we could come close to the rocks. Then one of my men took me out, gripped my hand fast, and slowly towed me upward over the seaweed-covered rocks, then the bare ones, then to rocky slopes, where the boats in summer are kept, then to higher ones to the winter boathouses, then to steps hewn from the solid rock, and so to the village path. I have never seen a more desolate place, or one which showed so forcibly the height and might of the winter seas.

Mykines village, as I found, is not a cheerful place. It has perhaps 150 inhabitants, and there are no houses elsewhere on the island. Around the rocky bed of a brook the cabins are built, and sticks and stones and bones lie about in confusion. There is no attempt at gardening and grass plots. The summer is cold and short, the winds are strong; potatoes barely grow, and are small and soggy; the few little patches of barley never fully ripen. But wherever the ground is drained and cleared of stones, there the grass grows thick and long; the one sweet and gracious thing in Mykines—fragrant as sweet clover and adorned with pink catchfly, daisies, and saxifrage. Good grass and puffins are the compensations which Mother Nature bestows upon her Mykineser children.

I am staying with Herr Joen Abrahamsen, one of the chief men of the village. The first evening after my arrival he and his brother Paol went with me to see the nearest bird cliffs; first to neighboring outfields, where thousands of puffins have their nests in burrows between great boulders, and in grassy hummocks. Others live in grassy ledges on the cliffs, and in dangerous, grassy slopes, and a rope is necessary with which to reach their nests. I pointed to a hole, and asked Herr Paol if he thought there was a nest in it. "We will soon see," he replied, and lying down flat he inserted a long arm. A puffin was at home. I heard Herr Paol's exclamation as he was bitten, and an instant later he wriggled up, holding a struggling bird, the prettiest thing, with snow-white breast, clean, little, shining feet, and a big bill, which was a "symphony" of violets and green-blues and soft reds. I admired it much, and stroked its back, when he wrung its neck before my horrified eyes. Of course I knew it is a puffin's fate to have its neck wrung, and I think I ate that one next day, and will probably eat thirty or forty more before I leave; but there is a sentiment about one's first puffin.

Then we went to see the homes of the *havhestur* or gray gulls, climbing a long, steep, grassy slope, where Herr Paol thoughtfully walked below me so I could step by the side of his big feet; and we lay down and put our heads over a sharply sliced-off cliff and looked over and down ledges where the beautiful gray and white birds sat on their nests. The fog was milling up from the sea I don't know how far below, and the sun struggling through the clouds turned it into a glory of fantastic wreaths. Then to the guillemot and "rita" or kittiwake cliffs, where hundreds of guillemots sat bolt upright in rows like china figures on a chimney piece. The dainty little kittiwakes were nesting above them and making an astonishing noise, quite at variance with their pretty looks and manners. "He makes as much noise as a rita of the rocks" is an expressive Faroe proverb, applied to a noisy, talkative man. Having taken a general survey of the neighboring bird cliffs, so I could know where and how to go another day, we all returned to the village, and I went to sleep under a feather puff containing what felt like ten pounds of puffin feathers, and had the most awful dreams of rolling down grassy slopes and going plop into the sea; of sitting on narrow ledges that crumbled and gave way beneath my weight; of catching at things that snapped in my hands, and having boulders whiz past my ears. Indeed every night I fell off of something in my dreams, and have come to dread these inevitable nocturnal adventures. After a week on Mykines one longs to be on a flat and flowery Western prairie and walk miles and miles in a straight line. I told my fears and dreams one day to an old sea dog of a Mykineser who was sitting on a cliff, and he assented sadly. I found afterward that I had better have confided in any other man, for this one man had one son killed on the cliffs a fortnight before, and another drowned at sea in April.

A fine set of men are the Mykinesers: hardy, athletic, brave, skilled cliff men, daring boatmen, proud and reserved to strangers, cheerful and very talkative among themselves. Their power of speech was a marvel to me; they had known each other intimately all their lives, are often weeks in the summer time and months in the winter time without one new idea coming from the outside world, and yet the stream of words can flow unceasingly for eighteen hours out of the twenty-four. It was, to me, one of the wonders of Mykines.

The young girls, who work out-of-doors a good deal, are bright and healthy, but most of the married women look worn and sad. Their anxiety about the men must weigh upon them. Storms are sudden and violent; the coast and the landing dangerous. Boats have gone out for a day's fishing, have been obliged to take refuge in Bøur or Sørvágur, and for weeks and sometimes months the women did not know if their men folk were alive or dead. Not long ago a boat's crew of men stayed three months and a half in Sørvágur before possible weather came, and the standard of a man of Mykines regarding the weather is not yours or mine. Bodies of men drowned in these waters are seldom found. But last spring when a boat was lost the fishing net drifted to the Vágar shore to tell the tale.

There is a little church here painted white, and sodded with turf on the roof. Service is held thrice a year, between April and October. A winter visit is not to be expected. Last autumn a young Mykineser was so inconsiderate as to plan to be married in November, so the Pastor ventured to go. But a great storm arose, the boat was crushed in landing, and the occupants had a narrow escape. As for the dead, the people sing a psalm or two at their graves, and there they lie until the Pastor's next visit, when a funeral sermon is preached and an "Earth Casting" takes place in the churchyard. No attention whatever is paid to the graves; there are no flowers, no grass, no headstones—only little posts with the numbers of their record in the church books. Over all, and growing high above the churchyard wall, is a rank growth of Angelica, and a bare spot where it has been cut away marks a new-made grave. Every Sunday the people meet in the church, and Herr Abrahamsen reads a sermon, and the people sing psalms. These sermons are appointed to last two years. At the end of that time it is supposed that the first sermons have been forgotten, and Herr Abrahamsen begins over again. Bare floors, bare bench seats, a little white-covered altar, a beautiful antique brass basin of fine repoussée work, large enough to hold triplets, two contribution boxes with handles, marked respectively "For the school" and "For the poor of the land"—this is all the church contains. In the entry I saw a little shovel with long, carved handle, which the Pastor uses in the burial service, casting earth on the graves three times, and saying, "From earth art thou come; to earth shalt thou go; from earth shalt thou rise again."

The school house is close to the church. We are having the June holidays of two weeks' duration, to enable the children to help in drying and bearing the peat. But if it is a stormy day, from my window I see the schoolmaster Samuel Niclassen (who keeps bachelor's hall above the school room) open the casement and toot on a nondescript tooter. Then, since the children cannot work, they must go to school and study. What would our young Americans think of such an arrangement?

In August they will have another two weeks of these so-called holidays, when haymaking begins.

As I stand by the churchyard gate I can see the small boys and girls climbing and descending the hills with the peat racks on their shoulders; their chattering sounds like a chorus of titlarks. They will grow up and emulate the conversational powers of their forebears. They are sturdy little men and women, and as they wear the same costume as the grown-ups, I am often deceived while watching the fjelds, thinking that a little boy not far away is a grown man at a greater distance. I would gladly spend much time on the peat moors, but there ranges a bull - an ungracious animal, quick to note and disapprove a "fremmand folk" or stranger. It is silly to be afraid of Faroe bulls, so my Faroe friends tell me, and then they forget me in talk among themselves.

"Do you remember that time Sigmund was chased to the edge of that precipice, and hung on as long as he could and then dropped?"

"Was he killed?" I gasp.

"No, not quite; he did live, but he was pretty badly smashed." And then they go on, "Was it last year that man was killed on Fugloy?"

"No; you're thinking of that case on Kunoy; Fugloy's was year before last," etc.

It was a beautiful, calm morning at eight o'clock today, and eight boats went to sea for fishing. Then in about two hours a great surf arose; no wind, but probably the after effects of a storm at sea. Back came the boats, hurrying to get to shore before it grew too strong; but it was too quick for them, and they retreated to the open sea beyond the reefs of the rift. And there, while waiting for a lull, the men sang the homecoming song. I could hear their voices rising above the roar of the sea:

> "Praise be to God,
> Father in Heaven,
> Who all things has created,
> And praise His Son forevermore,
> Who saves us all from danger;
> And praise be to the Holy Ghost,
> Who gives us of His Grace;
> This praise has been before all time,
> And shall be without end
> God us His mercy send."

Then the first boat charged in, neared the rocks, found it could not land, whirled back to the lea of a cliff; there watched the waves and rushed once more. Men on shore were waiting to help, the crew sprang out, all seized the boat, some being carried from their feet and dragged in the water, and it was swept on and over a ledge into a pool just as a mighty wave crashed down. One after another of the boats came in, the surf increasing, all on shore helping, watching the seas and giving the signal when to dash for the rocks. Then the women came trooping down with hot coffee, and the men sat down quietly, drenched as they were, and cleaned the fish they had caught.

Published in *Forest and Stream. The Journal of Rod and Gun,* October 26, 1901, 323.

Stormbound On Stóra Dímun

A tossing gray sea and fog driven by a north wind; that is what I saw when I woke early in Hvalba on Suðuroy Island and looked out my window. "No going to Stóra Dímun today," I thought, and was preparing for another nap when I heard a knock and a voice through the keyhole saying, "The boat will soon be ready."

"But can we go to Stóra Dímun in such weather?" I asked, surprised.

"Beautiful Dímun weather!" pronounced the voice with emphasis. "Two fishing boats have just come in and they say there is no surf at the southern end. We can 'make it' well."

Now there are two things I have learned in the Faroes: that "good weather" means what is safe, not what is pleasant; and that Faroe men know more about skies and seas than I do. So I meekly put on all the warm clothes I possessed, and in an hour we were on our way. The boat was an *áttamannafar*—an eight-man boat, built on the same lines as those of the old Viking ships, pointed and high, curving at both ends, the oars narrow and held in place by strips of whale skin. I had a crew of picked men warranted to contain no alcohol in any form. All wore the traditional Faroe dress and on the head the roomy hugva was convenient for holding black bread, tobacco, a piece of dried fish or dried mutton. I too wore hide moccasins fastened with purple thongs. Red and green are also allowed for women, but never white. Over them a pair of sandals knit of coarsest yarn with ribbed soles. Thus arrayed, my vanity was not flattered, but I could stand easily on treacherous paths and sea rocks slippery with tang.

Before we reached the open sea, one by one my men had put on their oilskins, and all was ready for the nine miles that lay before us and Stóra Dímun. It seemed rather dreadful to plunge on in the thick fog, steering only by compass, but there were no steamers or tugs to cut us down. The head sea was rough, and the boat proved how well it was shaped to ride the waves. Then, after more than two hours, came a change. We were in a confusion of broken water that bore down upon us from all sides, shaking and worrying the boat, and flinging it with a jerk to the top of the white-crested surges. The men stopped talking and worked with watchful eyes, and the foreman called out, "don't be afraid, thou blessed," a common form of address among the Faroe peasants. "We will soon be past. It is the stream running against the wind." Through the mist came a muffled clamor of seafowl, and the glint of white wings. It was strange to look up from the depth of a gray hollow and see scores of sleek heads peering down upon us, guillemots, puffins, and kittiwakes. Then the sea suddenly grew quieter, we passed to oily sucking water, the white fog before us darkened, and I saw above us a gray, perpendicular wall, the cliffs of Stóra Dímun. The summit was hidden in clouds, but, as I looked upward, I could make out row on row of white spots shining through the mists—the breasts of the guillemots on the cliff ledges.

There are two places where a landing can be made in good weather on Stóra Dímun—one a cleft in the rocks on the western coast, whence one must scramble over big boulders for a half mile under the cliffs to the ascent on the southwestern side; the other, a flat rock only a stone's throw from the ascent, where it is possible to land when the sea is quiet or the wind has blown some time from the north. We landed there without difficulty, the men hauled the boat up, made all secure, I kilted my skirts, and we began to climb.

The way up Stóra Dímun is neither easy nor safe. In many places a fall means certain death, and no one subject to dizziness should attempt it. But the difficulties have been exaggerated. Anyone of ordinary activity, who is able to keep a cool head, can make the ascent if he wears Faroe footgear, has a good helper behind, and takes thought for each footstep. My men had brought a rope for me, but I thought the use of it unnecessary. First, we climbed over great masses of rocks at the base of the cliff, then came a path about twelve inches wide, zigzagging up the ledges. In some places the trail was hollowed out a little, and there I could tread securely, but in others were slanting stones and sudden turns where it was hard to keep from looking over and down to the sea below. The most dangerous point was where steps had been hewn in the solid cliff, and these were worn and sloped downward. Here, a pastor from Sandoy fell, and was killed a score of years ago. Some say he was careless, others that he was "fey",—his time had come.

I had kept my eyes on the trail, and had not noted how high we had climbed. So, I was surprised when my helper exclaimed, "Now, thou blessed, we are up," and a few steps brought us over the summit of the cliff. A long stretch of grass meadow sloped gently to the edge, a steep fjeld rose beyond, and midway between fjeld and sea was a solitary house where lived the entire population of Stóra Dímun.

There are three of the Faroe islands which are especially difficult of access—Stóra Dímun, Mykines, and Fugloy. All can be entirely cut off from the outside world for weeks, even months at a time in winter. But Mykines has one little village and Fugloy two, while Stóra Dímun has but one house, with fourteen inmates.

And a gruesome kind of family it is that lives there—for often paupers, people who drink or for some failing or infirmity are not fit to live with their family or in a village are sent here by the Judge. They cannot get away from Dímun, and they work for the peasant as they can. Fourteen people, four with whooping cough, one with consumption, one blind, several brennivín addicts, several with doubtful antecedents. And indeed there were storms inside as well as out.

Twice a year, in May and August, the Pastor comes from Sandoy ten miles away, and holds service in the tiny, three-windowed, grass-roofed church. He remains but six hours, until the turn of the tide. The story is told about a priest, a good while ago, who for a long time could not visit Stóra Dímun where the ascent is dangerous, because of a dizziness in his head. And so it happened that when he did go, he confirmed a girl, gave her the sacrament, married her, baptized the baby, and churched her all at once.

Several times a year the peasant goes to Trongisvágur, eleven miles, and to Tórshavn, twenty-six miles away, to take the produce of the island and bring back necessary supplies. These journeys can be made only in the best of weather for the peasant has but a small, four-man boat and a crew of only three. If the seas are too rough to venture and the need imperative (as in case of serious illness), then he sends up a message of smoke from a certain headland and eight men come from Hvalba in their áttamanafar. There is little need to go often. This rock fortress has resources of its own for a long weather siege. Thirty-five head of cattle and 450 sheep graze on the upper fjeld. Potatoes of poor quality and almost enough barley are grown. Milk and seafowl are the staple food. Feathers are used for beds and for bed covering. Tools, implements, and single pieces of furniture are made at home; clothes are homespun and cowhides and sheepskins are tanned and made into moccasins. Petroleum, sugar, salt, coffee, and other household requisites are procured by the sale of feathers, butter, cheeses, dried mutton, wool, fresh seafowl, and seafowl eggs. All supplies must be on the island before the September storms begin. And how the winter gales must rage about this cliff set in mid-ocean in the stormiest part of the far North Atlantic! One sees signs of them in the old house built of stone, turf-roofed and moored at the corners by heavy chains. Wires are netted over the roof and fastened to iron hooks welded to large stones under the eaves. A seven-foot dike of earth and stones behind and one in front protect the foundations and break winds—and wings of stone three feet thick project from the ends; the living room, cowstalls, haysheds, and storehouses all open out to a narrow lane that can be barred at both ends by heavy high doors. Indeed an almost impregnable fortress.

A big, brave man is the "king's peasant" Jens Ole-Jacobsen of Stóra Dímun, steady of nerve and quick of eye, as he has need to be. He came to welcome us as we drew near the house, gave my crew coffee and thick milk, and in an hour they were on their homeward way and I settled down for a visit of (as I supposed) five or six days, long enough to see something of the bird life of the island.

There was plenty of it. I have never seen a birdier place. On three sides of the house at the edge of the grasslands, where the cliffs dropped down to the surf line, a cloud of seafowl soared and circled. Hooded crows strutted about, fat and bold from eating baby puffins; flocks of starlings chattered and gurgled on the earth dikes, titlarks, stonechats and wrens trilled all around the house. Stóra Dímun has no cats, rats, or mice and the peasant does not allow his boys to rob the nests. Marsh snipe, usually so shy, sat on the out-buildings and searched for food about the door. One actually had her nest on the house roof among the grasses.

And there were plenty of birds in the house. The great royk-stova—the kitchen and general living room—was the scene of great activity. Crates of plucked and of unplucked guillemots and puffins, of feathers and of refuse, stood on the floor and four women were hard at work. A good hand can pluck fifty guillemots or a hundred puffins a day. There were several hundred birds in that room and hundreds more outside the door. Three hundred guillemots had been lying under the cliffs for five or six days and were very "high," since the supply of salt had given out. But, all the same, they were to be split, hung up to dry in the sun and wind, and eaten in the autumn. Over the fire, in a great iron pot, fifty or sixty puffins were bubbling, when done they were put in a wooden trough on a stool in the middle of the room and the family, seated on benches fixed to the wall, ate dinner, a piece of black bread on the knee, a puffin in the left hand, sheath-knife in the other. Two puffins were carried to the guest room for me, and I repaired thither to eat my dinner with what philosophy I could summon to my aid. When only the breasts of the puffins are taken, skinned, soaked in milk for a day or two, then stewed or roasted slowly, with a brown sauce, they make a dish to be eaten with gratitude, but cooked whole in Stóra Dímun fashion, with skin, feet, head, and many feathers on, a puffin tastes of nothing but unrefined cod-liver oil.

I had hoped to see the men go down the cliffs with the line and was much disappointed to find that for the present they were taking birds in places too dangerous for me to visit. Four men, relatives of the peasant, had come from Sandoy to help, for on many cliffs five men are needed to hold the line, and the peasant had but two able men at his command. I watched their departure in the mornings full of bitterness that I was but a woman and must stay at home. Three men carried the great line, marching about five feet apart, each with a third of it coiled on his shoulders, another carried the fowling net, and all had portions of food, sandals, and fjeld staffs. Then, when their figures had disappeared over the crest of the fjeld, I went down to the cliffs near the house, lay flat on the grass, and, opera glass in hand, peered over the edge and consoled myself with the diverting ways of the inhabitants below.

Near the bottom, just above the highest point reached by the summer surf, were the guillemots in long rows on the ledges. In their vicinity the pretty kittiwakes had their nests, and a little apart, shunned by all, were the big havhestur (fulmars) the *Fulmarus glacialis*. Unpleasant neighbors they are, detested by the respectable, clean living guillemots for their disagreeable smell and for their habit of spouting offensive oil when disturbed. Sixty years ago these gulls were never known to breed in the Faroes. Now they are here in great numbers, unwelcome citizens. A few of the young are eaten, but eggs, adult birds, and feathers are too disagreeable to be used, and so the fulmars flourish, while worthier birds are destroyed. These gulls can cause a good deal of damage by squirting their oil over the guillemots; it mats their feathers, and the bird chills when in the sea and soon dies.

Near the summit of the cliffs the puffins—dear things—lived. Not all, however; perhaps a fifth of their number were scattered on the cliff sides, and among the debris at the base, wherever enough earth could be found for them to dig a burrow. The puffins were the only lodgers of this vast apartment house that I could observe closely. The lower stories were too distant, the walls too perpendicular to afford good vantage ground. Here and there a great mass of rock projected from the main wall, shaped like heads of sphinxes and of ogres. One that reminded me of a fairy book ogre of my childhood days had a peculiarly fierce glitter in its eye. This puzzled me until, with my glass, I found that it was a white kittiwake brooding on a nest in the hollow of the ogre's eye.

I was often at fault in judging the distance, as there was no tree or bush to serve as a measurement. At first the cliffs did not seem very high, until I discovered that a little white speck I thought was a daisy was really the breast of a big guillemot, and those small stones were huge masses of rock, hundreds of tons in weight, and that little pieces of driftwood was the peasant's four-man boat hauled up high on the boulders.

Lundaland—the puffinland proper, is the grassy slopes and coping of the cliffs. The grass grows thick and green from the fertilizing bird guano, but, close to the holes, it is brown and glistening from the trampling of webbed feet, and one should tread cautiously. A puffin is really a delightful bird (except when he is boiled with his skin on). He has such a diverting fashion of chuckling "ur-r-r-r-r!" to himself in a jolly fat voice as though enjoying some private joke; of paddling up and down, trotting gaily about in circles, and then suddenly falling into an attitude of pensive musing. And the pretty looks of him; when the sun shines his glossy back sparkles with blue and purple lights and his bright red feet cast reflections upon his snowy breast like spots of blood. The birds were not at all afraid of me and often made their toilets in little groups not more than eight or ten feet away. The beaks of the breeding birds were much larger and more brightly colored than those of the immature ones. The parent birds could also be distinguished by the little herrings which they were carrying to the young in the burrows. These stuck out on both sides of the curved beak, making the puffin look like a stout old gentleman with a fierce gray mustache. It is said that fifty of these tiny fish can be carried in this way, but it is difficult to determine the question, a number of times I counted twelve.

I much enjoyed these peaceful hours seated on the grass near the brink while the birds rose and sank in the air only a few feet away. There was a pleasing element of chance about it. What would pop up next—a puffin, folding his glossy wings with care, and throwing out his snow-white breast with a satisfied air as his red feet sought the ground? A dainty kittiwake flashing lightly, her long pointed wings in graceful flight? A guillemot, most dignified of birds on the ledges, most awkward as she scuttles through the air along the cliff's edge, steering herself with convulsive waggings of tail and feet, and spread flat like a Chinese pressed duck? A razor bill? A herring gull? A hooded crow? A big malmukke?

Very often it was a malmukke, and although he was not "simpatica" to me, I could not but admire his power and skill as, with outstretched wings, he silently rose and fell, circled and poised with only a slight tremor of the wing tips. And this not six feet from the level of my eyes; truly, I was a privileged person.

One day I saw an instance of the malmukke's nagging ways and mistaken idea of humor. A puffin, a quiet, respectable father of a family, was taking a little repose after arduous herring bearing, when a malmukke poised itself directly over his head and let down its big feet that looked like large sections of underdone pie, the claws almost grazed the puffin's head. He cocked up first one eye, then the other, shrugged his shoulders, fidgetted, looked up again, and saw always those disagreeable pale feet just above him. Finally it got on his nerves so that he flew away and the malmukke did likewise. After a little he returned, the malmukke came and tormented him again and the same scene was repeated five or six times, until the puffin was finally banished. The malmukke had no nest in the neighborhood, and the puffin had. It was clearly a case of "cussedness."

I had spent four days on Stóra Dímun and was beginning to think of leaving, when a fierce wind arose. In a few hours the great rollers were crashing along the coast and nothing but a balloon would have enabled one to leave the island. Even after the gale subsided the surf increased, and there was nothing to be done but wait, cheered by the promise of the peasant that in a few days they would begin bird-catching on the home cliffs where I could see it.

One afternoon I climbed about 600 feet above the house to the top of the island. Here graze the cows until late in September, when they come down to the more sheltered grazing lands near the house. On the fields a cowherd must stay with them to see that they do not stray to dangerous places and narrow ledges, where they cannot retrace their steps. The sheep live out all the year, never watched or fed. They have more intelligence than sheep of southern lands and are as nimble as a goat. A few are lost by snowslides and blowing from the cliffs, but the number seems small when one considers the exposures of winter.

It was on this eastern side of the field that a little eleven year old Stóra Dímuner went alone, many years ago, to "drag" puffins from their burrows. He clambered up and down the steep slopes and had collected a good number when he felt a strange dizziness and saw that the earth on which he stood was moving. The sod and thin layer of earth had broken loose and were sweeping down to the edge of the cliffs. With a bound he sprang up, and gained a ledge to which he clung—and saw the whole slope disappear over the brink. He was safe for the moment, but he could not descend, and no help could reach him where he stood. Creeping a little farther along the ledge, he saw a soft spot where grass grew, about 50 feet below. If he fell there it was possible that he might escape with his life. But midway between him and that one spot a jagged rock jutted out from the face of the cliff—if he fell he would be crushed on the rock. His only chance lay in springing as far as he could out into the air, clearing the rock, and falling to one place where there was grass and where his father might be able to descend and find him. And this the boy did, took his resolve, measured the distance with his eye, and sprang from the ledge. He was found unconscious and lived to be an old man, but always had a lame leg.

As I sat on the fjeld slope I could see a great stretch of sea around me. It was one of those days, rare in Faroes, when the arch of the heavens was clear—above, the blue of the sky; below, the deeper blue of the sea; not far away Lítla Dímun, the smaller of the twin islands, a rounded pyramid, inhabited only by wild fowl and wild sheep. Beyond, gleaming with intense blue and violets, the headlands of Suðuroy and Sandoy, then, far away, Streymoy, and, on the north, pale mists that might be the rugged mountains of the six northern islands.

But we seldom see the skies clear from dawn to sunset. Already, as I started down the home side of the fjeld, a little white cloud stole up around the shoulder of a headland. It looked like the traditional ghost maiden with arms uplifted and floating white draperies. A host of vaguer shapes followed in her train and suddenly I was enveloped in a pinky pearl cloud—house, sky, and sea quite out of sight. So, as no one could see me, I made a toboggan of myself and, regardless of decorum, slid down the grasses and white bed-straw and short buttercups, putting out a brake when necessary by clutching at the tufts of grass.

I had expected to remain on Stóra Dímun for five or six days, but I spent sixteen there before the surf permitted me to leave. It was dreary, those last ten days, cold and rain without and in the evenings the dense clouds that enveloped the house brought unusual darkness, and the winter supply of candles and petroleum had long since been exhausted. Occasionally, however, a short respite in the storms allowed the men to go to the distant guillemot cliffs, leaving one or two of their number to catch puffins in neighboring lands.

Puffins, it seems, have a fashion of staying three days on land and three days at sea. A dull day with a moderate wind blowing along the coast are the favorable conditions, for the puffin does not fly easily in perfectly still weather. The cliffs are a curious sight at such times. Round and round fly the birds springing from the cliffs, making a wide sweep seawards, and passing close to land as they swing back to their perches. It is on their return flight that they are captured. The fowling staff is about nine feet in length, at one end two slightly curved arms of hazelwood are bound and between them hangs the net made of sail twine or strong wool. The man sits on the edge of the cliff, sheltered from view by a large rock. As a puffin flies within reach, he swings the net upwards, back of the bird and over it, brings it in snapping and snarling, and wrings its neck. The net must not be passed over the bird from the front, or the momentum of its flight will tear out the meshes. When the birds are to be brought home, five are tied together by their necks into a bunch called a vorda and twenty or more vordur are bound together with a rope and borne on the man's shoulders. A clever catcher, if all circumstances are favorable, can take over 900 birds in a day, but usually half that number is considered a fair day's work.

Fatiguing as it is for back, arms, and eyes, the men enjoy the sport, and the small boys practice to fit themselves to go as soon as possible, one throwing his cap in the air, while another tries to catch it in the net.

When the slopes are treacherous two men go together. One sits above, bracing feet and fjeld staff in the earth. He has one end of a rope fastened around his waist, and at the other end his companion is tied, and works among the burrows dragging out the birds, wringing their necks, and slipping their heads under his belt. The danger is that the thin covering of earth may break away and slide down over the precipice, carrying the men with it.

I was sorry I could not come close to the guillemot ledges, but with my opera glass I had a fairly good view of them. The ways of reaching guillemot ledges and the high puffin lands are the same. Two men go together with rope and strong fjeld staffs. In ascending a man climbs with sandaled feet, hands and staff up to a ledge, his companion putting the iron point in his trousers belt and lifting him as he climbs. Once up he helps the man below with the rope, and in this way they ascend ledge after ledge to a great height. In descending the peril is greater—for as the last man leaves a ledge, he fastens the rope so lightly that a sharp twitch will set it free after he has gained a footing below.

In using the long line there is no danger from the line itself; it is strong and held by five cool and skillful men. The risk is in the cliffs from loose stones or from the giving away of a portion of the rock wall. Even a small stone falling from a great height can crush in a man's skull. A fatal accident of that kind took place here on Stóra Dímun two years ago. And some time before, while a man was working on a shelf half way down the cliff, a sharp wedge of rock fell on the line, cut it as if it were a piece of cotton thread, and man and line fell 600 feet into the sea. Another danger, hardly less, is of the ledges breaking down as the men pass over them collecting eggs and birds. As the men creep along the ledges or hang in the line, they snare the birds with the fowling net, and binding them together either send them up with the line or cast them down to the sea where men and boats are waiting for them.

✿❋❀

Last Sunday, in rain and fog, I performed the feat of leaving Stóra Dímun in a four-man boat, ten miles of open sea. Now I am being just lazy in Hans Kristoffer's cottage á Ryggi in Miðvágur. After Stóra Dímun everything is clean enough for me to be comfortable. I couldn't help laughing, though, when I looked in the mirror this morning and saw my sad and weary eyes as though I were carrying some secret grief or burden — the result of those sixteen days on Stóra Dímun, sixteen days of Puffins with their skins on.

I now mean to rest on my laurels and do nothing more of the kind in the future.

Published as "An Out-of-the-Way Island" in the *Morning Courier* (Buffalo, New York), October 26 and November 2, 1902.

In Puffinland

We have thirty species of birds nesting on Mykines, but in numbers the lundi or puffin takes an easy first. Sixty thousand are sometimes caught in a single season, but this year's catch will probably not exceed ten thousand. The birds are not as plentiful as usual, and north winds blowing steadily during the snaring time have kept them out at sea. I have stayed long enough at Mykines to see two of the methods of capturing the puffins—the taking of the females from the burrows before the eggs are hatched and the *fleyging* or snaring of the non-breeding birds with a net attached to a long pole as they fly to and from the crags. A few weeks later a man will descend from the summit of the cliffs, fastened to a line held by five men, and snare the birds as they pass him in midair, or creep along the ledges to the places where the birds are most numerous.

One morning the schoolmaster Niclassen and I went to lundaland, or puffinland, he warning me not to look seaward. Our foothold was secure enough, but it is well not to give one's thoughts rein, and wonder how far below the sea is and how steep the cliffs. Puffins are not particular about the location of their nests. All they ask is to be near the sea, and to have enough earth in which to dig a burrow. They live in the filled-up chinks of crags, in the debris at the base, in steep grassy slopes, or among the rugged hillsides. When the wind is in a favorable direction, thousands fill the air like a snowstorm of brown and white flakes. The schoolmaster and I sat down by the burrows in a sunny hollow, where pink and white catchfly, spotted orchis, buttercups, sea pinks, and white bedstraw grew in profusion, and soon the birds collected around us. No shooting is permitted in puffinland, and they are very tame. In double rows they sat on every stone and boulder, their round white breasts shining like strings of pearls, their glossy backs and wings reflecting the blues and violets of the sky. They chortled and chuckled, watched us with their heads on one side, and trotted about exchanging gossip about us. I found them most diverting and declared that I was coming to puffinland every day. But I never returned. The schoolmaster had neglected to tell me that puffins are afflicted with two kinds of ticks — one like the larger wood tick found in June in our American forests, and the other a little spidery creature that is very poisonous. We had rested long close to their burrows, and during the next twenty-four hours I thought hard thoughts of the schoolmaster; and how a puffin can seem so happy is a mystery.

Several men were at work near us taking the birds from the burrows. A bright little dog was giving assistance. If a hole was occupied, he scratched and dug at the entrance, and a man then inserted a short stick with a hook at the end, dragged out the puffin and wrung its neck. A painful bite can be given with the strong sharp beak, and without a *lundakrokur* a man's hands would be in bad condition after dragging out several hundred birds. I am told that when the ravens and hooded crows enter the burrows, the poor little mother shrinks back in helpless fright, allowing her eggs or young to be stolen without trying to defend them.

On a steep slope above the sea were two men, fastened together by a rope about thirty feet in length. One had seated himself on a secure bit of ground, bracing his field staff in the rocks or earth below him, while the other climbed about exploring the lower burrows. The grass was slippery with a recent shower, and they were near the verge of cliffs two hundred feet in height. It seemed very dangerous to me.

"But surely," I said to the schoolmaster, "one man could not hold up the other if he fell. At least four men would be needed to support his weight."

"Oh, he will not fall, really," replied the schoolmaster. "If he slips, he can save himself in time with the aid of the rope."

"But," I persisted, "if he should fall?"

I was given to understand, however, that this could not be taken into consideration. The business of a good field man is to make no blunders.

On these slopes, and in this way, the young Mykineser tries his 'prentice hand with a stout strong father or uncle at the other end of the rope. He begins when he is thirteen or fourteen, and later learns to wield the snaring net and pole, first from the crags and afterward suspended in midair by the line. He graduates, if he is brave and skillful, at eighteen or twenty, on the most dangerous of all bird-catching, that of the *sula* or gannet, at night, on the treacherous cliffs of Mykinesholmur, an island close to the main island of Mykines.

A few days ago I was shown the puffin snaring by a Mykineser called "Johannes of the Albatross" (and by that name hangs a tale I will get to later). I climbed with the assistance of Johannes to the edge of a precipice, where I sat, in much trepidation, though firmly wedged in between two rocks. Johannes was perched on a ledge close by me, and seemed quite fearless and at ease, though I could not see why he did not fall off every time he swooped at a puffin. He had need of a quick eye to enable him to take only bachelor and spinster puffins. If a bird held a little shining fish in its beak, that indicated that babies were at home waiting to be fed, and it must not be killed. When a puffin was brought in snarling and gurgling in the net, I looked the other way, and Johannes wrung its neck. In one morning he caught seventy-five, but had the wind been east or west, that is a 'long-shore breeze' several hundred might have been snared.

Mykines ranks perhaps first of all the Faroe bird islands, with puffins as her specialty. Stóra Dímun, a guillemot island, comes next. All the edible seafowl, except the gannet, are found in varying numbers on all the islands. A few years ago the annual catch was estimated at 235,000, but it must fall short of that at the present time.

Thirteen out of the thirty species of birds nesting on Mykines remain all the year—eider duck, marsh snipe, black-backed gull, black guillemot, cormorant, rock dove, hooded crow, raven, starling, northern wren, two kinds of titlarks, and common gull. The migratory breeding birds are the curlew, whimbrel, guillemot, oyster catcher, kittiwake, golden plover, razorbill, auk, stormy petrel, puffin, gannet, stonechat, white wagtail, jacksnipe, scoter, Arctic skua, and several species of gulls and terns. About forty other species are seen in the spring and autumn migrations, swans, geese, ducks, thrushes, and other small birds, hawks, loons and seafowl. This year a pair of corn crakes have favored Mykines with their presence. We are sure they must have a nest here, otherwise why should they spend June and July on the island? We can hear their "crake-crake" all night long, but the schoolmaster, in spite of his untiring watchings, has not caught a glimpse of him. The other Mykinesers, many of them keen observers, do not aid him in his vigils, for do they not know that whoever sees a corn crake will die within the year?

I notice that many of the birds go to rest about ten-thirty or eleven-o'clock and wake up at one-thirty or two. The titlarks, however, and the stonechats, marsh snipe, and our corn crake visitors seem never to sleep unless they take catnaps in the middle of the day. The schoolmaster says that about one-fourth of the kittiwakes are as busy as in the daytime. They seem to take turns in sleeping, and at any hour of night I can hear their peculiar barking and crying notes.

Mykinesholmur, the only breeding place in the Faroes of the gannet, is divided from the main island by a chasm twenty fathoms in width. The only landing place is perhaps an eighth of a mile away, and as the surf often prevents any going or coming for weeks at a time, a strong line has been stretched across the chasm to enable men to cross, and food to be sent at the seasons of birdcatching and sheep gathering. The island is about half a mile in length, and the grass grows unusually thick and sweet. Sheep live there all the year round, and twenty-five or thirty oxen from April until December. Then they are brought home to spend three months under shelter. In autumn, before the worst storms set in, several are killed and sent to Tórshavn where "Mykines beef" is held in high esteem.

I made the acquaintance of these oxen under painful circumstances. The schoolmaster had given me glowing accounts of the beauty of the gannets, and of course I wished to visit the holm. But we waited through ten days of storm and fog before the surf allowed us to venture. Then Herr Abrahamsen, the schoolmaster, and I set forth the first quiet morning with a fishing crew which had agreed to land us and call for us on their return from the cod grounds. We climbed over the tang-covered rocks and found ourselves in a nursery of Arctic terns or *terna*. In the middle of May the little terns arrive. It is said that long ago the ternas came much earlier than all other birds to the Faroes. But one day there burst a dreadful storm with sleet, and large numbers of the birds were frozen down as they sat huddled under the cliffs of the sea rocks. After it was over the miserable remnant held a meeting and it was resolved that "Whereas we, the little ternas, have heretofore been the first of all the birds to come to the Faroes, we will be the last." From that time they have arrived the middle of May. The nights then are too light for the stars to be seen, and the moon is only a pale presence in the sky, casting no shadow. So when the ternas come and the stars go, the short elusive summer is at hand.

On Mykineshólmur there were hundreds of tern nests and with difficulty we avoided treading on the olive and brown spotted eggs, so closely did they resemble the lichens and mosses around them. All along the coast were kittiwake colonies. I crept as near as I dared to the edge of the cliffs, and lying down and peering over, found myself close to the upper tiers of nests. Such pretty dainty creatures the kittiwakes are! I never tire of watching them as they sit on the nests, so spotless in their soft gray jackets and white hoods and bibs. I had just arisen from a kittiwake investigation when I heard a queer noise on the hill above us, and there were all the oxen galloping down, with eyes rolling and horns and tails high in the air, bellowing with joy at the sight of human beings again. Now, I ask if it is not trying for a timid woman to be on a grassy slope ten feet from the verge of a perpendicular precipice two hundred feet high, and landward twenty-five oxen charging down in a body? How was I to know just when those oxen, in the exuberance of their welcome, were going to pause? I skipped behind Herr Abrahamsen, and giving my fjeld staff to the schoolmaster, hurriedly told him that he had advised my coming to the holm and on his head rested the responsibility of my fate. So he went after them, and with the aid of the fjeld staff induced them to be a little less demonstrative. After that they followed us as a devoted bodyguard, standing in an anxious, troubled row when we climbed down to places where they could not follow, and gamboling around us like dogs when we went on again.

On the western end of Mykineshólmur live the gannets, or the "sula" as the Faroe folk call them. Their nests are crowded together on the cliff ledges, and on great masses of rock which have become detached from the island by the action of the waves. One of these *drangar* looked like an immense plum cake, the effect of glittering frosting on top being caused by hundreds of white gannets which covered the summit. Rows of guillemots were nesting in friendly fashion among the gannets. I noticed that the guillemots whose eggs are unhatched sat with their backs to the sea. When the little ones came out the mothers face about, looking like rows of prim, white-petticoated, hoop-skirted young ladies. Puffins flew to and fro, with their peculiar straight flight like shuttles in a loom, scores of oyster catchers, titlarks, curlews, and stonechats cried and quavered from the grass fields; now and then a pair of razor-billed auks passed, and flocks of eider ducks and a few pretty black guillemots (*Uria trolle*) bobbed up and down just beyond the breakers. It was a true bird paradise, and its inmates showed little fear, for the holm is seldom visited.

I doubt if among the seafowl a more successful bird than the gannet can be found. He is charming in looks, powerful in flight, graceful, confident, and accomplished. I had not expected to see such large birds. The males must have measured three feet in length, and weighed perhaps six or seven pounds. The snowy white plumage of the breeding birds shone like silver in the sunlight; we were near enough to see plainly their pale yellow eyes, blue eyelids, the black spot on their foreheads, and their dusky bills. Perhaps the prettiest of all were the three year olds—those which had attained the soft buff plumage of head and neck, and white body, but kept a little mottled gray and brown on their wings.

The breeding birds were more wary and watchful, but these carefree three year olds seemed quite fearless. They divided their time between the eating of anchovies and making the most careful and elaborate toilets. Three dandified young fellows seemed to be "showing off" for my special predilection. They sat on a ledge just below the crest of a cliff, and allowed me to approach within a distance of fifteen feet. They would preen each wing feather with their long beaks, laying it daintily in place, and then smoothing it down with the side and back of their sleek heads, turning their supple necks easily from side to side, and then glancing confidingly up at me, as if to say, "Are we not beautiful?" and I found myself nodding and smiling assent.

In April the fjeld men come to the holm to take the adult birds when they have made their nests, but have not laid their eggs. Then the birds are left undisturbed until September, when the young birds are almost ready for flight. In all, about one thousand are captured in a favorable season, but the Mykinesers do not encourage too large a booty. They are proud of possessing the only breeding place in the Faroes of the beautiful sula and wish to keep their colony in a flourishing condition.

The sula catching is very dangerous. It takes place always at night, and in April and September the Faroe nights are dark. Herr Abrahamsen showed me places above a cliff four hundred feet high, where four white flat stones in a row showed the men where to descend with the line. On the detached drangar no lines are used, and it makes one shudder to think of the men climbing in the darkness on those perilous crumbling ledges. No wonder that the sula catchers sing a special hymn—the "Sula Song"—as they leave Mykines at night for the holm. It has eight verses, and begins:

> "The light of day has passed away
> And night hangs over us,
> O Jesus Christ, Our Lord so dear,
> Be with us now,
> Cheer us, God in heaven."

And when all is in readiness, whether the men descend with lines or go down without them, all kneel on the edge of the cliffs and say a silent prayer.

Five years ago, on Mykineshólmur, an event occurred which made a stir among the ornithologists of Great Britain and Denmark. Johannes, my companion of the puffin-snaring morning, shot an albatross (*Diomedea melanophrys*) as it sat with the sula on one of the drangar at the west end of the holm. As the most northern limit of this species in the Atlantic is twenty-three degrees south latitude, and its usual habitat from forty degrees to fifty degrees south, this event was in itself of great interest. But this Mykineshólmur albatross had made itself an ornithological wonder by coming every February with the sula to the holm, spending the summer with them, and leaving with them in September, and doing this for thirty-four consecutive years. It was first observed in May, 1860, by a party of twelve men of Mykines, all keen, intelligent fjeld men. Thereafter, every year, it was seen on the holm, leading a solitary life, and it was never known to breed. There is some story about one queer-looking sula having been captured, with a strong large beak unlike that of the other birds, and some people think it may have been a young albatross, but this is only conjecture. The Mykinesers had never seen or heard of an albatross and thought this a very large sula. It was called *kongasula*, the "gannet king" and the men noticed that the other birds treated it with the greatest respect and made way for it when it approached.

Johannes did not mean to kill the kongasula. He happened to have his gun with him, and he fired, wishing only to make the bird fly up, so he could see its great wings, when to his surprise and regret it fell dead. It was sent to Peter F. Petersen, on Nólsoy, a local ornithologist and a skilled taxidermist, and later forwarded by him to Copenhagen. It was a female, well developed and in beautiful plumage. Inquiries were at once made, affidavits taken, and pamphlets written both in Danish and English, but no satisfactory explanation has been given of the motives that caused an albatross to forsake the sphere in which it had pleased Providence to place her, and spend thirty-four summers in solitary living among seafowl that granted to her at best only a respectful tolerance. Johannes did not know, and I of course did not tell him, how he had tempted Fate. He might, if he knew, think of it in some bad moment on the cliffs or at sea. But to kill an albatross, and such an albatross, makes it highly improbable that Johannes will ever die the "straw death" disdained by his Viking forefathers. A pity it is, for Johannes is a fine man among a race of fine men. He seems to have invisible wings attached to his Faroe moccasins, so lightly does he step. His face has a serious look, as befits one who looks so much on mighty seas, but his face and eyes light up with a bright quick smile.

Were creature comforts more plentiful, and Mother Nature less prodigal of storm, fog, and cold, a long summer stay on Mykines would be delightful. But I have been here twenty-two days, and in all that time we have had three days when the weather was fine from dawn to sunset. Little can be done when heavy fog makes all dismal, drenching the grass and shutting out from sight the fjelds and bird cliffs. So I end this letter at Bøur whither I came this morning with a crew of Bible-named Mykinesers—Abrahams, Isaacs, Zachariahs, and Mathiases. We had planned to start at nine, but at seven some of the men came to my door, and I heard that dreaded word *brim*; there would be surf, and I must come at once. I hurriedly packed my traps, and in half an hour was on my way to the boathouses. There was brim! I looked with dismay at the big waves surging over the reefs and flooding the embarking place.

"I dare not go!" I exclaimed to Herr Abrahamsen.

"Yes, yes," he replied reassuringly, "look at the sea outside. All will go well when you once get out, and every little while comes a quiet time."

"Don't be afraid," shouted up the men, "we can make it!"

So I climbed down and waited on the rocks for a lull, while the men kept the boat in a quiet spot under some cliffs across the inlet. "Now!" cried a man who was watching the sea. The boat shot forward to where I stood, I tumbled in anyhow, waved a farewell to those on shore, and in an instant we were tossing high in a whirl of white water between the reefs, cutting through masses of foam, and reaching the open sea just before the next big wave broke. There we were safe; there was little wind, and the great waves swept shoreward in unbroken lines. We could easily climb them and race down their outer slopes. It was a glorious day. No Venetian skies ever shimmered with more lovely tints than those that showed on the bare ranges of Vágar and Streymoy, while the sea gleamed with royal purples and intense blues. And yet with all this unusual display of color, we seemed to be in one of those "non-sounding areas" that puzzle the scientists. All round the coast the surf broke high against the cliffs, sending clouds of spray forty feet in the air. But it came to our ears only as a soft hushed thunder, and above it my men's voices rang clearly as they sang the "out-going song," "I turn now to Thy help."

Bøur smelt to heaven this morning with a mighty smell of pitch. The village, church and all, has just received its annual coat of tar, and shines like a polished stovepipe. And I had planned to make a sketch of the charming weatherworn houses here. Bøur has lost all interest for me. I will tarry here no longer, but return to Hans Kristoffer's comfortable house in Miðvágur, and see how my flower seeds have thrived that we planted in his pretty garden.

Published in *Forest and Stream. The Journal of Rod and Gun*, October 11, 1902, 283–284.

Fly-Fishing In The Faroes

Although I spent several weeks at Hans Kristoffer's, in Miðvágur, I fished only four or five times in nearby Sørvágsvatn. The lake was a mile from the house; it was the season for storing peats, when young and old are busy on the moors, and how can a woman fish alone with any pleasure when three bulls are grazing on the lake shores, and there are no fences or walls to climb over? I did not even try, but waited until the last peat was stacked in the grothus, and the very next night, Jógvan Jr., Heini, and I went fishing.

During the summer, the youth of Miðvágur seldom fish during the day. From eight in the evening until one in the morning in June and July, and from seven to ten at night and two to four in the morning during August are the hours preferred. An inconvenient time, one would think, but the Faroe people seem to lay up sleep in winter as a bear does his fat in summer, and they are able, without difficulty, to turn night into day. The tackle used consists of a stout pole, coarse white line, and large hooks baited with angleworms, and the trout are jerked violently from the water with no attempt to play them. Jógvan and Heini, however, had made much lighter rods and primitive reels, and they fished in more scientific fashion.

I left my fly-rod at home that evening and took a green-heart rod made by Hardy Brothers, of Alnwick, England. By changing the tips this served admirably for both bait-fishing and spinning. Jógvan and Heini were to take turns in rowing and fishing. Their method was to trail a rather small hook baited with angleworms, at a distance of about forty feet from the boat. I had a light braided silk line, stout leader, and a spinning coachman. Numbers was our object. It was not a time to experiment with fly-fishing at night. Frú Hans Kristoffer expected relatives from Bøur to dinner on the morrow—Sunday—and she had requested us to bring home enough trout to make a large dish of frikkadellir. Those are a glorified kind of fish cake. I

163

would give the recipe, except for my conviction that no native-born American would have the patience to pound and whisk the ingredients for two hours and a half, and so produce that creaminess and lightness indispensable to the ideal frikkadellir.

There is a charm and mystery about these night fishings. It is broad daylight until eleven o'clock, with wreaths of rosy mists above the bare fjelds, and the higher peaks glowing with flame and copper hues. Then for two hours is a clear silvery twilight, with every object distinctly visible. One waits, unconscious of the passing time, for it to grow darker, but it lightens instead and another day has come. As we pass, the ever-watchful curlews give the alarm, the oyster catchers answer, and the golden plover; there is a chatter of titlarks, wrens, and stonechats, and a few ravens and crows hurry from the cliffs to see what is the matter. The gulls, terns, and kittiwakes are all astir, eider ducks are taking little excursions in groups of five or six, and now and then a puffin flies over, straying from his quarters on the bird crags above the sea. It was so light that I am sure an expert fisherman could have taken many fish by using a small white or yellow miller, such as one would choose for early twilight fishing in America.

During the first hour I caught eight good trout, and Heini, whose turn it was to fish, not one. Heini (aged sixteen) is a born fisherman and something of a misogynist, considering woman of small account except as she provides food and clothes to man, and so enables him to live and fish. He had never spoken to me (Jógvan did the necessary talking), but I always had hopes of softening his heart. Heini takes his fishing seriously, and I realized that unless he could catch something soon, the situation would be critical. So I lent him a cappelin minnow. He caught five nice fish in half an hour, all larger than mine, and the danger was past. And that night when he returned the minnow, his lips were unsealed. "Thanks shall you have!" he said with haughty grace. "That's a remarkable good little fish!"

We came stealing into the silent house at one in the morning with twenty-eight trout, weighing from three-quarters of a pound to two pounds, every one a fighter and in fine condition. Our dish of frikkadellir was assured.

A few years ago a young Englishman spent a month in the

Faroes, and then wrote a book about them. In it he gave free rein to his imagination. This was a pity, for it caused inconvenience and disappointment to others who naturally wished to catch scores of trout averaging three pounds apiece, and to shoot large bags of curlew, oyster catchers, snipe, and plover during a short stroll. The courteous Governor of the Faroes has received and answered many letters asking if these tales be true. One less prudent sportsman, an Anglican clergyman, did not inquire, but came, shot a snipe the morning after his arrival and was promptly haled before the authorities. The above-named birds cannot be shot before September 15, too late for travel among the Faroes. As for the fish, "those finny monsters of Sørvágsvatn," Hans Kristoffer testifies that he has never seen anything bigger than two pounds and a half. The Sørvágsvatn fish, however, are not to be despised. They are the *Salmo fario* (the river trout of Europe), gamy, pink-fleshed and finely flavored, and under favorable conditions a large catch can be made. A few days after our first fishing, Heini had a regular fishing orgy, an all-night affair, and caught sixty, ranging from one-quarter to one and a half pounds.

As near as I can ascertain, there are nine or ten fishing lakes in the northern Faroes, not counting a number of tarns where small trout are often taken. Fjallavatn and Hvilvkinnavatn, two lakes in northern Vágar, have fish which, though not so numerous as those in Sørvágsvatn, are heavier—but there is no shelter at these lakes of any kind, and the way to them is rough and fatiguing. There are both sea and river trout at Leynar, Saksun, and Streymnes, at Eiðisvatn on Eysturoy Island, and Sandsvatn on Sandoy Island. I am sure there must be many an inlet and bay still unfished with light tackle, where sea trout might be taken. But the difficulties of Faroe travel are great. In many places steep fjelds prevent land excursions, and storms make excursions by sea impossible for weeks at a time. The life insurance companies of Copenhagen certainly do not underestimate the risks of a Faroe life. Their charges are five times greater for Faroes than for Denmark.

When I left Hans Kristoffer's it was to go to Leynar on the island of Streymoy. Here there are three small lakes connected with one another and with the sea. Waders and a boat were necessary here, and I had neither. There had been little rain, and the sea trout had not begun to run. Also, lest I do injustice to Faroe fishing, I might as well confess that I cannot cast a fly well. My line often falls on the water with a distressing splash, and I cannot cover much water with it. Had I been willing to use worms, I might have taken many little troutlets, but I persisted in fly-fishing, and the truth is I did not catch a thing. It was a time of humiliation, emphasized by the fact that the small boy who accompanied me, with a touching faith, always carried a bushel basket. It was some time before it occurred to me that this was intended to hold my fish.

To wait at Leynar for rains that might be long in coming, was not wise, and after two days I started over the hills to Streymnes, a halfway hamlet on the route to Saksun. No one who cannot take rough tramps can really see the Faroes. My walk that day was a typical one. Two men carried my traps in "leypar" on their backs, and I trudged on behind, with skirts kilted and fjeld staff in hand. We followed the brook and lakeshore for a mile and a half and then climbed slowly upward for an hour. A keen wind met us on the summit; the air was clean and fragrant with peat and wild grasses. We passed cow limit, then after a half-hour or so, the further sheep lands, and reached the lonely higher ranges, toiling over stones and hillocks, through matted grass and boggy spots where the feet sank deep in sphagnum mosses. For the first two hours I padded along in a state of active Nirvana, thinking of nothing in particular, vaguely conscious of the skirling of curlews and terns, and the plaintive "dee-e!" of the golden plover. The sweet rain whisks against my face and the sun lays a warm hand on my shoulder. I feel like a primitive person, a nomad, with none of the cares and worries of civilized life. The two figures on ahead are members of my tribe, bearing our few worldly possessions, only were I a true primitive person, I, as the woman and beast of burden, would be carrying the pots and skins and kettles.

Then this beatific mood passes, and tired muscles protest against the toilsome work. We stop to rest, and I curl up in a hollow and eat black bread and dried mutton, and find that the best "pick-me-up" is cold tea, East Indian tea, in a bottle with plenty of sweet cream in it. Then on again, feeling a kind of satisfaction (to quote Thomas Hughes) in "the consciousness of silent endurance, so dear to every Englishman, of standing out against something and not giving in."

It is slow work, over four hours for eight miles, and one's brain wearies of using one's judgment continually about the deepness of boggy spots and the wobbliness of hillocks. At last sheep come in sight again, then cows, and as we dip down to lower levels, from the fjord comes a breath of salt air, and peat smoke from cabins still hidden below the rocky ledges.

Though I have never heard Streymnes recommended as a good fishing place, I feel sure sea trout could be caught there. I dined from delicious fish which my hostess said were caught in her husband's herring nets—and there were all the conditions for sea trout, a sheltered fjord, a clear, swift stream and a tarn or two at its head among the hills.

Next day I left Streymnes and pushed on to Saksun, walking over easier ground for six miles. As we approached, dark fields closed in upon a narrow valley, a brook tumbled over and between boulders, flowed through a lake, and with many a fall and rapid to the sea. It looked very trouty except for the lowness of the water.

Saksun I found to be a three-house hamlet. The house where I stayed had its peculiarities. There was a rooster who crowed every two minutes after midnight; a cow homesick for the "outfields," and a calf whose lamentations had no beginning and no end, and all three lived directly under my bed, with only an open flooring between us. The number of exasperating things that calf did! He snuffled and snorted, thumped my floor with the top of his head, bellowed and grunted and rolled a wooden bucket about. In the morning I protested; my hostess suggested mildly that I "might get used to it," but I assured her that never while life remained could I get used to such a calf. They were kind people, and thereafter in the evening the calf and rooster were borne away to other quarters, the rooster protesting indignantly, and the cow and I put up with each other's society.

Then followed a tiresome week of waiting for the sea trout to come. The water near the lake was shallow and with no boat or waders there was small chance of any good-sized lake trout. The stream was shrunken, and the empty nets in the bay testified to the absence of sea trout. I had a gourmand's interest as well as that of a fisherwoman in catching fish, for I grew very tired of kittiwakes for dinner, and the only alternative was last year's whale's meat. Every day at eleven o'clock I heard the report of a gun, and soon a pretty kittiwake in a dying condition would be shown to me, and I ate it at two o'clock, feeling like a Moloch or a Juggernaut.

But at last came a mighty west wind, bringing with it the blessed rain, and all the burns and cliff waterfalls awoke and made a chorus up and down the glen. I took my rod and splashed through the puddles toward the inlet, glancing as I passed into a pool which had always seemed promising. Yes, there were fish in it, a little one, a larger one, and in the shadow of a boulder a vague shape that might be a large trout. The sea trout were coming from the sea. I quietly slipped on a grizzly-king and a professor, and cast across the pool. At the second cast a medium-sized fish took the fly and I landed him after a sharp fight, a beautiful pound and a half trout. A few minutes later there was a swirl and a big fellow darted out at the fly, but the little one was ahead of him and was taken in short order. Then I went away for twenty minutes, put on two new flies, tested the tackle, and did my very best to throw the flies lightly in the shadow of the boulder. In an instant I had him fast; he moved slowly away a few yards, then jumped high from the water, a great shining bar of silver, fell back heavily and diving under a sharp ledge seesawed the leader against the edge; at last it parted, the fish was away with my two flies, and I sat down on the ground and groaned and said unpleasant things to myself for hesitating to risk my light rod and force him out. An experienced angler might have done it, but my rod was a new one, and I did not know then how much it would bear.

That ended my day's fishing, but I dreamed of big trout, and next morning made extensive preparations, and with a small boy to help, stole softly down to that pool, hid behind a rock and peeped in. I could count twelve fine sea trout, all lying in the bed of the pool and swaying lightly to and fro in the strong current.

And then I began to fish. It was not easy work. The best place from which to cast was on a sloping boulder, where I was almost hidden behind a great mass of rock. I had to cast over this, wait to see that the fish was firmly hooked, and then in the few seconds which elapsed before he realized that fact, pass the rod over the rock, keeping the line taut as I climbed over several slippery rocks, and reaching the strand, face about just as he began to fight. I had never fished for sea trout before, and had always supposed that the Canadian Nipigon trout were the gamiest in the world. But I have never seen such wild rushes, high leaps, and lightning speed. I was no longer afraid to trust the rod and found I could check the fish as they made for the sea. But it was lively work. Such beautiful creatures they were!—like burnished silver with a little blue-green down the back. I had unfortunately left my landing net at Miðvágur, and I had to tire them out and then lead them cautiously up to one little piece of sandy strand where the small boy could go in the shallow water and secure the fish. And never have I seen a stupider specimen than Poul Jens. He stood each time like a graven image, not moving a finger until roused to action by my fierce wrath. He will never make a fisherman. Heini of Miðvágur, at the age of three, would have known just what to do and how to do it. There were times that morning when I had murder in my heart toward Poul Jens.

During the next two hours I caught seven of the twelve fish. In weight they ranged from one and a half to almost three pounds. I think I might have taken several more, but I was quite exhausted by that time, and had to go home for dinner. The largest and wariest fish were still in the pool, and I noticed that the heavier the fish the redder was its flesh. Even in the water one could see the pink and copper tints gleaming through the silver skin. They weighed probably from three to six pounds apiece. The water was very clear and I could see them distinctly as they poised themselves lightly in the current or made little tours around the pool, rising now and then at a midge or fly. I would return, I decided, in an hour, refreshed by my dinner, and try to catch at least three of those big fellows. But I reckoned without Poul Jens. While I was eating, that miserable boy awoke to a misplaced activity, took his heavy fishing pole, and thrashed the surface of that pool, scaring away every fish in the neighborhood.

I had but one day more to spend in Saksun, as I was obliged to be in Vestmanna on the following day in order to catch the little *Smyril*. Early next morning it blew a gale, but I was early at the pool, only to find that a man had stretched a net across it. Two beautiful sea trout, weighing five and six pounds, were in it, caught by the gills. Further up the stream I took three sea trout of a pound and a half apiece, and half a dozen river trout. But by that time the storm had increased, so that the flies were whisked high above the water and I almost blew away up the glen; and the men of the house sent word that the Frøkun must come home and rest; that she did not know what it was to walk from Saksun to Vestmanna.

✖✿✖

In leaving Saksun for Vestmanna, one can go twelve miles by sea, if the sea is calm, or nine miles over the fjelds. I had intended to take the former route, going in a large boat with eight oarsmen, on a serene day, the afternoon sun gilding the wonderful peaks and crags of western Streymoy, I taking kodaks and sketches on the way, and my men lifting up their voices in song. Three months of adverse experience had not taught me wisdom. Instead, I went, as might have been expected, by land, in a howling storm. All the waters were out, and four times one of my men, a giant of a Faroese, had to carry me through the streams, I rejoicing in the meantime in the bigness of his calves. There are, I believe, fine views to be seen en route in good weather, but I saw nothing but shifting gray walls of mist, and it rained "shoemaker's apprentices"—the Faroe equivalent of the English "cats and dogs."

A few days later found me on the way to Sandur on the southern island of Sandoy, where I hoped to catch one big trout before returning to Tórshavn. As we passed down the western side of the island, the captain of *Smyril* pointed out the place where the ill-fated *Principia* was lost in November some years ago. On that same night I had left Tórshavn on a Danish steamer. We had passed on the other side of the island at the very hour when, hidden from all help behind the cliffs of an uninhabited coast, the *Principia* was burning. Out of all the crew and passengers, only one was saved after drifting for thirteen hours lashed to a plank. And that same night a clergyman in Scotland, whose brother was on the ship, saw him in a dream; saw the fire amid-ship, the lifeboats burned, a hastily constructed raft overturned and wrecked in launching, and his brother jumping into the water. He woke with the words "Faroe Islands" sounding in his ears. But he knew nothing of the Faroe Islands, and thought the ship was hundreds of miles south, bound for America. He told his old housekeeper his dream next morning, and six weeks later when the post came from Faroes, he heard that a fire had broken out on the *Principia,* passengers and crew had fought it for three days; they could not steer the vessel, and a southwest gale had driven it far north; and there, burning, she was dashed to pieces against the cliffs of Sandoy. When I went to Miðvágur I found that it was Jógvan Sr. who had found the brother's body and helped to bury it. "A fine man, a sterkur [strong] man," said Jógvan, sadly. "He had a life belt on, but there was little chance for him; of all the wreck that came ashore, not one piece was big enough to use. It was in splinters. There was great surf that night. I have never seen worse."

I post this letter from Tórshavn. I accomplished my mission to Sandsvatn and caught my big trout. Only one big one, to be sure, among a number of small ones, but he was a fish to satisfy the most exacting, a beautiful sea trout, fresh from the bay, caught with my light rod and a small green-mantle fly. He weighed a full five pounds, and we had a long and fair fight. And then a fierce equinoctial storm arose, and little *Smyril* was due before it was over. Each day I watched the surf, and talked with old sea dogs, who were digging their potatoes, about the prospects of my being able to board her if she came. They were unpleasantly optimistic. "Don't be afraid, Frøkun," they said. "We'll get you on board somehow! Yes, unless it gets worse, though it won't be pleasant, we can do it!"

And I could only hope and pray it would get worse and so make the attempt impossible.

But *Smyril* came at last, the old sea dogs put me on board "somehow," and that trip to Tórshavn gave me a fellow feeling for the voyagers of the "Lotus-Eaters"—

> "Most weary seem'd the sea, weary the oar,
> Weary the wandering fields of barren foam."

The little capital, after my four months' absence among the lonely islands, looked cozy and hospitable. There was the hum of voices, the clatter of pattens in the narrow lanes; lights twinkled in the grass-covered cabins and on a fleet of fishing smacks from Iceland— Norse, Scotch, and Faroe—that had taken refuge from the storm.

The baker was making his Saturday evening crullers and little cakes. I could smell the spices in a whiff of land breeze. The cheerful voice of a friend greeted me in English as, chilled and tired, I stumbled out of the boat.

It is good to be back again.

Published in *Forest and Stream. The Journal of Rod and Gun,* November 8, 1902, 362–363.

Whales Aground!

A True Tale from the Faroe Islands

"Can He provide flesh for His people?"
PSALM LXXVIII, V.20

After an enforced sojourn of sixteen days on the top of an outlying island, "weather fast" by great surf, I have come, at last, to my desired haven,- the home and the garden of Hans Kristoffer á Ryggi. Haymaking, long delayed by storms, is in full swing. Hans Kristoffer, his brother, Elder Jógvan, Younger Jógvan, and Heini mow the grass, and six maids spread and toss it with their hands. My pleasant part it is to sit on a grassy hillock and watch the others. I need a little time of repose after my adventures on "difficult" islands. Every night, in dreams, I fell off those dizzy heights to thundering depths below, so now my weary eyes rest gratefully on peaceful fields where Arctic terns, like giant swallows, dart to and fro over the fragrant grasses. The sea is quiet, except at times when some larger wave meets the strand with a long-drawn sigh; and the distant islands gleam like jewels through opalescent mists that wander in from the lonely sea-wastes of the Northern Sixties. This is the so called "Grind weather," when *grinds* or flocks of pilot whales like to visit the Faroe group, for reasons that no one understands.

Not half an hour ago Frú Johanna Katrina, leaving her task of cooking for twelve hungry people, came hurrying from the cottage. Her eyes were bright, her breath came quickly and before she reached the men workers she called out "I believe,—*I do believe* I see out there, off Kolter, the flash of sunshine on spouting whales!" Rash Johanna Katrina! Even I could have told her what her reception would be. A burst of laughter reached my ears and scornful words. *"A Grindaflok!* A flock of whales indeed! And did she think that men-folk needed her, a mere woman, to tell them when whales were in sight?" And then followed, in old Norse, the equivalent of our homely saying, "Go teach your grandmother to suck eggs!"

Johanna Katrina returned to the cottage, her face a little flushed. Nevertheless, she was not the only one who had whales in mind that morning. I noticed that whenever the workers stopped to rest, all eyes were turned seawards, and when a young girl began to sing a dance ballad, it was "The Whale Song" that she sang and all joined in the refrain.

> Early, it was in the summer-time,
> (How pale the moon did shine!)
> The mists were fleeing before the sun
> That rose from the far sea-line.
> > *Refrain*
> Bold lads are we,—to kill the whales,—
> That is our joy.

A spirited ballad it is, telling in fifty-eight verses the story of a whale drive. No other song goes so well in the dances, or brings such a light to the eyes and such spring to the dancing feet.

Elder Jógvan paused near me to sharpen his scythe. "That song was written back in Grandfather's time by a Governor of the Faroes. He was often here, for ours is a fine strand for a killing. Over on that Streymoy coast the fishing grounds far and wide can be seen. Some one is always watching and if he spies a fishing shirt fastened to the top of a mast, he knows that it is a signal meaning that whales have been discovered and men and boats must come at once. Then a *Glaða*, or smoking fire, is made as a signal. All goes by rule. We know from the position of the Glaða in what direction the whales are; and a man whose appointed duty it is, lights an answering fire that means, 'We have seen your message and sent it forward.' For already a man is running towards Sorvágur, four miles away over the hills. He doesn't need to go the whole way. That man has a mighty voice and a mile from the village he stops on a height and bellows, '*Grindaboð!*' and down on the fjord he is heard and a man hurries on to Bøur, a hamlet two miles farther on. It's a long and weary way here by sea and many come overland just to help at the land-going."

"There's a man in the Northern Isles who always knows when the whales are coming. Perhaps, during months, he has not thought of them, but when he begins to think of whales, dream of whales, when he can not put them out of his mind, then he knows that the Grindaboð will come within two or three days. It never fails. I'd like to have that man here to-day."

Then Elder Jógvan went back to his mowing, and I sat awhile longer on the grassy slopes that his forebears have mown during more than five centuries. The fields overlook the garden of Hans Kristoffer, where even on this day of calm a half gale seems to be blowing, so bowed down are the little trees, so curved and tossed the twisted branches.

The next day, Sunday, was so warm and serene that Johanna Katrina declared I must have breakfast in the "Summer House," a little enclosure at the foot of the garden, wherein table and benches stand always ready. Little trees and big elderberry and currant bushes encompass it so closely that we seldom stay long within its chilly precincts, but that delectable morning we sat at ease,—Hans Kristoffer, Johanna Katrina, and I,—and ate our breakfast to the singing of a "Mouse's Brother," as the Faroe wren is called. Miðvágur village still slept in the Sunday calm and only a few wreaths of blue peat smoke rose from grassy roofs.

Suddenly came a loud shout, close by,—"Grindaboð!" An old man on the strand was pointing towards the Streymoy coast, where a column of smoke rose high in the quiet air. "Grindaboð!" again, and as if by magic, a peaceful village became pandemonium. A great wave of sound swept around the bay. Men's deep voices shouted the message. Women and children cried it shrilly, babies screamed with fright. Ducks, chickens, and dogs added to the tumult. Three minutes had not passed when a group of young men raced by, grind knives in hand, their eyes blazing with excitement. The younger Jógvan was among them. Close behind Elder Jógvan followed his firstborn, and both went in the same boat. In eight minutes nine men living in cottages here and there around the bay had met at the boat house, launched the boat, and put to sea with the full whale outfit on board. In fifteen minutes nine boats had started,—Miðvágur's quota to the drive. They passed at full speed out of the bay, turned under high cliffs to the open sea, and were lost to sight.

Boys of fifteen and sixteen years were not allowed to go, for some of the drives make a terrible strain on heart and lungs; but while lamenting their hard lot, they had hope that at the last they might take some part in the slaughter.

"What next?" I asked Johanna Katrina. She made no reply. Her head was held high, her lips compressed, her blue eyes wide open, but unseeing. So might some leader have looked when rallying his forces for a coming fray. Then her lips parted and she murmured, "Put salt sausage and mutton to soak, brown coffee, make rye bread, sweep, bring in dried meat, send to the shop for tea, sugar, spices, white flour, raisins, prunes, rice, and sago." Then she became aware that I stood near. "And perhaps Frøkun will dust a little and bring in fresh flowers? The Grind may escape, of course, but it is not the custom to make white bread or put sweet soups on to cook until the whales have been driven past that far-off point that we call 'The Pastor's Point.'"

Soon the men of Sorvágur and of Bøur were seen coming over the hill. They dropped down breathless on the grass, sharpened their knives, and waited.

The hours passed slowly. I ate my dinner standing or walking to and fro between the window and the table. At last I saw, far away, in a shining belt of water, boats, like tiny, black specks, in three shallow crescents, one behind the other; and now and then, a flash of silver showed where a whale was spouting. "They seem uneasy," said Johanna Katrina. "They may yet break away." And the men of Sorvágur and of Bøur rose to their feet and watched in anxious silence. Six boats then left the others and made their way cautiously along the rocks of the outer bay. "They have come to get more small stones to use in the drive," explained Johanna Katrina. "It won't be long now before it begins." And I hurried away to the opposite side of the bay, where the whales must pass. Here and there I could see a round black head bobbing above the surface. "They seem very few to me," I said to an old man who stood above me. "Oh, where you see one head," he explained, "there will be twenty down below."

All was quiet, no woman on the strand (women are "unlucky" creatures), no sound from the drive. Through the day the flock had been herded in from far out to sea. Now and then, the whales had

seen a little way from them, on one side, a light splash on the water
and bubbles rising, as a small stone fastened to a fishing line was
thrown from a boat. The leader was not alarmed, but it looked
strange and he didn't care for it, so he led the flock more to the other
side as they slowly swam forward. Then came a splash and bubbles
there, also, and again the whales turned from them. So, gently
guided while yet they had no knowledge of that guidance, the
whales approached the entrance to the bay. The water was still deep,
the leader not yet afraid; but at any moment he might take alarm,
dive, turn seaward and the whole flock escape. Then, as they drew
near to the shallow water, the foreman gave a signal, and one boat
dashed forward, a man with a harpoon wounded a whale in the sen-
sitive spot above the tail, and, as the creature mad with pain and
fright rushed into the middle of the flock, the boats charged forward
with loud shouts, the clanging of metal on metal, and blows on the
gunwales. Alarmed, bewildered by the sudden uproar and the charge
of the wounded whale, the whales were seized with a panic and
swept at full speed up the bay. A large band of Eider ducks, generally
so fearless, became frightened and made for the shore, turning their
heads from side to side, reluctant, even in flight, to leave the water.
From the sea came sounds like an Indian powwow, the hoarse, staccato cries of weary men, "*Ah ha! ha! ha! Ah hoy! hoy! hoy!*" There was
a gathering roar from the sea. The whales were hidden by the storm
of white water that preceded them. Six great rollers came crashing
along the coast. I heard the old man above me crying, "Come up
higher, Frøkun, you're in danger there!" The whales tried to turn
seaward and were met by the boats; they rushed to the other side
and, unable to stop, struck the rocks with a shock that made them
tremble. One big whale, upheaved by its fellows, was thrown clear
from the water and fell where I had been standing. The first row of
boats closed in and the slaughter began.

With long lances and knives the men fought, using hooks attached to lines to draw the boats within striking distance; and as the
blood flowed freely from the wounded whales, their comrades
would not leave them. Even if they reached clear water, they turned
again, "seeking the blood." The large whales seemed to be trying to
protect the small ones. Some of the whales, maddened by lance

wounds, rushed forward and were stranded in the shallows, where they were met by the men of Sorvágur and of Bøur, who, breast deep in blood and water, struck again and again with their grind-knives to sever the spinal cord. One large whale, made fast to a boat, dragged it close to high rocks, hemmed it in, and threw such quantities of blood and water over the men that they were helpless. It was like a great red fountain through which I saw dimly the men, blinded by blood, afraid to strike, lest they should injure one another. The boat was being shattered to pieces and other boats had to come to the rescue. The whales made little active resistance, but in their dying flurry they were dangerous. I saw one boat crushed like an egg-shell between two whales, and as it sank, the men flew from it, like rubber balls, to other boats nearby. I saw little boys of six and seven years running into the shallows and jabbing at stranded whales with their little knives until seen by irate great-grandfathers, who sprang in, seized them by the scruffs of their necks, threw them up on the shore, and then ran back to do a little killing of their own.

At last it was over. Not one whale escaped. A hot, heavy odor filled the air; two hundred and eighty-six whales lay dead and dying on Miðvágur's strand, and high above the lessening clamor rose the voice of the *Sysselmand*, summoning all hands to aid in dragging the whales as near the shore as possible, there to be stranded by the outgoing tide.

That night the sun went down in a fiery glory, turning the sky above blood-red, making the bare fjelds glow as though with inner fires. Lambent flames played along the basalt ledges and gleamed from the bare rock beds of little watercourses, but of a deeper red than the sky's angry hue was the bay from shore to shore, not tinged with red, but red as flowing blood, while on the strand the surf beat in a long, crimson line. Rank on rank lay the whales in pools of blood, their smooth, dark skins reflecting the sky colors. Their broad, thick lips curved backward in a grotesque smile, disclosing the small, white teeth clenched fast. There lay the leader of the flock, and there,—oh the pity of it!—were poor, little baby whales lying by their mothers, born in the agony of panic and of death.

There was no sleep for Miðvágur's house-mothers that night. Four hundred men must have food, rest, and shelter. Hans Kristoffer's cottage was the centre of activities. Within the guarded "best room," the Sysselmand and four assistants were to work during the night, apportioning the Grind. When I returned to the cottage, I found them there, neat and trim in changed clothing, eating sweet soup and other good things. The family living-room was full to overflowing with men from the drive. They were having hot coffee and some simple food, then quickly giving place to others. Later, all would have a heartier meal. In the *Roykstova*, or outer kitchen, Hans Kristoffer had spread a thick layer of hay on the earth floor, leaving only narrow passageways between the fire, peat box, doors, and water buckets. Here, twenty-six weary men found grateful warmth and sleep. Their faces were haggard, their clothes drenched with blood and water, their faces and hair plastered with caked blood. Too exhausted to eat, they drank a little hot coffee, took a bit of bread, dropped down on the hay, and slept at once. In closely packed rows they lay, the steam rising from their bodies in the warm air. After a few hours' sleep they could have more food and go out to give place to others in like need.

That night, for the first time, I paid full homage to Johanna Katrina. I had never before seen her during great stress; and in a garden, as a would-be assistant, she could make trouble. Now, however, I saw her as house-mother and hostess, cheerful, capable, attending these tired men as a mother might do and bearing herself with such gentle, smiling dignity as befitted the wife of a "King's Peasant",— one on whom the Danish King had bestowed the Cross of the Danebrog.

The Sysselmand and his helpers showed much thoughtfulness for the "guest lady" in the little room close by. Not once did their voices rise above a deep rumble, and the many men who came and went on mysterious business, trod softly with moccasined feet.

It was dusk at midnight in late August, and through the interlacing branches of the little garden trees I could see the glimmer of lanterns on the strand. There, sober and watchful, four men guarded the Grind. From three houses I heard the sound of singing and the tread of dancing feet. Tired though the men were, it was better to dance, in their wet clothes, while awaiting their turn to sleep. I could distinguish from the confusion of sound many of the ballads. The Whale Song, of course, a song of Charlemagne, one from the Nibelungenlied, an old Danish war song, the story of Sigmundur Brestisson, the Faroe hero, as told in the Faroe Saga, and then more soberly,—gently,—sounded the ballad of the death of Queen Dagmar, with a pensive lilt in the refrain, "In Ringsted rests Queen Dagmar."

The brief dusk had passed. There seemed to be much activity on the shore. Without waiting for early tea, I went down through the garden and opened the gate near the sea. Scores of men were cutting up the Grind. The heavy smell of flesh was in the air. From side to side of the bay, the strand was a shambles. Compared with the larger whales,—the Blue, the Humpback, and the Finner,—the Grind whale is small. The largest one I saw was twenty-one feet in length. But there were so many,—two hundred and eighty-six! The sight of the great piles of meat, bones, blubber, the incredible mass of refuse, were too much for nerves made shaky by a sleepless night and all that had gone before. I retreated in disorder, was met by Johanna Katrina at the cottage door, haled into the vacated best room, put in a chair, and told to swallow at once a piping hot cup of coffee. That

"Scores of men were cutting up the Grind. The heavy smell of flesh was in the air. From side to side of the bay, the strand was a shambles." Photograph by Elizabeth Taylor on Vágar island.

helped, and I then noticed by the side of my plate at the breakfast table, a piece of paper. My name was on it, and strange legal phrases unknown to me, signatures and figures. A vague apprehension filled my mind. Had I unwittingly transgressed the law? I went in search of Hans Kristoffer and showed him the paper. "Yes," he said placidly, "just show that to one of the men in charge of the Grind and you will be given your portion."

"Am I to have a piece of whale?" I queried weakly.

"Certainly," said Hans Kristoffer. "Even if you had been only a chance visitor for the day, you would be entitled to a share. But," he added, "if you don't care to take your portion with you when you leave here, it can be auctioned off to-day, with other lots, by Sysselmand."

A little later, I went down again to the strand and found that many boats had come from distant islands. Over piles of blubber and vertebrae I exchanged greetings with men who had gone with me over fjelds, rowed and fished and climbed with me. In Faroe fashion, they shook hands and said, "Thanks for our last meeting," and I, remembering *my* manners, responded cordially, "The thanks are to you." All were in good spirits. There had been no serious accidents, there was a calm sea for the heavily laden boats. One old man said, "There is good food here for the winter. The Lord *has* provided flesh for His people."

Boat after boat put to sea in the twilight and as the men reached the outer bay and settled down to their work at the oars, many began to sing the thanksgiving Psalm.

It is two days since the Grind and the waters of the bay are still thick and red. We long for strong winds and tides to bring in fresh seas and purify us again. People are still busy salting meat, cutting it in strips to dry in the salt-laden air, making oar straps from the hide of the back fins, tanning and blowing up stomachs to use as buoys for the fishing nets, and boiling whale heads to extract the prized oil they contain. Moreover, there is the refuse to be carried out to sea, for a wise law requires all to be removed within seventy-two hours.

Elder Jógvan has been telling me of the great Grind of 1898, when fifteen hundred whales were killed here. The people toiled night and day so that the enormous amount of meat should not be spoiled. A dreadful sight the strand must have been.

I am weary of whales. I have eaten whale boiled, fried, and minced; the liver, heart, brains, and kidneys of young whale; and best of all, head fin boiled, cut in thin slices when cold, and eaten with thin slices of dry bread. It has a firm, white substance and a pleasant, nutty flavor.

Our pastor was to have held service and christened several babies at Sanðavágur, a mile away, but there could be no christening when the fathers and all the godfathers were on the high seas. So he preached a very short sermon to the rest of the congregation, hurried home, changed to his oldest clothing, seized his grind knife, ran along the coast to the outer bay, climbed down a cliff, was taken on board a boat just before the "land-going" began and was in the midst of the fight with nine of his flock.

I asked Hans Kristoffer what happens when the whale message comes to a village and the people, unaware of it, are in church. He told me that a messenger goes to the church, opens the door quietly, and whispers "Grindaboð" to the nearest man. He, in turn, whispers to the neighbor and tiptoes softly from the church, and so the message is passed on to all who are to take part in the drive. Generally, the pastor shortens the service and often goes too, but when the Sacrament is being administered, no message is sent to the church. No man would leave the Lord's Table to join in a Grind. Should he dare to do so, no blessing would follow him or his.

Elder Jógvan tells me that many believe in the supernatural powers of the hooded crows, that they know when the whales are near, and often they will come boldly to the very windows of a cottage, peer in and say "Bu! bu!" meaning to give the whale message; but they lack the words to tell more.

Many are the little stories connected with the Grind. I heard of a man who eight times had found a Grind and eight times it had escaped. So he came at last to fear that he was under a ban and to dread the sight of his own shirt at the mast's top (as a signal to other boats or to shore watchers that he had seen a Grind). Then he found the ninth Grind. In an agony of suspense, he awaited the signal of the foreman, and just before the final charge, he called out, *"For God in Heaven's sake, Rasmus, don't lose this Grind!"* But the ninth Grind (nine is a blessed number) was taken and the ban was lifted.

Just one more little tale that illustrates the high spirit of the old Faroe men. It was old Jorgen's dearest wish always to be in the first boat that left shore after the Grindaboð was heard in the village. Not once had he failed during almost sixty years. Then, one peaceful Sunday morning, early, when weary men were sleeping, sounded the Grindaboð. The first shout awakened old Jorgen. He sprang from his bed, seized his grind-knife, and started headlong for the shore. His old wife pursued him, calling and waving his trousers, but Jorgen only shook his head impatiently and raced onwards. He didn't want his trousers, he wanted to go in the *first* boat,—and went in the first boat. His trousers went in the *second* boat, and they met,—hours later,—far out at sea.

Published in *Forum*, August, 1927, 214–225.

My Party

Dansibod! i prestagardinum!—Dance message! In the parsonage! A small boy was going from house to house throughout the hamlet of Viðareiði, opening the doors of the little turf-covered cottages and making this announcement to the people who were eating their Sunday dinners in the *roykstova*. No need to ask the time of the dance; as the day was Sunday, it would of course be given that evening. And, in truth, the sending of the Dansibod was a mere formality, for everyone knew all about it, even to the fact that Drikka had baked little cakes all Saturday afternoon and had bought several pounds of sweets.

It was my party that the Dansibod proclaimed. The fishing boats had returned from Iceland; the young men, the dancers, were at home again; the Pastor and Pastorinde had gone to Denmark, And I was living in solitary state in the front of the parsonage, with Drikka and Sigga at the other end and visiting cats ranging between. After years of nomadic life, it was a pleasure to assume the role of "housemother" and *pro tempore* to have a house all my own. Hospitable instincts, long dormant, awoke to life—all the circumstances pointed towards a party. When could I, a wandering American, have such an opportunity of entertaining the youth of a church capital? It was not a case of the mice playing in the Pussy's absence. It is the custom to dance from September until Lent, every Sunday. Often had the Pastor loaned the big kitchen to his parish children for a dance on a Sabbath evening, making only this stipulation—that they bring no brennivín.

There were no puzzling queries "who to invite" to my party. All that wished to dance were free to come. The matter of music, too, was a simple one. It would be furnished by the strong lungs and vocal chords of the dancers themselves, for these Faroe Islands, preserved by storms and dangerous seas from the changes of lands "down below," have guarded one precious heritage—the chain dance accompanied by the singing of medieval ballads.

After days of storms the sea was at rest, the surf sighing gently at the base of the cliffs. The peace, the silence, were welcome to ears weary of the long uproar, and the parsonage doors stood open to admit the quiet air. Above Malinsfjall's snowy cone the full moon mounted, touching with silver the little watercourses and the hoarfrost on the wild outfields. Within the big roykstova all was in readiness. Decorous clean curtains drawn before the wall beds, fishing rods, milk stool, lanterns and lamps hung high to leave clear space for the dancers. A fragrant whiff of coffee came through the inner kitchen door, and in the dining room Drikka was cutting cake and Sigga laying plates. By half past seven o'clock all the guests had assembled, but no sounds of festivity were heard in the roykstova. Little groups of girls whispered and giggled softly on one side of the room; on the other sat a long line of men puffing gravely on their pipes and from time to time growling out a few words. The men wore the true Faroe dress: dark homespun knee breeches, a row of brass buttons at the knee left unbuttoned to display the gay striped garters, brown or dark gray woolen stockings, low Danish shoes that on holidays replace the sheepskin moccasins, homespun coats of brown wool with stitched upstanding collar, on their heads red and blue striped "Brownie" caps, and around their necks thick woolen scarves.

Suddenly a tall broad-shouldered man rose, stepped out on the floor and sang loudly:

> "Wilt thou listen to my song?
> Then I will sing to Thee;
> Of the rich and mighty kings
> Shall the story be."

Instantly the dancers were on their feet and joining hands formed a close circle that, too large for the room, bowed in upon itself in chainlike loops that wound and slipped smoothly from right to left while all sang the refrain:

> "Grane bore the gold from the heath;
> Sigerd in wrath swung his sword;

Victory over the serpent he won;
Grane bore the gold from the heath."

It was the ballad of Siegfried (Sigerd in Faerosk speech) and the dusky old roykstova was echoing with the story of Sigerd's youth, his charger Grane, of Regin the Blacksmith, the welding of the sword, the combat of Fafnir the serpent and the bearing away of the Golden Treasure—tales of the Niebelungenlied that had found their way to these faraway islands five centuries ago. In verses of four lines sang the leader or *skipari*, many of the dancers singing with him, while all joined in the refrain.

"Grane bore the gold from the heath." Only the first part (there are five in all) of the Sigerd ballad was sung. This is called Regin Smedur (Regin the Blacksmith) and has 125 verses. The other four parts treat of Brunhild, her wooing and desertion, Gudrun's marriage, Sigerd's murder, Gudrun's revenge, and so on to the locking of Atte in the Golden Mountain.

The dance step was simple, the left foot took one step to the left, and the right foot joined it, being placed a little behind, then the left foot took another step and the right foot joined it. These steps formed the whole figure. The hands were clasped and held usually on the level with the chest, but as the ballad expressed violent action or excitement they were raised shoulder high and moved backward and forward with quick jerks. In perfect time they moved, the singing giving the beat and the shoes marking it on the floor with perfect precision. Not a pause or a break was there in the whole 125 verses. As the refrain died away, the dancers still standing with clasped hands, two voices began two ballads, one an old Norse ballad and the other a whale song written only fifty years ago. For a moment all was confusion, some voices joined one, some the other, but the whale song was the victor—the opposing voices died away. Whales, the grind or driving whales, are dear to every Faroinger's heart. With enthusiasm swelled the voices, every man singing with might and main, eyes flashing, faces flushed. The floor shook. The whole house seemed to tremble. The sound of the singing floated out in the quiet moonlight. One heard of the peaceful day, the calm morning, the solitary fishermen at sea; the sight of the distant flock, the message flashing from island to island, the pursuit, the killing. The men leap up in the air and stamp hard, then the battle is over. The Thanksgiving is heard:

"Great is God in the works of man
And wonderful is His law;
Though He had made the whales so strong,
They must to mankind bow.

Far to the south, high in the north,
Doth He His blessings send.
I see them on mountain, dale, and fjord,
Wherever my eyes I bend."

And the refrain was:

"Strong lads are we!
To kill the whales,
That is our joy!"

I thought surely the dancers would rest now after this stirring song of more than half a hundred verses; but no, a young lad began softly the song of Queen Dagmar's death:

"Queen Dagmar lies in Ribe sick
To Ringsted they wait for her,
All the dames that in Denmark dwell."

And the refrain:

"In Ringsted rests Queen Dagmar."

Slowly, gravely, the clasped hands hanging low, parallel with the hips, this ballad was danced. Three others followed before the dancers separated to rest for a few minutes. There was more life, more chatter now. The men filled their pipes.

There are differences in custom on the different islands. In some places, all, old and young, dance. Here in Viðareiði only the young men and girls participate, and the half-grown children, though a bride may dance for a while after her marriage and occasionally a middle aged man will too, a few times. I remember seeing a gray-haired woman, a grandmother but still graceful and light of foot. She had under pressure taken part in one rather staid dance and had come back to my side. "I am too old for this kind of thing," she said sedately, "my dancing days are over." Just then a skipari struck up a lively seaman's song with a gay rollicking refrain of "fol de rol rol, fol de rol." The grandmother sprang to her feet, all her resolutions thrown to the winds, her eyes flashing: "Farvael, I must go, I cannot hold out," she said, and in a moment I saw her in the circle dancing as lightly as the youngest there.

❦

Two o'clock—It is time to break up. One by one my guests come up, bow, shake hands, and say thanks for the evening; and I respond, bow and answer, "Sjalvtakk" [to you the thanks]. At last only a few men are left and they are the Pastor's Seydamenn that have general supervision of the half-wild flocks in the fields. This is the morning of the first "mountain-going," the first slaughter of the year. It is not worth while to go to bed—the men will go home to change to their old clothes and then meet to start off for the distant fjelds.

❦

Viðareiði, Viðoy

Dear Helen:

I have given my party and it was a great success. You could have heard it for half a mile. It began at seven-thirty and ended at two-fifteen A.M., leading off with a dance of 125 verses. Fifty people were here, thirty-eight grownups and the rest large children. The folks had coffee, jolakokka [Christmas cake], American Scotch crackers, candies, tobacco for pipes, and cigars. The whole thing cost three dollars and a half and was considered a handsome affair. With it I acknowledged a good many little courtesies from the men here in helping carry up luggage, taking messages, &c.

Elizabeth Taylor Papers, Minnesota Historical Society.

Odd Way to Get a Wife

Between Christmas and Lent dancing in the Faroe Islands reaches its culmination in frequency. On Christmas night the great saga of "Oluva Kvadet" is sung. The unhappy Queen Oluva's faithfulness to the King, which is the theme of the song, is doubtless intended as a reminder to young couples who engage themselves during dancing time.

There being no parlors in Faroe cottages, nor corners to hide in and tell the fairy tales of the heart, the young people are obliged to do their courting in the open, that is, as the dance goes on and under the eyes of every one partaking. If you have been courting a Faroe girl for some time and wish to get her "yes" or "no," you will have to line up alongside her in the dance and make your proposal then.

Take care that sharp eyes do not detect your secret, and your purpose before you have got what you want—the girl's "yes." If they find you out before you succeed they will point their fingers at you, and sing ditties with sarcastic little flings at you.

At the same time, the tempo of the dance will be increased, and if you don't withdraw it is likely to develop into a sort of native can-can. Of course, as soon as the ditty making sport of you begins to circulate among the crowd the girls all prick up their ears, and the particular girl you may be heading for gets out of your reach at once.

If you are a shrewd man you will retreat; you can always try again. If you are obstinate you may always be sure of a refusal, for no Faroese girl will take a man who is too clumsy to get hold of her hand without other people noticing it.

Absolutely nothing is said during the courting. The man says nothing, and the girl says nothing. If he can but get hold of her hand—that is his only chance. A slight pressure from hers, and he is accepted. Then both are supposed to blush and clasp hands.

The dance stops. With smiling faces and expectant looks the

crowd faces the lovers in deep silence to see that the first kiss is bestowed according to Faroese rule. The dance is then renewed with vigor.

That is a neat and handy and straightforward way of courting. The Faroese style is well suited to people who know their own mind, and marriages there are happy, divorces exceedingly scarce.

A refusal is even more prompt. The young man, having secured the girl's hand, she quickly snatches it away from him, and turns her back on him. There he stands then, the target for a shower of sarcastic speeches, the blushing, awkward victim of the cold shoulder literally.

A Faroese wedding without dancing before and after was never heard of. Not infrequently the priest gathers up his long sable robe and joins the dancers. The dancing and singing are sometimes kept up for several days after the wedding, but no orgies ever occur, as the Faroese is a very sensible man and a moderate drinker.

Current Literature, 32 (June, 1902) 678–679. Originally published in *Chicago Inter-Ocean*.

Weddings and Sheep

The return of the Pastor was made necessary by sheep, those of the outfields and those of the church where there are those to be married. There is a close connection between the two. During my first visit to the Faroes I expressed to the Pastorinde a wish to see a wedding. "My dear," she turned to the Pastor, "When does the slaughter begin?" I was not pleased by the flippant cynicism of this remark, but I was soon enlightened. Fresh meat is absolutely essential at a wedding and in autumn only is it to be had in sufficient quantity and quality so the weddings are generally arranged to take place between the time of the first sheep slaughter in early October and late November.

Elizabeth Taylor Papers, Minnesota Historical Society.

The Baptizing of the Baby

The Baby arrived at Viðareiði in a howling nor'easter. The fjelds were white with driving snow, the sea was white with the spindrift of gale-lashed waves, when the little procession filed into the Parsonage courtyard. There were a father, five godfathers, two godmothers, and a few non-official friends. No baby was visible, but a muffled gurgle betrayed her presence. One of the godfathers, a fine young Viking of a lad, had a woman's dress-skirt buttoned around his neck and hanging down in front. Within its warm folds was the Baby.

The Baby's age was but four weeks, and this her first journey into the outside world. Custom has decreed that a Faroe Island baby must not pass its parents' threshold until it goes to the Pastor to be received into the Church, and so made secure from the Powers of Darkness. Having once left its home, it cannot return with the sacred rite unperformed.

Imagine, then, the dismay that fell upon the Baby's escorts when they learned that the Pastor had gone to the Capital, several days before, on important church business. To Tórshavn! Not many miles away, by sea, to be sure, but, with that gale, it might as well be seventy. What to do now? The Baby could not be taken back unbaptized. And there was the baptismal feast all arranged: sweet soup, hung mutton, potatoes, coffee, little cakes, with card playing in the afternoon, and rice porridge and sandwiches in the evening. The Baby's mother was putting the sweet soup over the fire when they left that morning. Five miles by fjord they had come; then, as the gale increased, and they neared the open sea, they had "set up" on land, and trudged the remaining three miles through deep snow.

"Oh well," sighed the father, "we may as well take it with quiet. The women folk are too weary, anyhow, to go through those drifts again. We had better send one man home to explain matters, while the rest of us visit our friends. The storm may lessen at any time, so we can go to Tórshavn and bring home the Pastor."

But the Baby—And here the Pastorinde was called upon to advise. Yes the Pastorinde *did* know of a newly-arrived baby in Viðareiði village, and she doubted not that its mother would kindly permit the stranger-baby to share and share alike with her own.

I, too, was "weather-fast." From Tórshavn I had come, twelve days before, to "hold Yule" at the parsonage, intending to return two days after Christmas. Then came this long storm. No going to Tórshavn by sea; but in a roundabout way, by fjord and fjeld, it might be done in a case of necessity, like this church meeting that the Pastor must attend.

The foreman of the eight-man boat, however, flatly refused to take me. "The Herr Pastor," he explained patiently, "has strong legs. He can jump and stand fast in surf, climb cliffs, and go through deep snow. But it is no journey for women folk in high winter time."

So I was left behind when the Pastor went to Tórshavn.

One must start before daylight these short winter days to enable the boats to return before dark. For eight days I had been living as much packed up as possible, sleeping lightly, waking in the blackness of morning at the sound of voices in the kitchen below. Groping to the head of the stairway, I could hear the decision of the foreman: "Not possible today, Frú Pastorinde. There is *ribbingur i sjonum* [dangerous sea] outside."—And back I would creep shivering, sure of one day more in the parsonage.

"What is the Baby's name to be?" I asked one of the godfathers, as we chanced to meet the next day. An embarrassed silence was followed by an abrupt change of subject, and I felt that I had made a *faux pas*. Later, I was told that a baby's name must never be asked, never be told before baptism. I knew, already, some bits of baby-lore. For instance, if a child cries while it is being baptized, it will have a good voice and sing well at the ballad dances. The water must never be allowed to run down into the baby's eyes, or it will have "second-sight." This is not a happy gift, and I notice that the godmother holding the child, tilts it at the right moment so that the water flows back over the forehead. I know, too, that the man who carries a baby boy to and from the church goes as fast as possible, so that the boy will be strong at the oar, sure-footed on the fjelds. This, you observe, for the boy baby. No such trouble is taken for a mere girl. But, for both alike, there is this precaution: never leave a child alone before it is baptized. Until then it falls easily into the power of evil spirits, and is in danger of being carried away by Huldufólk. These underground creatures are not "the little people," or the brownies. In size and appearance they resemble human beings. They have boats and go to the fishery; they have cows, sheep (that are always gray), dogs (large black hounds that often have a light on the end of their tails); but one thing the Huldufólk lack, and that is souls. If, however, they can take away a Faroe baby and substitute one of their own, and it is baptized, then that child will have a soul.

I know a peasant woman whose daughter died in childbirth not long ago, leaving her baby to her mother's care. The father of the baby was fishing in Iceland, and the old woman lived alone in her little cottage. I went to see her, and during my visit, she wished to show me some articles in another part of the house. Wherever we went she took the cradle with her. I understood the reason and said to her, "but, Sanna, living by yourself as you do, are you not obliged sometimes to leave the baby alone?"

"Yes, Frøken," she replied sadly, "several times I have had to leave him just for a few minutes. But I put the Psalm book under his pillow, I mark him with the sign of the Cross, and *I run my best!*"

Another story I have heard lately is about a Huldu-child on Viðoy. A peasant and his wife had a baby boy, a good happy healthy child, that never cried or made trouble. One day the mother had to leave him alone a little while. When she returned she found the baby crying and fretting. Its face seemed changed, somehow, and yet she could not say that it was not their child. From that time it cried night and day until the parents were worn out, and they took it to the Pastor to ask his advice. Now the Pastor "knew more than his Paternoster," as the saying is; that is, he had studied Black Art. He examined the child and said he feared it *was* a *bytisbarn* [changeling]. "Now," said he, "go home and build a great brewing fire in the fireplace. In each of the four corners put a limpet shell filled with milk. Then hide yourselves, so you can see and hear the child, but it will not know you are there. If it says or does anything that shows it is a Huldu-child, then you may hope to get your own baby back again."

The parents followed carefully the Pastor's instructions, and, trembling with anxiety, awaited the result. As the fire roared and crackled, the child stirred uneasily and stopped crying. Then it raised itself on its elbow and watched the fire and the four limpet shells that were sizzling away in the corners. Then they heard the child laugh scornfully, and saw it point at the limpets. "Huh!" it exclaimed, "how can a child be expected to thrive in a house where they have such things for kettles! They should just see the great kettles—the great brewing pots, in the house of my father, Buin!" The Huldu-child had betrayed itself! That night there was no crying, the parents slept in peace and woke to find their own good happy baby in the cradle.

What are the cradlesongs this Baby will hear in the cabin where she first saw the gray light of December? Verses from the old Kingos Psalm book, ballads of the Long Serpent and King Olaf, of Queen Dagmar's death, the Whale Song, stories from the Iceland Sagas and the Nibelungenlied. Little verses, too, Mother Goosey jingles, one that is sung in Norwegian to babies in all the Scandinavian lands:—

> Row, row to the fishing ground,
> How many fishes have you found?
> One for Father,
> One for Mother,
> One for Sister,
> One for Brother,
> One for him that drew the nets,
> One for my little Baby.

Here is a little Faroe verse:—

> Down comes the Puffin to the sea,
> With his head carried high.
> "Little Gray-titlark, lend me thy boat?"
> "Small is my boat, short are my legs
> But come thee on board";
> And the oars rattle in the oarlocks.

When the Baby grows a little bigger, she will not be taught that "the Bossy-cow says "Mo-o-o," the Pussy-cat says "Me-ow." No, she will learn what the *birds* say:—

> The Puffin says, "*Ur-r! UR-R! UR-R!*"
> The Raven says, "*Kronk! KRONK! KRONK!*"
> The Crow says, "*Kra! KRA! KRA!*"
> The Eider-duck says, "Ah-oo! AH-OO! AH-OO!"
> The Wheatear says, "*Tck! TCK! TCK! None so pretty as I!*"

and so on through a long list of the birds of field and sea.

Summer and winter the birds will be the Baby's neighbors. From her father's cabin she can hear the eider-ducks cooing softly as they rise and fall just beyond the white crest of the breakers. Starlings bubble and chortle on the grassy house roof; from the dark cliffs sounds the raven's clarion cry, and there are always sea gulls near. With spring come all the seafowl to the bird cliffs, and curlew, golden plover and Arctic jaegers, "plaintive creatures that pity themselves on moorlands." All through the long dark winter the wren and titlark sing cheerfully. The "mouse's brother" the Baby will call the Faroe wren, and she will know one fact of which grave scientists are ignorant, that the "mouse's brother" and the titlark sing a bird-translation of a verse from the old Kingos Psalm book. She will know, too, how the eider duck won her down, the story of the naughty shag and the Apostle Peter, why the cormorant has no tongue, and that the great black-backed gull once struck our Lord upon the Cross and thenceforth bore a blood-red spot on his bill. Well can the Baby say in the words of the Kalevala, "The birds of Heaven, the waves of the sea, have spoken and sung to me; the music of many waters has been my master."

She will also sing a less prosaic "rain, rain, go away" when she wants good weather:

> Gentle Mary, Jesus, let the sun appear
> Call up the mists from every peaked hill;
> Follow sunshine, then, and bid the wind be still.

Few will the Baby's pleasures be. She will never have a Christmas tree, nor hang up her stocking, nor have other presents than a pair of mittens or a woolen kerchief for her head. The day before Christmas she will help her mother to scrub everything that can be scrubbed, indoors and out, working far into Jolanatt, so that all shall be sweet and clean for the birthday of our Lord. And next morning, in the sod-roofed church where never was a fire made, she will sit with her mother on the women's side, waiting meekly after service until the last man and the last boy have left their seats. She will dance lightly on the sea rocks, her fair hair blowing in the wind, retreating as the big waves crash down, and singing something which sounds like "*Alda kann ekko taka meg*" ["The wave cannot catch me!"] She sings it to the same little tune I sang as a child when dancing back and forth across the danger line of Taffy's land, mocking the rushes of an agile Taffy.

From seven to fourteen years she will go to school two weeks out of every six (the schoolmaster must be shared between three hamlets), and when fourteen years old, she will be confirmed, if she has learned enough Danish to pass the examinations and to say the prayers and creed. On that morning of confirmation she will turn up her hair, and wear a dress skirt that will flap about her little heels. And that afternoon there will be chocolate and cakes in her father's cabin, with friends coming and going.

She will know suspense and fear and sickening dread when "the boats are out," and the great gales burst without warning. From every hamlet the sea has taken many; not one home has been spared. She cannot escape the common lot; of grief she shall have her share.

Three days of storm passed and the Baby was not thriving. She needed her mother, and a consultation was held, the old sea dogs of the hamlet advising. The gale was surely lessening, and with nine picked men, eight to row and one to steer, it could and should be done. The passage was to be made to Tórshavn to bring the Pastor home. So off they went in the early morning.

I was in my room, upstairs, about eleven o'clock, when I noticed that the roar of the wind, and the creaking and groaning of the timbers overhead had ceased. I went to the window in time to see a great mass of snow gathered up from the ground and hurled against the house. In that short pause the wind had changed, and now blew from the west with redoubled fury. I hurried downstairs, and one glance at the Pastorinde's face confirmed my fears. She knew only too well where the returning boat was at that hour; far out, off the worst place on the coast, in fierce sea-currents, and in the full sweep of this new offshore gale. The men were in peril. Many boats the Pastorinde had known to "go away" in such a storm, after hours of desperate struggle to hold the boat in place and make some headway toward land. Then, as strength failed, there would be a slipping seaward, faster and faster, till men and boat went under, overwhelmed by a mighty cross-sea—"the drowning wave."

Hour after hour went by; the Pastorinde paced the rooms, pale and silent. Under the shelter of walls and boathouses were groups of men looking seaward. At last a shout, and men pointing; out in a smother of flying foam a dark spot had been seen, then lost, then seen again far away under the cliffs of distant Streymoy. The boat was slowly making its way to a point due west, where it could blow in with the gale. All the men and boys who could stand on their legs were down in the surf to meet it, and with a rush the boat was borne up on land.

All was ready in the Parsonage. The rug in the dining room rolled up, hot coffee made, food on the table; and the Pastorinde was standing in the doorway as the men toiled feebly up, their clothes streaming with sea water. *Nine* men only! Where was the *tenth*— where was the Pastor? And, all together, the tale was told. The Pastor, they had found, was not in Tórshavn; two days ago the Danish gunboat had carried him off to Trongisvágur on some church affair, and nothing had been seen of him since. Higher and higher rose the voices, trembling with the irritation and unreasoning anger of utter exhaustion. The storm had struck them at the worst place; for four hours they had struggled just to hold their own, and were drifting seaward, when a short lull came, and with hope renewed they fought again and at last reached the sheltering cliffs of Streymoy. Their eyes were wild and glassy, their hair matted, their hands swollen and bleeding from straining at the oars. The Pastorinde—wise woman— wasted no words of sympathy: she poured coffee, hot fragrant coffee with plenty of cream in it. The men drank and the talking quieted to grateful mumbles, and the cups were filled again, while their clothes dripped sea water and the floor was all afloat.

Two mornings later, before dawn, I heard a knock on my door, and the Pastorinde's voice calling, "The storm has ceased and they are going to take the Baby to Tórshavn, to be baptized by the Tórshavn pastor. They will take you, too, if you can be ready in half an hour."

We were ready, all the baptismal party, plus myself and the borrowed "maternal font." One of the men came for me with a lantern and I clutched his strong hand and slipped and slid over the icy rocks. Lights flared here and there, and land, sea, and sky were all one blackness; only a faint gray line showed where the sea was breaking. The surf was still high, covering the usual landing place. One by one, we women were carried to a group of rocks that rose above the surf. Beyond, the boat was pitching and tossing, two men in the rowing seats keeping the high sharp prow pointing toward the land. It was no easy matter to get on board, but we stood not upon the order of our going but jumped at once. At one moment I was on top of two godmothers, the next moment five godfathers scrambled over me to their places at the oars. Muffled shrieks arose and ejaculations: "Ak gud bevare os!" "Ak Herre Jesus!" The boat swept out into the darkness, and we womenfolk picked ourselves up and sorted ourselves out.

It was bitterly cold, and it rained—oh, how it rained! But we didn't care, we were going to Tórshavn at last, and there was a good sea. The change of wind, the downpour, had flattened the broken surges. Only the great ground swells swept landward, rank on rank, crashing along the coast. We mounted slowly to their summits and glided down the outer slopes with the motion of a bird in flight. Gayly rose the talk in the boat, and there was a lighting of little pipes, one at a time, so that the rowing need not be hindered. Now a faint yellow gleam on the southern horizon beyond the downdropping veils of mist, then, dimly seen, the snow-crowned heights of Nólsoy rising eighteen hundred feet from the sea. The danger point on Streymoy passed, and then in the distance, twinkling lights, and a breath from shore bearing the fragrance of peat smoke.—"So he bringeth them to their desired haven."

Out on the fjord the Danish gunboat rose and fell, and on the wet shore rocks was a lonely figure gazing out to sea, like the pictures of Napoleon on Elba. It had a familiar look—it was yes, it was the Pastor!

They laid hands on the Pastor, as though they expected him to vanish from their sight. The Baby would be baptized then and there. Scant time was given to the godmothers to change their shoes, skirts, and stockings, and to prink.

Clang! Clang! Clang! rang the church bell in treble, staccato notes. There was a clattering of pattens in the stony lanes as children hurried to the Baptism. The Pastor, a dignified priestly figure in his long black robes and Elizabethan ruff, left the Tórshavn parsonage, passed through the side gate to the church portal, and the bell ringing died away.

I was down at the landing an hour later to say "farvael" to the Pastor and the baptismal party. And, as the boat left shore I turned away to my little cabin home with a sigh of relief. The Baby *Karin Marin Malene Elsebet Jakobina Jakobson*—was baptized.

Published in *Atlantic Monthly*, 109 (February, 1912) 278–283. Reprinted in *Atlantic Classics,* Second Series, Boston: The Atlantic Monthly Press (1918).

Absalom's Wreath

I am having a picnic, a solitary picnic in Dalin. Our milk girl, Sigga, escorted me past the bull that lives in the outfields, and then I tramped on alone for an hour and reached the Valley of the Delectable Mountains. In a semicircle stand the fjelds facing the rising of the September sun, their highest ridges lightly powdered with the first snow, their lower slopes seamed by scores of little brooks "that tumble as they run." When peat is to be cut, and the wild sheep captured for wool-pulling and for the autumn slaughter, then people come to Dalin. But today I see only a few black sheep, the kittiwakes and gulls on the sea rocks, and curlew quavering above the heather. Dalin is exclusive, reserved, and has an undefinable charm. Nowhere else has afternoon tea, made over a fire of peat, so fine a flavor; in no other valley does one feel that mingled sense of mystery and of brooding peace. The only disturbing element is a *Nykur* who lives in neighboring waters. His attributes vary according to the narrator's fancy, but all agree on the length of his tail, his black hue, and his disagreeable habit of appearing suddenly, snatching up some unhappy man or woman, and diving with his victim to the bottom of the sea. One saving idiosyncrasy he has, however. He cannot "thole" to hear his own name. Can you but look him in the eye, and say calmly, but firmly "Nykur!" he will recoil in affright down to his fishy home.

But this is a digression. The reason of my solitary picnic is that little Absalom is dead and will be buried tomorrow, and some wreath or cross should lie on his coffin. In Viðoy, the most northern island of the Faroes, there is not a tree or shrub or square foot of garden; it is the 15th of September, and we are near sixty-three degrees north latitude. But of heather there is a plenty in sheltered Dalin, where it dares to grow a foot high, and surely, I thought, some last flowers can be found there, also, for little Absalom's wreath.

I stopped on my way to shake hands with the father and mother.

Absalom lay in an unpainted pine coffin, a cross marked in ink on the lid. He wore his best fur cap and a muslin shroud with a cross made of pink ribbon stitched above his breast. The pastor is in far-away Denmark, but tomorrow Absalom will be carried to the grave-yard on the sea cliffs, we singing psalms all the way, and next month, when the pastor returns, he will pray and cast earth on the grave, saying, "From earth art thou come; to earth shalt thou go; from earth shalt thou rise again."

When I first looked about me in Dalin the prospect was discouraging. The heather bells hung brown and dry; only the bent, turning to russet and ochre, gave color to the slopes. But kneeling down by the little burns, I found, under the overhanging banks, some scanty heather blossoms, belated by the shade and the proximity of the cold water. Then I scrambled up to a small ravine that looked promising, and slid down its steep sides, holding fast to heather twigs. I explored that ravine *au fond*, finding a flower here and there in the clefts and among the heather, and now, tired and hungry, I am perched on the hill-side, and with an appreciative appetite, eating barley bread and cheese and cold fried cod, my treasures by my side. Here are tiny pink polygalas and intensely blue ones like a scrap of southern sky; that cosmopolitan, the crowberry, golden tormentillas (my sheepskin moccasins are tanned with tormentilla roots), a narrow-leaved polypody fern called by the Faroe folk *Trollakampur*: under it the "little people" are supposed to dwell, and prudence dictates that we tread softly where it grows, for they are quick of temper and malicious when annoyed. Here is an arctic form of the field gentian (*Gentiana campestris*), dull lilac in color; the common lady's-mantle and the alpine species (*Alchemilla alpina*), little St. John's-wort, stonecrop, the calluna heather, and the crimson bells of the cinerea heather. Not a bad display for the middle of September in latitude sixty-three.

And yet it is not the latitude that limits the flora so much as the storms. Iceland, farther north, has a greater number of both species and individuals. Her summers are warmer, and she is large enough to afford some protection from the sea winds. But these islands in a storm district well up toward the Circle have conditions peculiarly their own. The Gulf Stream, mingling with the Icelandic polar current, causes dense fogs; it rains on three hundred days of the year, and the area is too small to check the momentum of the gales. They rush through the fjords, searching out every nook and cranny; through openings in the fjelds they fall, writhing and whirling down upon the lowlands as the dreaded *kastivindur*, and where can the poor plants find shelter? And not only the sea gales, but the sea itself, for when the air is filled with flying spray, and even the brooks run brackish, many species are cut down as by a frost.

The first flower of spring, however, cares nothing for the salt spray. Were you to come to Dalin on May Day you would find the white cochlearia, hardy and honey-scented, growing in clefts of the shore crags. The little English daisy is open about the same time in the home fields and on the grassy boathouse roofs. A few days later, open the sweet-scented marsh violet, the dog violet (*Viola sylvestris*), polygalas, shepherd's purse, a veronica, lady's-smock (*Cardamine pratensis*), the little starry saxifrage, and the moss campion, a charming flower, which I fancy grows on the highest of our White Mountains. It has an innocent, wide-eyed look, and varies in color from bluish white to deep crimson; I have seen a thousand growing in a space of twelve inches on a cushion of moss-green leaves, and not a blossom more than half an inch in height.

Soon after the middle of May the show of the marsh marigold begins. Never have I seen such big fat ones; many have eight, nine, or ten petals, and are two inches and a half in diameter. They grow usually in the *gravir*, or little ditches that drain the infields. Most of the cultivated land in the Faroes is divided into long strips from eight to twelve feet in width, extending down the hill slopes. These, for better drainage, are made about two feet higher on one side than on the other, so that a cross section of a field would have the shape of a saw. Between these strips run the gravir, and when the flowers are in full bloom and, as often happens, there is a bit of marsh land at the bottom, the effect is of little golden brooks running down to a pond of gold. "Pure color is rest of heart," wrote Richard Jefferies. After the long dusk of winter this radiance of yellow and orange delights the eye and cheers the soul. It makes the most striking color note of the round year, in fact, the only bright one except when the gay, flaunting ragged robins in June blossom also in the gravir.

As the season advances it is interesting to see how the wave of plant life mounts from the sea to the fields. By St. John's Day, all the lower levels have their fullest bloom; the first part of July it is summer on the *Brekkur*, or grassy slopes that crown the terraces of basaltic rocks on the fjeld sides. These terraces, or *Hamrar* as they are called, begin generally at a height of from six hundred to a thousand feet. In the latter part of July and the first week of August the flowers have opened on the summits. The plants grow leisurely, and remain in bloom much longer than with us, for there are no hot days to hasten their departure. The largest, tallest species are those of "high summertide," the wild geraniums, angelica, hawkweeds, buttercups, spiraea, ragged robin, sorrels, yarrow, red campion, *Matricaria inodora var. borealis*, or "Baldur's flower," and an orchid (*Orchis maculata*) that grows slim and tall in the gravir and stockyard, but only about two inches high in the open. The sea-thrift also adapts itself to circumstances. It sometimes has a height of six inches at sea level, and on exposed heights is a mere button of a flower, with no appreciable stem. Mother Nature exercises great prudence in her arrangements, the juicy angelica she puts in the gravir and ravines, the polypody fern under heather and among thick grasses, the aspidium ferns in clefts and under overhanging rocks. She seldom permits a flower to be more than three inches high in the wide exposed places. Wild thyme, white bedstraw, yellow rattle, eyebright, bird's-foot trefoil, brunella, buttercups, saxifrages, all grow there in dwarfed form, and the plants that are exposed to all the winds of heaven on the fjeld tops open during the quietest time of the year. Upon the brekkur we find in their season many of the flowers of lower levels, together with many alpines and other small inconspicuous plants. The pretty and rare *Dryas octopetala* and the Iceland poppy are found from 800 feet upwards.

All these Arctic species grow also on the summits of the fjelds either on rocky wastes, well fastened down by strong roots, or in the protecting grimmia heath, a close thick carpet composed of the moss *Grimmia patens* and other kinds.

Considering all disadvantages of climate, latitude, and small area, the number of species of native vascular plants, 277, is a goodly one. In addition there are forty species that have been introduced by man.

The flora resembles that of northern Scotland; indeed only ten of the Faroe species are lacking in Scotland. Many, however, that are rare there, and found only on the highest mountains, are here very common and grow at low levels.

There are many small plants which a botanist would at once notice, but only the flowers I have mentioned would attract the attention of the non-scientific observer. I have a speaking acquaintance with but a few of the grasses, I regret to say, and as for the 338 kinds of mosses, no one could be more densely ignorant than I. Yet even an ignoramus can admire their graceful forms and charming tones. They grow most luxuriantly over the hidden little rills, and shine with vivid green far up the fjeld sides. There are always pretty things to be found among them: butterwort, and saxifrages, epilobiums, rodiola, etc. One must tread cautiously where they grow. Today I was about to step on a firm-looking green patch when a sudden impulse prompted me to test the spot first with my field staff. "Plup!" sank the staff, with an ugly sucking sound, over the top as I held it in my fingers. How much deeper it would have gone I do not know, but the staff measures five feet two inches, one inch above my head.

None of the Faroe fields is of great altitude. The highest, Slaettaratindur on Eysturoy, is only 2894 feet high. The Delectable Mountains (that is not their Faroe name) are from 2000 to 2450 feet. But the effect of a mountain is largely dependent on its latitude and the distance above the spectator's eye. Here they are usually seen from sea level, and the utter absence of trees and bushes adds to their apparent height. And when snow rests upon sea cliffs that rise 2000 perpendicular feet from the surf-line, with mists wreathing their rugged summits, and the observer is looking upwards from a little four-man boat tossing in the sea below, I think he would not care to have one cubit added to their stature.

Dalin is almost silent these September days. From the sea rocks, softened by distance, comes a confused babble of kittiwakes; "*whippoor-will!*" they cry shrilly, with tremendous emphasis on the first and last syllables. From time to time I have heard the cry of a raven, clearer, more metallic, than that of the hooded crows. Both are thieves and murderers of the young and of the helpless. Were one of these wild sheep to fall on her back in a little hollow, so that she could not raise herself, it would not be long before her eyes would be plucked out and her stomach torn open. Only a month ago, a full-grown healthy sheep was brought in dying, her side mangled by a raven. I am glad to see that an anxious father, a black-backed gull, is harrying the raven out of Dalin. He, too, occasionally kills lambs, but does not torture a helpless sheep. A beautiful bird he is, with shining white breast, black back, and white wing tips. He has a red spot by his lower bill. The legend says that once he ate a dead man's flesh, and ever since he has borne this blood-red spot. Now he has come back, laughing with a monotonous bass voice, and is so flushed with victory that he must needs pretend to take umbrage at my opera glass and swoop down close to my face with a rush that makes me wince. The young bird is almost as large as his father, but has gray plumage. "*Phe-a! Phe-a!*" he cries in his baby voice, circling slowly in mid-air, a powerful, broad-winged bird.

There is one inhabitant of the outfield who leads a peaceful life for the reason that, though he prefers harmony and order, he is always prepared for war and always ready to take the initiative in case of any "unpleasantness." That is the *tjaldur*, or oyster catcher. The Faroe folk do not kill him, because he nests in the same wild uplands where the mother sheep graze and the lambs are born. If any raven approaches he is attacked by the valiant oyster catcher and routed ignominiously. Altogether he is a successful bird: he is good eating (though on no account would we eat him); he is striking in his good looks, cheerful, brave, and a defender of his young and, incidentally, of the weaklings of the flocks. Were he less warlike in disposition and of weaker build, I suppose he would assume like the curlew, rock pipits, snipe, etc., the general tones of the outfields, their grays and browns and russets. But as it is, his vermilion legs and long strong bill, and dazzling black and white plumage, can be seen far afield. One must note also that the other warrior, the black-backed gull, has the same conspicuous plumage. What matters it if they are seen of all men? They are well able to take care of themselves.

Dalin is a favorite place for the *myra-snipa*, or marsh snipe. They are quiet now, and make no sign until I almost tread upon them, when they burst up through the heather like a bomb and scurry away with a fretful cry. In June, however, we can see and hear them at night, and during the day in still, foggy weather. Then they make that peculiar noise which a year ago I thought was a cry or call. A friend, writing from America, first enlightened me. She quotes, I think, from Frank M. Chapman's *Handbook*:

> "In the springtime, and occasionally in the autumn also, Wilson's snipe mounts to a considerable height above his favorite meadows, and darts downward with great velocity, making at each descent a low yet penetrating tremulous sound that suggests the winnowing of a domestic pigeon's wings, or, if heard at a distance, the bleating of a goat, and which is thought to be produced by the rushing of the air through the wings of the snipe."

This is written of the *Gallinago delicata*, and the Faroe species is called *Gallinago media*, but the intricacies of comparative nomenclature are not to be unraveled in this remote island with no books at command. One day last June while resting in the heather, and looking upwards, I saw a myra-snipa flying overhead in a series of vertical V's. Part of the time his flight was noiseless, but occasionally he descended with great velocity, and then came that peculiar ventriloquistic sound, "as though the air laughed" I wrote at the time in my notebook. Only yesterday, in a story by the Danish author Herr Sophus Bauditz, I read in a description of the heaths of Jutland this passage: "If you lie down near the edge of the marsh you will hear suddenly over you, around you, now on one side, now on the other, an infinitely weak and infinitely penetrating sound; you know not whence it comes; it is as though the air itself laughed around you."

What a wreath we could have made in Dalin on one of those days in June; then only the frequent rains and the distance from the base of food supplies prevented us from becoming a "permanency" in Dalin. As it was, "Our Lady" (as the peasants call the Pastorinde) and I have several times returned home reluctantly at midnight, I humming sadly,—

> "And does it not seem hard to you
> When all the sky is clear and blue,
> And I should like so much to play,
> To have to go to bed by day?"

As we passed close to the sea cliffs we could hear the eider-ducks cooing just beyond the surf, and the puffins on the sea cliffs chuckling to themselves with a jolly fat "ur-r-r-r!" and could see them moving about in circles with careful dancing steps, and then falling suddenly into quiet and solemn musings. Who that ever had the privilege of knowing a puffin did not love him?

Yet were you to come here even in June I doubt if you would feel the spell. "Grim, barren, desolate." I can fancy these words your judgment. Can we ever give the full measure of appreciation to the unfamiliar? Washington Irving looking for the first time on Sir Walter's beloved hills was impressed only by their sadness. And yet, compared to the Faroes, the Border land is a land of fatness.

"Where shilfas sing and cushats croon," the flowery shrubs and stately trees follow the courses of the burns. To appreciate our "marcies" here, a certain lapse of time is required wherein to forget those of other lands. We must look to sea and sky for grace of form and motion and beauty of color, and put from mind the thought of forests and gardens and freely growing green things. Trees,—they are the hardest to forget; trees and the glory of the changing foliage, the pageant of Indian summer that is beginning now at home: and oh, to scuffle up leaves again and smell their crisp and pungent fragrance, and in November blasts to see them "march a million strong."

Of all the birds of summer, about twenty-one will remain with us during the long, dark winter that is closing in upon us. The hooded crows will wax bold and impudent, and wrangle over bones at the cottage doors. The ravens are more wary; perhaps they have an inherited distrust of man from the old days of the *nevtollur*, the bill tax, when every man between the ages of fifteen and fifty was required to give every year a raven's bill to the magistrates, or pay a fine.

Black-backed gulls, the lesser black-backed, the common and the herring gulls, a few kittiwakes, the fulmar petrel, and the land-rail winter here.

The pretty rock doves live all the year round up among the cliff recesses; wrens, starlings, rock pipits, snowbirds, cormorants, eider ducks, black guillemots, a few red-throated divers, northern divers, dunlins, mallards, and myra-snipa make up the list of the assured winter residents. In addition there will be strays, blown here by gales; not rarely the English blackbird appears, the blackcap, the bullfinch, and the little golden-crested kinglet. Last winter in Tórshavn I found myself thinking (with no apparent connection in the train of ideas) of Tewkesbury Abbey; suddenly I became conscious of a robin's song, and looking from my window saw a storm-driven waif singing as sweet a song as that I heard on the April morning when I saw my first English church and first English robin in Tewkesbury, the old village of John Halifax, Gentleman. The courage and endurance of these tiny birds is one of the marvels of nature. The seas rage and the gales howl, and there are all kinds of tragic experiences, and suddenly a round ball of fluffy feathers appears out of the commotion and sings a careless, cheerful song.

The dark days will soon be here: each morning the sun takes a step toward the south, and a November day will come when we shall see a bright and winking eye peeping for one moment above the eastern ridge of Malinsfjall; two hours later another wink above the western ridge, and the next day only a brightness in the sky. "Baldur the Beautiful" will be—not dead,—but very, very low, and for two months and a half not one glimpse of his face shall we see, not one sunbeam will fall upon the little turf-covered Parsonage of "Onagerði."

But a chill creeps over Dalin, and I find that I am sitting in shadow; the sun shines now only on the cliffs of distant Fugloy. Sigga will be waiting at the dike to escort me past the bull again. The Delectable Mountains are turning black, the clouds are falling low, the curlew are silent, the kittiwakes have put to sea. Now if Nykur should appear would I have the nerve to confront him, and put him to flight by the terror of his own name? Decidedly it is time for me to join Sigga at the dike.

❋❋❋

"Ak du! Ak du!" exclaims Sigga, peering into my basket, "what a beautiful wreath we shall make for little Absalom!"

Published in *Atlantic Monthly*, 91 (February, 1903) 248–254.

A Day On Nólsoy Island

After a week of tempest, the morning dawns serene and clear. The inhabitants of our little town of Tórshavn hail with delight their release from long imprisonment. There is a feeling of exhilaration, the sound of happy bustle in the air. The laughter of children echoes through the narrow lanes. Neighbors greet each other gaily, as they bring out the family garments to be dried, and festoon the rocks and turf-covered cabins with stockings, shirts, and trousers. From the shore, boat after boat starts for the fishing grounds; I can hear the rattling of the long slender oars, and the singing of an old Norse ballad, as the men settle down to their powerful sweeping stroke. Seated on a rocky ledge overlooking the bay, I am trying to finish a long deferred sketch. But this is not a morning for steady work. For days my ears have been filled with the thunder of surf, from the windows of the lonely little parsonage I have seen only low scudding clouds and angry waters. And now these clear, quiet spaces above, this peace and sunshine, cause a lightness of spirit with which my feet sympathize, and I long to run, to jump, or to climb to the snowy heights which encircle the harbor.

The fjelds, usually so silent and grim, this morning resound with the shouts of men, barking of dogs, and plaintive bleating of half-wild sheep being driven down to slaughter. One man, who has preceded the others, bears on his shoulder a shaggy black sheep. He puts his burden down a few yards away, and leans up against a boulder to rest. What a subject for a painting he would make in his picturesque Faroe dress. He has loosened his red neckscarf, and pushed back his long striped cap, showing the tawny hair which lies in close wet rings about his handsome flushed face. At his feet lies the bound sheep, against his knee presses his dog, glancing up at his master with loving eyes. Whether the background of the picture be the snowy fields, or the wide stretches of sea, either would be appropriate. A hill sheep and a codfish represent his sources of livelihood. He is a mountaineer and fisherman, and this dual existence has preserved for him the splendid physique which is his rightful inheritance from Norse ancestors. For the Faroe folk are true Norsemen, descendants of those proud old Vikings who, not powerful enough to resist the assumption of royal authority by Harald, the fair-haired, fled from Norway to these islands, and to Iceland during the ninth century. The poverty of the Faroes and their isolated position midway between Scotland and Iceland have prevented much intercourse with the outside world, and the peasants, in their mode of living and thinking, have changed far less than those of Continental countries.

I watch the men and sheep until they disappear down the steep trail, and am just settling down to work again when I see a little Faroe boy approaching, jumping lightly from rock to rock. As he reaches me, he pulls off his cap, murmurs bashfully "Godan morgun," and hands me a note. I divine at once its contents. It concerns a long talked of trip to the neighboring island of Nólsoy. Three weeks ago Louis Bergh, the Hovedlaerer or head-teacher, asked me to accompany him "the first pleasant day." He is to hold an examination in a small village, and while he is engaged I can explore the neighborhood.

An hour later the Hovedlaerer's boat is fairly flying over the sea, rowed by six stalwart oarsmen. I must confess that as I embark some doubts come to mind. Have I not heard of that clergyman who, intending to make a call on Fugloy, an island in the north, was stormbound there for fourteen weeks; and of another clergyman who, going forth confidently to take a midday dinner with a parishioner on another island, was separated from home and family more than four months. Then there was the story of a Pastor, visiting a distant island, who could not resist the last meal before departure of a smoking hot dish of Vaelling. Now the Pastor dearly loved the Danish gruel Vaelling and he was loath to leave it. Just then the men of his crew appeared.

"Herr Pastor must come at once! We cannot make it if he waits." Bad weather was threatening.

"Oh, it cannot be as bad as that," said the Pastor. "Just five minutes while I eat this Vaelling."

"As the Herr Pastor pleases," they replied, "but he stays at his own risk." And stay he did, for eleven weeks, and had Vaelling every day, that being the only dish his peasant hostess knew how to cook well. It is said that when the Pastor succeeded in getting away from the island, he was never, no never, known to eat Vaelling again.

But these were "outlying islands," surrounded by dangerous seas, whereas Nólsoy is in sight, only five miles away.

As we leave the harbor, Tórshavn seems to disappear as if by magic. Nine-tenths of the little capital is composed of weatherworn cabins, built on and among ledges of basaltic rock. The roofs are covered with turf, the grasses growing long and thick, so that the town harmonizes with the surrounding fields, and at a short distance one can define its limits only by the curling blue smoke of peat fires.

The sea today is still rough, but with these skilled boatmen one need not feel afraid. Midway they rest on their oars, and pass around a tin can filled with corn brandy. As they drink, each man shouts the old Norse pledge "Skal!" while "Takk!" [thanks] reply his companions.

Nólsoy, or "Needle Island," gets its name from a curious hole in the solid rock at the southern end, through which one can pass in a boat when the sea is calm. On Sandoy, an island some miles to the southwest, is a similar opening. In the old giant days a mischief-making lady giant put a strong band through both of these holes, tied the ends together, slipped the band over her head, and essayed to draw both islands up to a larger one in the north. Strong as she was, she found her task a difficult one, and in straining and tugging her head flew off, tumbling into the sea north of Sandoy where it is still to be seen rising like a great dome of basaltic rock above the fierce tidal currents.

The close affinity between the Faroes and Norway is seen in their folklore. One finds there the same Havfrugv or mermaids, trolls or mountain witches, the sometimes harmless Huldufólk, hideous Marras, that in the night strangle people with their long bony fingers, and malignant water spirits called Nykur. Perhaps the Nykur are identical with a water spirit of which one peasant told me. He said it lives in mountain lakes, and is "not good." Half its body is shaped like that of a man, the other half is like a boat. It lives on the bottom of lakes in a rather unreasonable fashion, considering its boat-like form, but it rises occasionally in search of human victims which it pulls beneath the water and drowns. There are dwarfs also, which live in the rocks, and are blacksmiths by trade. Through them man first learned the craft, and how to temper steel. And nearer the houses live good-natured little goblins, which seem to correspond to the kindly "Brownie" of Scotch kitchens. They often bring good fortune, and perform useful "chores" about the household during the night time.

Among the Faroe proverbs or sayings are a number which are common to many countries; such as, "A burnt child dreads the fire;" "One calamity shakes hands with another" (Misfortunes never come singly); "One can lead an ox to the water, but one cannot make him drink;" and "It is hard to teach an old dog new tricks." Other sayings indicate the natural surroundings and occupations of the people: "Where there has been one mountain slide another may be expected;" "A black sheep often has a white lamb;" "It is not easy to build the plank strong against the wave;" "Bound is the man who has no boat." One can picture readily from the last saying the mountainous islands, rugged, trackless, and swept by fierce seas.

Some of the riddles recall those cited by Paul Du Chaillu in his *Viking Age*. "I know a gray goose with white feathers on its neck; it is idle in still weather; is not fed with corn" (A sail ship). "A house full of meat (food) and no door to it" (An egg). "Fed in winter, starved in summer" (The wick of a lamp). This saying would be understood only in a country of high latitude, where no lights are needed during the summer months.

My small stock of Danish is adequate only to the simple needs of a traveler; but the Hovedlaerer, who speaks English admirably is invaluable as an interpreter, and our trip to Nólsoy resolves itself into a session for folklore investigation. I find the Faroe peasant sometimes franker than the Icelanders in speaking of their own customs and superstitions. In Iceland I seldom met a peasant who would confess even to a knowledge of a flower superstition or childish play. I remember the struggle I had in extracting a "counting-out rhyme" from a charming young Icelandic girl. With many blushes, she declared that it was too foolish to tell; that I would laugh at her if she told it, and she consented to do so only after I, to encourage her, had solemnly chanted, "Eeny, meeny, miny, mo," "Onery, Oo-ery, Ickery, Ann," and other counting-out rhymes employed during my tender years.

Our landing place at Nólsoy is like most of the tiny Faroe villages. There is a church, where a sermon is preached by the Tórshavn Pastor once in three weeks, a shop or two, and a cluster of houses, several being of fair size, and less primitive in arrangement. In one of these we receive a pleasant welcome from a pretty Faroe woman whose husband Peter F. Petersen is not only a skilled fisherman, but an excellent taxidermist, and wise in matters pertaining to life on the bird crags.

The preliminary step in the transaction of Faroe business is to partake of coffee and small cakes. This having been done to the satisfaction of all parties, the Hovedlaerer repairs to the examination, while I sally forth in search of the picturesque. In three minutes I find it in the shape of an old Viking, who has just returned from some festive occasion in the capital. He greets me as an old friend, calls me "Thou blessed," shakes hands cordially, and insists upon showing me the dreadful remains of a recently stranded whale. On the way he warbles gleefully fragments of a ballad about "Torkolls dotur," and, being unsteady on his legs, urges me to sit down and have a chat, indicating an especially marshy bit of ground. Having seen the whale, which surpasses my worst expectations, I craftily manage to lose my escort in the labyrinths of village lanes, and escape to the "infield," the cultivated lands bordering the houses.

Among the rocky fields stand several cabins built of rough stones and turf, used for drying barley. The cold summers here never ripen the grain, and after it is cut in October, it must be subjected to a strong heat for from twenty-four to thirty-six hours. A great fire of peats is built on a high raised hearth of stone, about five feet above it wooden beams support laths fastened several inches apart. These are covered with a layer of straw, on which unthreshed barley is spread to the depth of several inches, and allowed to dry. Passing near a cabin, I venture to peep in, and there see a group worthy of Millet's brush. Three women, with skirts kilted high and heads bound up like Millet's "Gleaners," are treading out the grain with their bare feet. Their bodies slightly bending, and hands resting on their hips, they trot to and fro, singing as they go snatches of some Faroe peasant song. The air is luminous with golden dust, and the firelight flashes over their strong supple bodies and large fair faces. It is a charming picture, and a rare one in these days of machine labor.

But this treading of the barley does not sufficiently separate the grain from the husk. The next step is to beat it with flails; not the jointed flails formerly used in America, but treskja, which resemble a baseball bat, flattened a little towards the end. I was fortunate enough to see the whole process, for the women, after questioning me curiously for several minutes, confer among themselves, and I hear them say, "She is from America, and there they do not know the way of Faroe folk; we must show it all to her." After treading vigorously for perhaps fifteen minutes, they bring out the flails and, kneeling on the floor, wield them, the blows falling, one, two, three—one, two, three, in perfect time. Later, they take down large shallow trays of wood from the walls, and putting the grain in them, separate the chaff by shaking the trays from side to side.

I find the whole affair so fascinating, and the company of my kindly entertainers so pleasant, that an hour slips away unnoticed, and I have little time for further explorations before the Hovedlaerer is ready to return to Tórshavn. The Faroe days are very short in early November, and as we cross the fjord again, the sunset clouds have turned to violet above the Streymoy mountains. In the fast gathering dusk we pass under the small fort, where a solitary figure paces up and down. He is one of the six marines that comprise the military strength of Tórshavn. Today the man's duty is to watch for an overdue steamer coming from Iceland, and, when seen, to run up the Danish flag at the tall flagstaff as a signal to Tórshavn of the coming vessel.

The codfish boats are returning in a straggling line as we reach the landing. Here we cannot see the fort, but the men in the farthest boat have just spied the signal, and faintly across the water sounds a voice, "*Damperen kommer!*" [the steamer comes!]. From boat to boat sweeps the sound like an incoming wave, as sonorous voices join the chorus, and "*Damperen kommer!*" cry the children's shrill voices up and down the steep lanes.

Were the steamer coming from Denmark bearing the mails and supplies, half of Tórshavn would soon besiege the Post Office. But she is homeward bound, her swept decks and crushed boats showing what a struggle she has had with Icelandic gales. So the Post Office is neglected, and I climb with the Hovedlaerer up to his pleasant grass-roofed house where Frú Bergh is superintending the serving of codfish fresh from the sea, potatoes, and Katrine-blomme pudding, or "budding," as the Dane hath it. The enthusiasm with which I receive these delectable viands is not displeasing to the Frú Hovedlaerer's hospitable soul. Afterwards, in the drawing room, creamy coffee and kiks are served, and a half hour later I start homewards under my host's kindly guidance.

The streets are silent and dark, and few lights glimmer in the cabin windows. But from one large house came a blaze of light, a sound of singing, and the tread of dancing feet. "There has been a wedding today," remarks the Hovedlaerer, "and now they are dancing the 'Bride's dance.' Shall we go in for a few minutes?" and he leads the way up a crooked staircase. In an empty room threescore people, young and old, form a great circle, dancing hand in hand, and singing the words of an old Danish song called, "Isaach's Giftermaal." The bride, a yellow-haired peasant girl, has forsaken her pretty native costume, and wears a tasteless imitation of modern wedding finery. On her head, instead of a veil, there is a clumsy wreath of crudely colored artificial flowers and leaves. One hand is held by the bridegroom, and the other by the Pastor, for he must dance and sing "Isaach's Giftermaal" with every bride, or give serious offence. The music in these Faroe dances is always vocal, and the whole company join in singing the legendary ballads of love, war, and adventure. Round and round glides the circle sedately, almost solemn for this is a semi-religious rite; "Isaach's Giftermaal," or "Wedding," being the Bible story of Rebecca's courtship, in thirty-two verses. As we enter the room they have reached verse the thirteenth, and Eleazer is talking with Rebecca at the well.

> "He said, 'I pray thee, my damsel dear,
> Tell me who is thy father and kindred;
> And where shall I find lodging and food

For myself, my men, and my camels?'
She answered, 'Bethuel's daughter am I,
With us there is room for thy people and thee,
And fodder for thy camels.'"

To the sound of shuffling feet the love story unfolds in quaint old phrases. Eleazer's mission is successfully accomplished, and the last verses find Isaac leading Rebecca to his mother's tent, "there to become his only wife, beloved all her days." The dance ends with a blessing for the bride and bridegroom, and the wish that they may see around them a crowd of their children's children before death shall divide them.

Then comes a pause, and we are turning to leave, when the handsome young fjeldman I saw in the morning starts another song. This time it is the fine old ballad of Sigmundur Brestisson, the true hero of the *Faereyinga Saga*.

"In Norway there dwells a christianed man,
Ye Norway men, dance so fair and free!
And Olav Trigvasson is his name,
Hold your peace, ye good knights all!
Ye Norway men, dance so fair and free!"

As he sings, one voice after another joins in until the room fairly rings when he reaches the couplet:

"Sigmund falls on his bended knee,
Christ sain thee, Lord! what wilt with me?"

We leave them rehearsing the events of Sigmundur's career, and descend to the deserted streets. The pathway to "Sandagerði," the little parsonage where I am staying, winds close to the rugged seacoast. On the open fjord we can see dimly the black hull of the steamer. As we mount from the hollows of the road to higher ground, a burst of song comes clearly to our ears. In fancy we follow the dancers through Sigmundur's adventurous life, through storm voyage and Viking battle, murder and treachery, to his tragic death.

"South in Suðuroy was he slain,
And north in Skúvoy was buried again."

Then silence, the ballad is over, and the tired dancers are resting.

In the north the Aurora flashes to the zenith in streamers of white and red. Seaward a black mass of clouds is spreading and mounting slowly. The Aurora and the coming storm suggest two vast forces arrayed against each other, and preparing for conflict. And who can doubt which will conquer? Tomorrow will see the loosed storm raging furiously over the Faroes. Our respite has been a short one. From the dark crags below sounds another precursor of tempest, a wailing sound like that of a suffering woman. I hear it often along these wild shores. It is not the wind, nor the surf, and there are no trees or shrubs to serve as harp strings for the wind to play upon. I have tried in vain to account for it, to find some tangible practical reason for its existence. The Faroe peasant has no such need of investigation. He knows it is the Huldufólk quitting their homes in caves among the rocks to bemoan their soulless state, and it behooves the listener not to speak lightly of them, but to say a little prayer for the gentle Huldufólk.

And now, turning from the darkening sea, the bright windows of "Sandagerði" send long rays along the path, and the opening door admits me to light and warmth and cozy shelter.

Published as "A Day in the Faroes," *Good Words* 42 (1901) 414–419.

Folklore From a Faroe Praestegaard

This is the praestegaard of Viðareiði on the northern end of the most northern island of the Faroe group. If you climb a little way up the fjeld slope north of the parsonage, you can see the headlands of six islands that form the parish of the Pastor; Fugloy and Svínoy on the east, this island, Viðoy, and on the west Borðoy, Kunoy, and Kalsoy. Their mighty promontories brave the northern seas that stretch, without a break, to the ice floes of the Pole. Only young and strong men can serve in such a parish, in a storm center where Gulf Stream and polar current strive for mastery.

The praestegaard "Onagerði" is built of driftwood that is well tarred every June and roofed with birch bark from Norway and grass sods from the fields. The Pastor and Pastorinde are in faraway Denmark, but I have permission to stay here as a charge of the maids, Sigga and Drikka. I live in the seaward gable of the great attic, called the Maidens' Bower. A *nisse*—a kind of Danish brownie, lives next to the Maidens' Bower in a secluded northwest corner. As nisses are not indigenous to the Faroes, it is supposed that this one was a stowaway among the Pastor's belongings when he came from Denmark six years ago.

The first year I made little progress in collecting bits of folklore. I knew no Old Norse (the language of the people) and not enough Danish to talk freely. The peasants have a fear of ridicule, and if I had asked bluntly, "Do you believe in Huldufólk?" the answer would have been, "The Lord preserve us, no! How could Frøkun think I could be so foolish!" I found it best to adopt the methods of Robert Louis Stevenson when he trotted out his native brownies and kelpies in order to extract from some reluctant South Sea islander his own particular spooks.

The few accounts of the Faroes that have been published in English speak of Huldufólk as fairies, brownies, and the little people, but those who write about fairies in the islands are strangely unobservant. Where are the sylvan glades and bosky dells, the warmth and sunshine, the freely growing green things beloved of fairies and butterflies? Not a tree, not a shrub grows wild in the Faroes. There are

*Pastor Lorentz Peter Heilmann and his artist wife Flora
are joined by Elizabeth Taylor (wrapped in a blanket),
in front of the parsonage of Onagerði in 1901.*

no butterflies, bees, or wasps. They would blow out to sea, or be drenched and battered by the cold storms that often last long even in the summer time. One fact I can affirm with confidence. *Where there are no butterflies there are no fairies.*

The nearest approach to fairies in size are the *veittrir*—little creatures that live in cow sheds or under houses, and, in good weather, often sit under the eaves, or after dark climb up and peer into the windows. They are associated with Christian service, while Huldufólk are of the Devil. They stay only where there are God-fearing, peaceloving people. Quarrelling and profanity drive them away. Even now I think that some of the old women, remembering the little veittrir, pause in the doorway before they throw hot water into the dark, and call out a warning, "Take care, you who sit thereout!"

Some writers have also given the name Huldufólk to giants and giant trolls, but at the present time—and indeed as long ago as 1670, when Pastor Lucas Debes wrote about them in his book about the Faroes—Huldufólk are said to resemble human beings in size and appearance. They have homes underground in the wild outfields, in ravines and clefts up among the fjelds or near the sea. They have boats like those of the Faroe folk, and go to the fishery; they have cows, sheep, dogs. Not always are the Huldufólk harmful. Many stories are also told of kindly services rendered. But if offended they take revenge, preferably on the anniversary of the day the offence was given. Usually they are invisible, though at will they can reveal themselves. One who has second-sight can see them, and if you should go to the wild outfields with such a *Framsyntur* [one who has second-sight] be careful not to tread in his footsteps, or touch his arm or his shoulder if you walk by his side. If you do, you will see what he sees.

Huldu-children have been seen playing with the children of this hamlet, though only once has a Huldu-child been known to enter a house. Then a little Huldu-boy ventured inside, but soon a voice was heard calling, "Reuben! Reuben!" The child burst into tears and ran out quickly. He was never seen again.

It would seem that (as with humans) there are good Huldufólk and bad ones. Why, if all serve the Powers of Evil, should many

Huldu-parents desire *souls* for their babies? A Faroe baby is in danger until it is christened. Huldufólk will lie in wait to smuggle a Huldu-baby into the cradle, hoping that the change will not be detected. If the Huldu-baby is christened, it will possess a soul.

There are stories, too, of Huldu-women in travail who could not be delivered unless aid was given by a *Christian* midwife. One New Year's Eve, a Faroe midwife stood by her fire stirring barley por-ridge. In came a black hound and pulled at her skirts, indicating by signs that she must come outside with him. She did so and there stood a Huldu-man waiting. He begged her to come and help his wife. Her eyes were bandaged, and she was led away up on the fjeld-side to the Huldu-man's home. There she helped a young Huldu-woman in dire need. Afterwards she was led back to her own home. Dawn had come before she reached her cottage, and all asked where she had been, but all she answered was, "A large head has come into the world this day." From that they knew she had been absent on a midwife errand, but more she never told. She received a handsome present also, but was bound to silence about it.

❀✿❀

Lately, stormbound by really terrible gales, I have passed many hours in the great attic looking over old books and records of the olden times when the pastors spent a lifetime in the remoter parishes. One extract from the records determines the time when two men lived who were rivals in the mystic arts of sorcery.

> "1706–66. Klement Jensen, Pastor in Viðareiði, Viðoy, during 60 years. This was "The Wise Priest," who, for the reason that he has gone in "The Black School," was equal in sorcery to Guttorm of Muli."

Guttorm of Muli, and his wise old father, Rasmus of Haraldsson —how the personality of some men survives through many genera-tions! So vivid are the stories told about Rasmus and Guttorm, so often are their sayings repeated, that at first I thought they had died but a short time ago.

Rasmus was a kind of chief in the six Northern Isles, and not al-ways amenable to the tyranny and oppression of the trade monopoly and the Danish officials in Tórshavn. Both father and son were noted as powerful sorcerers, they had studied the Black Art; but they used their wisdom only for the good of their fellow men. Here is a little tale about a fight the old man had with the Powers of Darkness made manifest in the Huldufólk who lived in the clefts and hollows of the island of Borðoy.

Rasmus had five sons, clever lads, at sea. One morning, before the dawn, as they rowed seawards, they saw a boat in a rock cleft on Borðoy, where Huldufólk are said to dwell. The lads thought it was a boat from Strond, where the folk have big noses, and one of them called out mockingly, "Always late for the fishing, Big Noses!" and other mocking words.

"*That shall be revenged!*" a voice answered from the shadows; but the lads only laughed and rowed on. They told their father about it when they returned.

"A troublesome nose that shall be to you," mused Rasmus, and wrinkled up his own.

A year from that time, Rasmus, saying nothing to his sons, went down to the boathouse in the night, and hid himself in the boat, under the sail. He knew his sons would not permit him, old as he was, to go with them, and he feared that his power in sorcery would be needed that day. Towards morning the sons came, dragged out the boat, took their places at the oars, and rowed seawards. As they passed that unlucky cleft where they had seen the men the year before, out came a boat right towards them, so fast that the foam flew high from the prow. Straight towards them it came as though to cut them down. A Huldu-boat it was, with Huldu-men in it. Then the sail was thrown aside, and Rasmus sprang up. They had need of him! Against such foes only the power of sorcery could avail. Rasmus reached out, seized the prow, and with his strong arm wrenched it to one side, so that it struck only a slanting blow. A Huldu-man in the prow seized one of the boys. Rasmus planted his foot on his son's sea-shirt, so that he could not be dragged away. "Lord save us!" cried Rasmus, and gripped the Huldu-man, and they fought as the boats went on. The sons of Rasmus rowed with all their might. A dark cloud hid Rasmus and the Huldu-man. Within its gloom the two were still struggling as the boats came north of Muli, and there came in sight of the church of Viðareiði, with the cross on it, and beyond it the dawn breaking. At the same instant the Huldu-man cried out, "Knis-knas! The Red Cock in the East!" that is to say, "My strength is gone, for now rises the sun!" "Risras!" gasped Rasmus, and in a twinkling vanished the huldu-boat. When Rasmus and his sons came home, the old man told them that they must never again call out mocking words to a boat in the dusk.

From my window in the Maidens' Bower I can see across the water the tiny hamlet of Muli, under the grim heights of Borðoy. There lived Guttorm, son of Rasmus. It is said of him, "a rare man, advanced in wisdom, trustworthy in every way." He is connected with this old praestegaard by tales that show his power of sorcery—stories of Guttorm going out in a great gale to save life at sea, and calming the waves as the boat advanced; of Guttorm laying the troubled spirit of an unbaptised murdered child who had returned in the dreaded form of a *nidagrisur*, demanding the right to lie in sanctified earth. Of the many stories of Barbara of Sumba (a village on the southernmost island of Suðuroy) I like best the one of how she came north to see which was the stronger in sorcery, Guttorm of Muli or herself Barbara the fair, who once had been tried for her life as a witch, and would have been burned had not the judge said *she was too beautiful to be tarred*. When she arrived Guttorm was with his sons at sea. She began to mix and to brew. She put limpet shells on the stream Matara, and said that the number that sank should be the number of the boats that were lost at sea. Such a storm Barbara raised by her spells that Guttorm and his sons barely escaped with their lives. As they rowed homewards the spindrift was like flying ashes, the waves blood-red to see.

"What is this?" cried one of his sons. "The waves are on fire!"

"I know what it is," Guttorm answered. "*Row thou, row! All is not well at home!*"

As they came near the Muli landing cliffs they saw Barbara sitting on the hillside by the stream, her long yellow hair flowing free about her. Then came the punishment of Barbara. Guttorm took his woollen mitten, put in it a stone weight from the fishing nets, and struck her across the nose. He cut off those yellow locks, and with them much of her power vanished. He bound her to a seat close to the open hearth, and built thereon a great brewing fire. He conjured her up on the house roof, and brought on a northeast storm with snow. Finally, at dawn, he let her go, more dead than alive. She had learned only too well—poor wicked Barbara—who in the Faroes was strongest in sorcery.

Nevertheless, Barbara had some power left. She vowed that no grass should ever grow on the place where Guttorm had conjured her, and to this day the sods on the Muli roof are bare where Barbara sat that night.

Guttorm's youngest son was called after his father. Guttorm told his wife that she must never let the little one go out in the hagi [the wild outfields] fasting, or without his knife. At last, when he was almost grown up, he did go, fasting, and without his knife, and from that day he was lost. Many years later a Pastor of Viðareiði, who had second-sight, was going by sea around Mulin in with a crew of Viðareiði men. Looking landward, he saw young Guttorm crossing a grassy fjeld slope.

"There goes a lost sheep of my flock," said the Pastor.

The men asked, "Would it not be possible to get young Guttorm back?"

"No," said the Pastor with sorrow. "He is a lost soul."

Rasmus and Guttorm live, not alone in musty records and old legends, but in the lives of those around me. In my wanderings about these six northern islands, if I meet someone, man or woman, who has a bright, full eye, a keen intelligence, who tells a story modestly and yet with a certain dramatic power, who is not ashamed to speak of the old customs and beliefs, then I query, "You are, I believe, of the family of Guttorm of Muli?" and almost invariably the answer is, "Yes, I am, but how did the Frøkun know?"

One old woman I met in a distant hamlet, worn, bowed over with rheumatism, but I fancied I saw in her signs of the old race. So I did not ask her for stories, but, at a venture, I told her a little about a descendant of Guttorm of Muli who had second-sight, and was thought to be almost equal in sorcery to Guttorm. It was his custom to remain in the church on New Year's Day after service, and, while sitting there quietly in the silent church, he would see the shapes of those who were to die in the coming year pass by him, go up the aisle, and stand before the altar. One New Year's Day he saw his old wife going up the aisle, and closely following her he saw himself. She died in the first week of the new year, and, seven days later, he died also.

As I ended my little tale I saw the face of the old woman light up with pride and pleasure. "Frøkun," she cried, "that old man was my grandfather!"

A woman who was also a descendant of Guttorm of Muli had second-sight from her eighth year. One summer morning she was playing outside her father's cottage, when she saw before her eyes, like a vision, bird cliffs, seafowl, the sea below, and a man in the ancient Faroe dress falling to his death. Frightened, she cried aloud, and ran to the cottage. Later in the day news came that on a distant island, at the same time a man had been killed on the bird cliffs. It was his custom to wear the old style Faroe dress that had long ago passed from use. The child had never before seen or heard of the man.

The gift of second-sight is not a happy one, and at the christening of a baby the godmother is careful so that the water will not flow into the eyes and the child have second-sight. Jonas Lie calls second-sight a malady of the soul that no reflection, no reason, no remedy can cure. One is born with a third window in the house of the soul in addition to one's two sound eyes — a window that opens out to a world of which others only dream. When the impulse comes one is forced to approach and gaze therefrom.

Many stories told me are of great age, but what shall one think of tales like the following one, that belong to the last generation?

It is the custom, during church services, for those who cannot attend to sit quietly at home, and not allow their children to play outside. One Sunday morning, a day of bright weather, a father and mother permitted their little three-year-old boy to play near the cottage door. Suddenly a black cloud came before the window, hiding all without; it vanished in a moment, and the parents ran out, but the child had gone. Search was made at once, the help of the Pastor and district sheriff besought, and for three days parties of men looked far and wide for the child. The morning of the fourth day, a woman living ten miles away saw a child standing near her cottage. She asked him how he came there. He answered that "the white man" had brought him. He was warm and clean, was not hungry or thirsty. Now, how could the child have traversed ten miles of rough country, bogs, fjeld streams, and difficult rocky trails? Even his little sheepskin moccasins were quite clean.

The man who told this tale (it dates from his mother's time, and she dwelt near the place where the child lived) was a reliable man of much intelligence. He evidently believed this to be the work of Huldufólk. It was done to punish the parents for their neglect of Sunday customs, but the Huldufólk would not let the *child* suffer.

The Pastorinde, when speaking of the Huldufólk, told me that in lonely parishes where there is no companionship with men of education and varied interests, a stay of more than six years is unwise. Often, to men of imagination and sympathy, there comes a time when they query, "Is it not possible that the Creator, in His inscrutable wisdom, permits these creatures to exist?" That is when their wives decide it is high time to take steps towards a move to prosaic workaday Denmark.

A Pastor confessed to me that on one wild and lonely trail over fjeld and moor that he had to traverse alone he always felt a presence that accompanied him, heard a soft footfall just one step behind him and a little to one side, that again and again he has reasoned with himself, saying, "It is only an echo—a nervous fancy; I will *not* turn and look!" Yet at last he has wheeled about suddenly, desperately, to find—nothing, and to go on unhappily, feeling again that invisible presence, hearing again that hushed footfall.

There is a Faroe saying, "A knifeless man is a lifeless man," or, in other words, "A man with no knife loses his life." Steel protects against evil, both on land and at sea. Even now, a man will not go to the fishery or to the wild hagi without his knife—nor would he call it *knivur*. It is always *hvast*, "the sharp one." If questioned about it he will make some jest about foolish old customs. In calm weather on a sunny day one can laugh at silly superstitions, but in darkness and storm, with dangers on fjelds and sea, the old beliefs wake to life again.

✿✿✿

Last Christmas Eve, in a terrible gale from the northwest, a young man tried to return to his home to "hold Yule" with his family. The rocky trail passes around, in where Huldufólk were said to dwell. On those rugged slopes young Guttorm had gone "fasting and without his knife," and never returned to the homes of men. All that night the gale raged. In the late dawn, the young man's body was found close to his father's door. His clothes were in tatters, his face, hands, feet, and knees cruelly lacerated. . . . A little group of men were talking together the next evening. One said gravely, *"All was not as it should be"* (an expression that signifies that supernatural powers had a part therein). "That is true," was the general assent. Then a man questioned. "You heard? *He had no knife with him."* "Ay, we heard," was the answer. That was all. Now these men knew well the mighty power of the dreaded "castwind," the echo wind, confined in great gales up in the hollows and clefts of the high fjelds in gathering force, until it bursts down with a report of a gun on the lands below. These men had seen the carcasses of sheep whirled up and cast down again and again on sharp ice and jagged rocks until they were a mass of broken bones and crushed flesh. Yet they gave no thought to the castwind as the cause of that tragic death. No, the lad, passing over those slopes where the Huldufólk dwelt, had no protecting steel with him; he had met the Huldufólk, had striven with them — and they had conquered.

The strange stories one hears of those echo blasts are a tax on the credulity, but I lend the ear of truth to their recital since my acquaintance with a norther a few weeks ago. The gale had been blowing fiercely but evenly all day from the northwest. But after dark it shifted to the north. At once began irregular blasts from the south. The oftener they came, the weaker was their force, and now and then came a long calm; not a sound to be heard but the hoarse roar of the sea. You might have carried a lighted candle. Suddenly a rushing sound is heard, the heavens overhead snap loudly. A violent blow strikes the house which shakes to and fro as if in the hands of a giant. The lamp flares, the beams groan and creak and complain as a ship in a heavy sea. Drikka and Sigga, the handmaidens, go on with their work and the Pastor draws on his storm hood, puts on his boots, and sallies forth to see if all the roofs have held fast against the on-slaught of the Huldufólk.

❦❧❦

Someone (I think it is Henry Buckle) wrote that when men are wit-ness to great danger they cannot avoid or understand, they are im-pressed by their helplessness and insignificance, their fantasy is excited, and their faith in the supernatural is called to life. How true this is seven men of Faroe can bear witness, men still living who go with a lifelong burden on their hearts. It was a night of storm, and six boats were far away on the fishing grounds. Five of the boats started homewards from Suðuroy. In the fifth one to leave was one who was a famous swimmer. None could compare with him. After some delay the sixth boat started. In it were seven grown men and one young lad. The sea was bad and dusk had fallen. An hour or so passed when the men heard faraway shouts and cries for help. At least they sounded like voices, but one hears such strange sounds at sea never knowing what they might be. The sea was rough and the waves breaking. The boat came to a smoother stretch, where the waves rolled as though oil had been cast on them. Then from the sea rose an arm, and the hand clutched the gunwale. In horror the men sat staring at it. They were in the grip of the Powers of Darkness, malignant spirits that would drag them down to destruction. One of the crew sprang forward, seized the giant hook with which big hal-ibut are killed, and struck again and again. The hand loosened its clutch and sank beneath the calmed water. When the men reached land they found that the fifth boat, wherein was the strong swim-mer, had not come in; only then did they know what they had done.

In the Faroes the equivalent of the Evil Eye is *Spirstunga*—the unlucky tongue. When one who has it makes a remark such as, "We will have good fishing today," look him in the eyes and say quickly, "It shall be as you say." That will avert the coming evil, but bring you in another plight: for he will then know that you believe him to be a Spirstunga. The following story (true it is) illustrates the undesir-ability of having a Spirstunga as a companion. It was the day before

Easter, a good day after a fortnight of storm. Food was much needed in the village, but the men had caught nothing after two hours' fishing. Then a great halibut was taken, one that weighed fully two hundred pounds. It was dispatched in the usual way with the heavy iron-bound implement used for that purpose, and then tied securely to the prow of the boat. So large was it that as the body rested in the bottom of the boat, the head and tail projected above the gunwales on either side. The men went on with their fishing for two hours more when the Spirstunga turned to one of the crew.

"That's a grand halibut we've got there, what a fine Easter dinner there will be tomorrow." Instantly the great halibut that everyone thought dead, heaved itself up, snapped the lines that bound it, was over the boat's side, and in a twinkling to the bottom of the sea. "Oh hold thy accursed jaw!" cried the exasperated crew.

Even if you are not a real Spirstunga, it is best to avoid praising the thriving appearance of a calf or a patch of potatoes and especially the health of a child, though I think it is allowable to call him "pretty."

Two Faroe men went into a cottage where a mother was feeding her baby boy with porridge. He was a fat, sturdy little fellow and was gobbling down the porridge as fast as his mother could stuff it in. The woman saw the men looking at her child, and feared that some comment would be made about his fine appearance. "Ak ja!" she sighed. "Poor thing! He has no appetite. It's all I can do to get him to pick a little now and then,"—all the time ladling in the porridge. "Poor thing," said the men with sympathy, knowing what was expected of them.

❧❧❧

A land of storms, yet there is a charm in high latitudes that the South cannot know; the mystery of starless summer nights, when the pale moon casts no shadows; the wonderful cloud and mist effects; the purity of color in the dust-free air and deep sub-Arctic sea. There are nights of coming storm when fishermen in home-hurrying boats see long lines of fjelds glowing as with inner fires. Not seldom have the older men spoken to me of those calm and solemn hours at sea when the sunset and sunrise colors together linger in the North. Their eyes "behold the beauty of the night," and in the peace that broods over land and sea, they feel that the Powers of Darkness have no might.

Published in *Chamber's Journal*, December 13, 1924, 29–32.

Up Viðareiði's Mountain

Haraldssund, Kunoy, 12 July, 1903
Dear Helen,
This is a little five-house hamlet, eight miles from Viðareiði and three from Klaksvík. As it is very important that I take *Botnia* day after tomorrow from Klaksvík to Tórshavn, it seemed prudent to leave that very uncertain place Viðareiði for one where there is less surf. If a journey is important it is best to come in good time to a nearer and quieter place. So I came here yesterday with six men, in a pouring rain, and this was wise, for as I listen to the wind howling outside I know that Viðareiði is stormbound today.

It was my turn to pay for the men and boat, but the Pastor arranged his church duties so he could have passage with me and hold *altergang*, communion, at Kunoy village across the fjelds. There is no church here or at Skard, another hamlet we passed on the way, so the *Messubod*, literally the sacrament or communion message, must be delivered in both places. At Skard we rowed close to land under the cliffs and signalled for someone to come down. All seemed deserted except for a small boy and a puppy. But at last an old man appeared and climbed over the sea rocks to a place high above where our boat lay.

The Pastor stood up and shouted, "Good day, Messubod in Kunoy tomorrow."

"So-o-o?" answered the man.

"Will you take the message?" said the Pastor.

"Yes, that I will," and off we went again.

After two months of fierce, dry nor'easters and no rain, the weather, which does nothing by halves, has changed to steady cold rains and heavy masses of clouds covering two-thirds of the fjelds. This is better for the grass than the nor'easters, but the grass needs sunshine and warmth.

232

Another reason for my coming here to Haraldssund was the wish to climb the high fjeld to get some rare flowers, but the heavy clouds are wrapped tightly about them as if they had no idea of departing during my two-day stay. As usual, I am having a series of disappointments.

I have long wished to go up Villingadalsfjall north of Viðareiði but the weather has prevented it. Last Thursday, however, before leaving for here, I decided to try it, though the day was not promising. I had a nimble and strong old man as companion, all the younger ones being at work with the peat. Villingadalsfjall is 2770 feet high and as we started from sea level it was quite a climb, a direct ascent, no winding in direct trails. Everything was wet and soft and slippery and we had to go carefully. Those flowers that were due the middle of June were still in bud on July 9th so I found fewer blossoms than I had expected. At 2000 feet I discovered, after much search, fine Iceland poppies in bud (which I am trying to nurse into bloom). At this point it began to rain hard, but, being so high, it seemed a pity to turn back.

Here we saw ptarmigan—the *rypa*—, three beautiful creatures almost snow white, only a few rich brown spots. They sprang up with a hoarse "*gekk-gekk-gekk!*" and a whirr of wings exactly like grouse on the high moors. They are Greenland ptarmigan that some years ago

Six stalwart oarsmen shown in a boat from Viðareiði.
Photograph by Elizabeth Taylor.

were brought to Tórshavn and there set free. They showed their dis-
approval of Tórshavn's climate by coming at once to the highest,
bleakest ranges of the northern islands' fjelds where it more resem-
bled their Greenland home. They increase slowly, but so slowly that
their growth is hardly appreciable from year to year. I do not think
the climate is especially unfavorable. It is the great number of birds
of prey that keep their numbers down: the ravens come up from
below and the black-backed gull nests just where the ptarmigan live.

I did not get above 2550 or 2600 feet. Those few remaining feet
would have brought me to a level where a carpet of *grimmia* moss
would have had treasures of rare flowers. But I could not do it. A
sudden half-gale swept down upon us, clutching at my clothes as if
they would be torn from me. It rained furiously and was cold as winter; and I could see nothing from the rain on my specs. So my guide
and I crawled under a ledge and sat crumpled up until the worst was
over. Then, as it threatened to come on again and might prevent our
return, I beat a retreat back to Viðareiði and have had regrets ever
since. But what can a poor womanfolk do? Nowhere else that I
know of does one have sea gales on mountain tops.

So here there is no going up any fjeld for me. And now my mental heights are clouded by a persistent and disagreeable feeling—that
degree of nausea which makes one lose interest in life's duties and
pleasures.

I have written this on dreadfully shabby scraps and I am hastily
scribbling on a knee on board *Botnia*. We leave in half an hour. The
tourists are peacefully sleeping, but I hope they will wake up soon so
I can stare at them awhile before we come to Tórshavn. Why are
most tourists ridiculous? I hope by giving the matter my close attention to eliminate my most offensive tourist features—even if I do
not go to the length of one person I knew who covered her Baedeker
in gray linen and labelled it "Macaulay's Essays!"

Elizabeth Taylor Papers, Minnesota Historical Society.

The Valley of the Others

I have come to Dalin to spend the whole night alone. The Pastorinde and I have often talked of coming—just we two,—to see what goes on here during the sub-Arctic summer night, how the birds and flowers conduct themselves through the hours that are dark in more southern lands. Dalin is a great, lonely valley, two miles from the Parsonage called "Onagerði." On three sides are high, rugged fjelds but the fourth is open to the northern seas to distant islands, and to wonderful shore-cliffs. The Pastor affirms that his best sermons are composed here on snipe shooting days, and I know that when I come here fishing I return a much better woman than when I left home, even though midges bite and trout do not. When a rare guest visits the Parsonage in the summer, the Pastorinde brings him here as the best her hospitality can offer. If he grumbles at the rocky, boggy trail and looks with a cold eye on Dalin, finding her desolate, then the Pastorinde knows that to one chamber of her heart that guest will have no key. It is a great heart, that of the Pastorinde, and I have learned to know its strength and sweetness during my winter in the little parsonage of Viðareiði.

In August, ten months ago, I did my Christmas shopping, talked my last English to the Danish officials in Tórshavn, the capital of the Faroes. Then I sailed away to this northern island where Danish is the language of the Parsonage, old Norse that of the little turf-covered cottages.

The last boat of the year came in November. After that we were shut off from the outside world. No telegraph, no cable, no post! Truly I had need of the Pastorinde, and she has not failed me. There are no children at the Parsonage, but long ago the Pastorinde learned to call me her 'Plejebarn'—her foster child; and I call her 'Plejemoder'—foster mother.

It is because the Pastorinde slipped and sprained her ankle that I am here all by myself to spend the night in Dalin. Viktorinus and Jakob Johan, small boys of my acquaintance, bore on their sturdy shoulders provisions, spirit lamps, warm wraps, and sketching things, and I have made a little camp not far from the sea cliffs. The boys have shaken hands and said in Danish, "Farewell," and "A pleasant night to you," and I have answered, "Thanks for thy friendly assistance." As they left me, I heard Jakob Johan say in old Norse (thinking I would not understand) that he was glad it wasn't he who was to spend the night in Dalin, and Viktorinus murmured something about a *Nykur* that is supposed to dwell in a tarn up on the hillside. The sentiment of the village is expressed: in the words of old Sigurd, said, not to me, but to the Pastor's milk girl. "Dalin in the daytime," said Sigurd, "is for Men, there to cut and dry the peat, or to hunt down the sheep from the fjelds. The daylight is theirs, but Dalin at night is for *the Others*. They would think the Frøkun [Miss] had come to spy on them; they are easily offended, and might take revenge. No, that the Frøkun should not do. But to *me* the peasant women say only, "Will not the Frøkun catch cold?" "Is not the Frøkun afraid of cows?"

It has been what we call a *myrisnipa* day, the kind that the myrisnipa or marsh snipe love, and the air seems to vibrate with their curious bleating sound; a day when the mild southwest wind blows gently and all is bathed in luminous mists. There are many rainbows, distant arches, and fragments close by that spring out of a straw-covered chimney, a big boulder, the prow of a boat, or the cliff's edge. Clouds are bowled softly in from the sea-levels, and wander in a casual fashion over the home-fjelds and between the houses. As I sit in sunshine one envelops me in damp gray walls, then flashes by and whisks in a great hurry round a corner. In rose and violet and gold they come, some stately and full-breasted, others frolicking along like a band of playing children. On every side rises the happy chorus of bird song. Though many of the notes are harsh and plaintive, they are softened to the ear by the mellow air. A curlew is not a cheerful bird, but he has one sweet contented croon, "*To-whee-e! to-whee-e! to-whee-e!*" On a myrisnipa day it tells the joy of living as well as the song of the bobolink.

Ten o'clock, and a change is coming. The clouds have risen, colors are darker, outlines harder. The sheep are slowly mounting, grazing as they go. That is a sign of bad weather. Far out at sea is a heavy bank of cloud. Only the upper fjelds are in sunshine now. There is wind up there. The braided clouds writhe and toss, and from each blood-red peak swings up and away a mighty fiery banner like that of a volcano in eruption. It will not be a friendly night in Dalin; but I cannot go home now, lest the cows invade my camp. Curious beyond the common wont of cows, they rend and trample objects that are new to them, and some cows will eat garments of cotton and of wool. I am told that a true Faroe cow is never guilty of such evil. When it occurs, it is due to a vicious strain of *Danish* blood. The Faroe attitude toward things Danish always reminds me of Kipling's conviction that Canadian political morals and private principles would be of a snowy whiteness if it were not for the contaminating influence of Americans.

I have just remembered that it is the twenty-fourth of June, Midsummer night, when evil spirits are freed to fare abroad at will. In Norway the fires of Saint John are burning now; but how can one keep the feast in this treeless land? The Norse forbears of the Faroe folk found here, a thousand years ago, a scanty growth of juniper and willows,—and bonfires burned for Baldur, God of Light. Now, not a tree or a shrub breaks the outline of the hills.

The old pagan beliefs died slowly here in the Faroes, isolated as the islands were by distance and by dangerous seas. On land and water lingered a host of evil, malignant spirits, jealous of the faith that had supplanted Thor and Odin. Even yet an uneasy belief in the supernatural dwells curiously with the religion taught by the Pastor and accepted by his flock; and with the exception of the two at the Parsonage there is probably not a soul in Viðareiði who could be persuaded to spend Midsummer Night alone in Dalin.

Eleven o'clock, and I have just had a visit from a messenger, but whether for good or for evil, I do not know, since he could not tell his message to me. Sitting under the shelter of a huge rock, huddled in my warm wraps and half-musing, day-dreaming, in the silvery light that is neither day nor night, I saw a hooded crow, usually one of the most wary and timid of birds, flutter to the ground just beyond my reach. He did not caw as usual, but looking up at me intently, he bobbed his head up and down and said, *"Boo-a! Boo-a!"* Now in this way the old Norse word "buð" is pronounced, and buð means "a message."

Both ravens and crows, as all the Faroe folk know, have gone far in the Black Art. They can foretell events, and know when the flocks of driving whales are in neighboring waters; but alas, they lack human speech in which to give their warnings. Last winter a crow came to the cabin of an old woman in Viðareiði, looked in at the window and gave the message-call. "Now what does this betide?" said old Ranaa. An hour later a column of smoke on distant Borðoy told that whales had been seen off the coast and that men and boats must come at once. "Ah, so ol-o!" said old Ranaa; *"that* is what the message bird was trying to tell me."

It is pleasant to sit here in camp, mulling over in my mind fragments of story and Faroe memories, but I had better go a-fishing if, as I promised, the Pastorinde is to have Dalin trout for her breakfast tomorrow. Up among the fjelds that inclose Dalin like an enormous semicircular amphitheatre, a brook takes its rise and comes leaping and foaming down between the rocks, to run, gathering other little brooks to itself as it goes across the grassy slopes of the valley, to cliffs where it plunges downward to the sea. And in that brook there are trout such as anglers dream of when their sleep is sweet; beautiful trout like those of the Scottish streams. One can easily catch a string of fish weighing from one eighth to one fourth of a pound. Larger than that I have never caught in Dalin, but one day, when I wandered through the valley without my fishing tackle,—a warm day with little midges swarming in the air, I saw in the brook, rising for the midges, great lusty trout such as I had never seen before in Dalin,—trout of fully two pounds, and I without so much as a string and a bent pin!

Gray or white Millers, or perhaps a Royal Coachman, are the flies to use tonight. They resemble the thousands of moths that are flying over thousands of little pink-and-white orchids in the marshy grasses. I must crush the flowers' waxen petals beneath my feet as I fish along the banks, and a delicate fragrance of bitter almonds will fill the air. These little orchids are potent in love charms and have, it is said, power as whale charms. If the white hand-shaped root,

"Mary's Hand" is cast into the water, it will drive away whales; and if the black, withered root, the "Devil's Hand," is used, it will attract them. There are blue-and-white speedwells, eye-brights, yellow tormentillas, and buttercups growing with the orchids, but the rarer plants are high on the fjeld slopes.

Midnight now, and in the north the sunset colors lingering. Nature seems painted with a large brush, forms and colors showing, but insignificant detail omitted. Far away, on the heights of Villingadalsfjall, the clamor of the seafowl has almost died away. From the ledges under the sea cliffs comes that monotonous droning that often precedes a storm at sea. A pair of ravens are playing and turning in the air above the dark crags of Myrnafjall. Now and then an oyster catcher scurries by, but the birds are strangely still. In friendly weather they would be heard the whole night through. In the hush of bird life other voices are calling—the little brooks of Dalin. On the black cliffs they show like strands of silver. They bubble up from the peaty soil, cold, sweet, undefiled. Shrill notes are heard on pebbly beaches, deeper murmurs from overhanging banks. Here and there one gushes up from a mossy basin, swirls over a flat rock, and buries itself with a chuckle beneath the heather. I walk on grassy slopes and hear the rushing of water below my feet, and all around the rumor of waters hurrying to the sea.

I had planned to climb high on the fjeld-side to see what the little alpine flowers are doing, which ones are sleeping, which keeping their petals and leaves unfolded in the midnight hour; but somehow, I feel reluctant to go far from my camp. Not that I am afraid. No, one feels such confidence in islands. There is no mysterious interior as on the mainland, where terrors may lurk. The only danger would be from falling stones loosened by the winter's frosts and dislodged by the hoofs of grazing sheep.

There are over a hundred thousand sheep in the Faroes, hardy, active creatures that scramble like goats along those terraces where I would not dare venture. They live out, uncared for, all the year. The ordinary winter storms they bear well enough. Early spring is the time of danger, when sometimes a cruel northeast wind blows for many days. It comes from the Arctic ice floes, the glaciers and snow fields of Spitzbergen, often bringing with it a bitter fog that whirls drearily over the land, obscuring the light. The freshly springing grass is seared and withers away, the grass that the mother sheep need if they are to have milk for the coming lambs. And so the babies die—by thousands they die—not only from starvation, but killed at birth by the ravens and crows. The birds linger near. They know the approach of travail, await the event, and the lamb is killed before the mother's eyes when she is too weak to rise and defend her young.

A great boulder has just fallen from the heights of Breiðeskarð, bounding from ledge to ledge, and disappearing over the cliff's edge; and as the clamor of the echoes died away, a loud cry rang out, so wild and despairing that I sprang to my feet in dismay. Then came a crazy laugh, and I laughed, too, though a little shakily, for I recognized the voice of a loon—the northern diver. That laugh is strange enough, but it is cheerful beside the rarer doleful cry like that of a woman in extremity. Night hours in Dalin seem to strain even stout nerves slightly. I know that frost and sheep are responsible for that boulder, but, in spite of sturdy common sense, I find running through my head fragments of queer tales heard beside cottage hearths, or in the boats, or on the trails.

Dalin is said to be *ibygdur*—inhabited—not by human beings but by Huldufólk, underground creatures who look like men and women, and pursue various avocations by land and sea, as do the Faroe folk. And now is the time of the Huldufólk. From midnight until three o'clock there is danger in the fjelds, and on the bird cliffs. Landslides come often. Boulders fall from the heights upon unwary human intruders in the hours of the Huldufólk.

These creatures are usually invisible, but, at will, they can appear to human eyes. A *Framsyntur*, or one who has second-sight, can see them, and so can those who follow in his footsteps or go side by side with him in the wild outfjelds.

The Huldufólk, though they are heathen spirits and in league with the powers of evil, sometimes perform kindly deeds. Stories are told of their coming to the rescue of milk girls lost at night in the fog, and leading them safely to the village boundaries. They have given warning of dangerous seas, have provided a Faroe man with food for weeks when he was stormbound on an uninhabited island. Sometimes they are present at a wedding, hidden in a dark corner, or dancing, seen by the Framsyntur, in the Bride's dance. Once, before a wedding, a woman who had second-sight saw a pretty girl, a stranger to her, stepping from one of the arriving guest boats. She turned to ask a companion who the girl was, but she had disappeared when they looked for her. She saw the girl again dancing in the Bride's dance. "Who is the pretty girl with the blue kerchief and apron?" she asked a man who stood near, "the one who is dancing in the ring between Drikka and Sunnuva?" "But there is no one dancing between Drikka and Sunnuva, they dance hand in hand." "Why, don't you see her?" the woman cried. "Wait until the girls pass us and I'll take hold of her skirt so you can see which girl I mean." Across the room she saw her plainly, but as the girls danced by, behold Drikka and Sunnuva danced hand in hand.

An old woman told me of an experience she had had when a child of nine years. She was walking in the outfjelds with her uncle one Sunday afternoon when she saw a pretty bunch of ribbons hanging on a rock, and near it a handful of sweets. Delighted, she took the treasures and ran to show them to her uncle. He looked at her in a puzzled way and asked her what she meant. "Why, don't you see the pretty ribbons?" But he saw nothing in her hand. "And these?" showing him the sweets. To him her fingers seemed empty. Then a fear seized her and she threw the things away, for she knew they were a temptation of the Huldufólk, and had she worn the ribbons and eaten the sweets, from that day the Huldufólk would have been visible to her and she would have been in their power.

A man living in Sandur on Sandoy Island went one day east to Skálavík to a wedding. He was on horseback, and as he passed under the heights of Tróndardalslið he heard a voice crying, "Hear thou, man that rides by! Take word to the house where the wedding shall be, that Bembil is dead, and the child is burned." When the man came to the house where the wedding was, he opened the door, and standing in the doorway called out, "Bembil is dead, and the child is burned." Then sprang one who was not of the invited guests, out from under the table and ran out, crying, "*That was my son!*"

And there was a peasant of Sunnbøur, who found a little Huldu-maiden under a rock, and he brought her home with him. He set her to spinning night and day, giving her no rest. On one condition could he keep her, but I do not understand how or by whom the condition was made. It was that no one should call her by name. If he did she would vanish away. Titil-tata was her name. One Christmas Eve she was dead tired of spinning and she began to sing to herself as she worked,

Titil-tata is my name
Titil-tata is my name.

Over and over again she sang it, hoping to make some one speak to her. No one paid any attention to her, but she sang on and on. At last one of the working women suddenly lost patience, whirled around and cried, "There she sits gabbling away! Don't we all know your name is Titil-tata?" *Z-z-z-z-p!* Titil-tata vanished away and was never heard from again.

Here is another tale, but whether it is about the Huldufólk, who shall say? Rossva is a big red setter, powerful, conceited, and fearless. He has thrashed every dog on the island, and carries himself with a lofty superciliousness which is almost more than they can bear. We can trace his progress round the scattered hamlet by the vituperative chorus of his victims. But lately Rossva has known fear. One calm clear evening, the Pastor was crossing the island, Rossva, as usual, careering on in front. Suddenly Rossva stopped, his eyes fixed on the way before him. His hair bristled on crest and back, his tail drooped, and turning, he fled whimpering, and took refuge between the Pastor's legs. Then, wondering, the Pastor saw his trembling dog's eyes, dilated with fear, watching, following an invisible something that approached, passed close by, and went its way. Then Rossva, with a sigh, emerged from his shelter, and the two went homeward,—the Pastor much "shaken," as the Pastorinde confessed to me later with a twinkle in her eye.

One o'clock, and now the storm is here, bringing the northeast fog. Between the flying scud are glimpses of a leaden sea with great white surges. The surf thunders at the base of the cliffs, and from the brink the spray blows landward like a cloud.

Dalin is very strange tonight, unfriendly, inhospitable. I am not afraid, but never, I think, have I been more wide-awake. All my senses are alert, and all kinds of things that I half believed in as a child all at once seem possible. If I should see a little troll, gray, hairy, misshapen, seated cross-legged among my possessions, or if a queer face peeped at me from behind a boulder, or a line of odd little creatures ran past me down the hill, I am sure I should not be frightened. It would all seem fitting, seemly, what we would naturally expect to see tonight in Dalin.

There is really no relation between the degrees of a thermometer and the sensation of cold in the Faroes. One suffers greatly at a comparatively high temperature, from the violence of the salt winds and the penetrating dampness of the air. I doubt if it is colder now than thirty-five or forty degrees Fahrenheit, and the passage of the hours has been marked by the assumption of many warm and woolly garments, and yet I shiver miserably, and must often leave my camp to tramp vigorously up and down to get warm, a teapot full of hot water clasped fondly to my heart.

A few minutes ago I heard distinctly the voices of women and children chattering not far away. I was glad, surprisingly glad. My lonely uncomfortable vigil was ended. The Pastorinde had grown anxious in the storm and had sent some women to bring me home — but why had they dragged their children from their beds to travel the long, hard way? Hurriedly, happily, I ran forward to a point from which I could overlook the Viðareiði trail and see my relief party as soon as it came out of the fog. As I stood waiting, listening, the wind tossed the fog aside. The gay voices died away. There was no one on the trail.

Queer things happen in Dalin.

I have had more visitors. The first contingent came waddling from the cliff's edge,—low, clumsy shapes, emerging gradually from the fog, mottled gray and brown creatures that stood in a row and stared solemnly at me and said, "*Kwa-a-a!*" in low guttural notes. Eider ducks they were, that probably came to the spot every night and were vastly surprised to find a human being here in Dalin. "*Kwa-a-a!*" they exclaimed again, looked at one another as though to say, "Did you ever see the like?" and so backed away into the mists.

Hardly had they disappeared when I heard a gasping sound from a bank behind me, and turning, I saw, half obscured by the clinging fog, a great gray object. It was about seven feet tall. Its shape was not that of a beast,—rather a grotesque caricature of a woman's form. The face was oval, the features indistinguishable through the fog, the neck very long and thin, the shoulders sloping. From the head long hair blew in the wind. The body was clothed in a loose tunic or blouse, and short skirts whirled about, disclosing two thin ankles. I was not frightened. It was all too wonderful to admit of fear. Only a mighty curiosity possessed me. "*What is it? Oh, what is it?*" The creature tossed its head and stamped its foot. It gasped again, and it looked like nothing of which I had ever heard or dreamed.

Then the storm-fog parted and there stood a large gray-white sheep. I could see that it was a sheep, yet so unnatural, so fantastic, was the figure that it seemed hardly less wonderful than before. It had escaped the men and dogs at the two "mountain-goings" of June when the wool is taken. The long, heavy fleece, with the straight outer hair, had come off on neck and shoulders, leaving them quite bare. The hair on the head was still fast, and at the ends other hair had tangled, lengthening it to eighteen or twenty inches. On the body, part of the fleece had come out, caught in the ends of the fast hair, and had been carded and raveled by rocks and heather, making a great fluffy mass like a woman's draperies. Dimly seen through the fog, the illusion was perfect. The creature faced me, and as the skirt tossed in the gale, two slim legs were revealed. The gasp I heard was the alarm note given by these half-wild sheep.

And the size? Have you ever heard of the peculiar magnifying effect of fog under certain conditions? Warburton Pike in his book on the Barren Lands of Canada tells of one foggy evening in camp when some large animal, presumably a timber wolf, was vaguely seen charging on the camp. The men seized their weapons and sprang to their feet as into the circle of the fire's light ran a little field mouse. And Sir Martin Conway's party in Spitzbergen, on such a day, hastily prepared for an encounter with a polar bear whose form was dimly distinguished through the mists. A few steps farther on and they met that bear—a little scrap of white paper skating along the frozen snow.

But there is something about my apparition that I cannot understand. There are hundreds of sheep high on the fjelds tonight, and surely not another one among them like this curious caricature of a human form. Why should this one sheep have left its fellows and sought my little camp down on the sea cliffs? Is this also "a sending" from "the Others?"

It is four o'clock. The storm is lessening. I am too tired to tramp any longer. Rolled up in as small a compass as possible I will rest a while in the shelter of this big boulder.

"Good-day, Thou Blessed. Is all well with thee?"

I open dazed eyes and there stands old Sigurd looking at me anxiously. It is six o'clock. He has come, he explains, to work on the peat, as the sea is too stormy to go a-fishing. So he says, but I know that he has risen three hours earlier than usual, made his own coffee, and come to Dalin to look after me. He will carry my things home when he leaves work, and I am free to go when I will.

The way is long and weary. The surf, thundering far below, the sea birds' cries make a sleepy confusion of sound; and as I drowse and stumble over rocks and rouse to clearer consciousness, it seems as though I had been going on for hours and hours. At last I reach the outer dike of the hamlet. The homes of men are a pleasant sight after my night in Dalin. In the quiet air the blue peat smoke lingers in wreaths above the grassy roofs. I hear the pounding of coffee in the little black mortars. The fragrance of coffee is in the air. Half-dressed babies are sitting in the sunshine. Friendly faces greet me as I pass the open doors. "Ah! God be praised, it is the Frøkun!" "And what kind of a night did the Frøkun have?" "I could not sleep all night for thinking of the Frøkun!"

On again over the Pastor's glebe lands, and there at the foot of a grassy slope is the Parsonage. Rossva comes cavorting and barking to meet me. Grä-mis [gray puss] follows, picking her way daintily, her tail held carefully erect. "The Frøkun is coming!" I hear Sigga's voice calling within; and there is the Pastorinde hopping on one foot to the door, and waving a dish towel. "Welcome!" she calls in her clear ringing voice, "Welcome home, my plejebarn" and she takes me in her motherly arms. Within that shelter I make confession. "Yes, plejemoder, Sigurd was right. Dalin at night is for 'the Others.'"

Published in *Atlantic Monthly* (December, 1912), 825–832.

A Night With The Mouse's Brother

"And houseless men, who have lain down with the fowls,
open their dim eyes and behold the beauty of the night."

Hans Kristoffer had stacked the last piece of peat in the Gróthús. I
had caught trout enough for breakfast, and we were resting from
our labors, seated on the banks of Sørvágsvatn. It was eleven o'clock
at night; but that matters little in sixty-three degrees north latitude.
The sun disappears for a few hours behind the northern mountains,
and there is a clear, silvery twilight, just the right light for fishing.
Hans Kristoffer glanced at my string of trout. "They are good fish,"
he said, "but you could get larger ones at Fjallavatn, seven miles to
the north. But it is a lonely place, there is no shelter, and you could
not go and return the same day." And Hans Kristoffer shook his head
doubtfully; for I was convalescing after a long illness in Italy, and so
far a three-mile tramp had been the extent of my powers.

"But we can go two of the seven miles by boat on this lake," I
pleaded, "and if the weather is good, we need not return the same
day. I can curl up in a sheltered hollow, with plenty of wraps, and
rest most of the night, and then it would not be too hard." I added
craftily, "Heini too would enjoy the fishing." (Heini is our youngest,
and a born fisherman.) So before we started homewards it was decided that we would go the first sure day.

"A sure day!" That was the difficulty; for this group of mountain
islands, the Faroes, moored in mid-ocean between Iceland and Norway, draw to their rugged summits the wandering mists, and there
are influences, not yet well understood, which make them the land
of sudden changes and fierce storms.

But only three mornings afterward I was awakened by a voice
saying in Faroese, "Konufolkaveður." [Real woman-folk weather.] In
a twinkling I was at the window. Hans Kristoffer and his brother

Jógvan were examining sea, sky, and fjord with a critical eye, and the above phrase was their verdict. "Can we go, Herr Hans?" I called.

"Yes," answered Hans Kristoffer. "It is a clear day, dry and warm; the glass is high and rising. One seldom sees such a day in Faroes."

"I can be ready in an hour!" I exclaimed. "Please ask Heini to dig some worms."

Women knitting and carding wool. Photograph by Elizabeth Taylor.

"He's digging them now," replied Hans Kristoffer as he disappeared around the corner.

We made quite a procession as we started, two hours later,—Hans Kristoffer, Jógvan, Heini and his friend Sigmund, Frú Hans and Frú Jógvan, who, according to the Faroe custom, were to go "a piece of way" with us, knitting long gray stockings as they walked. Provisions and wraps were packed in two *Leypar*, or oblong wooden crates, borne on the shoulders, and supported by a broad woolen band around the brow. Heini carried all the fishing ropes, and I was in light marching order with Fjeldstaff in hand. So we filed out through the bøur and passed into the hagi.

The bøur and hagi—the infield and outfield—these are the two divisions of land in the Faroes, seen best when looking from the sea. The bøur shows as a patch of lively green surrounding a cluster of turf-covered cottages. Here grow grass, potatoes, and a little barley. All the rest is the hagi, a confusion of rocks, short grasses, peat bogs, and marshy pools up to the bare summits of basaltic rock. On the nearer slopes live the cows six months of the year. Beyond are the half-wild sheep, never watched, never fed, living or dying as the storms determine. Desolate as death in the winter, the hagi on a fine summer day is joy enough for sinful human nature.

"Provisions and wraps were packed in two Leypar, or oblong wooden crates, borne on the shoulders and supported by a broad woolen band around the prow."

Perhaps some weak souls amongst us know that peculiar light-ness of spirit that comes when a rather bad-tempered loved one is pleased, for the hour, to be in jocund mood. So one feels on a fine day in the Faroes. One knows it will storm tomorrow, but now how good to feel the warm hand of the sun, to see the fog drawn back across the sea levels, and the fjelds clear-cut against the sky! Below my window a northern wren is pouring out his soul in thanksgiv-ing. The "mouse's brother" the Faroe folk call him, and indeed, ex-cept as to tail, he is much like a mouse in size and color; the same bright eyes and darting motions; the same fashion, too, of whisking in and out between the slats of the *hjallur*, or outside store, and stealing the dried meat. He is seen on the moors and fjelds and bird crags as well as near the houses, and more than any other Faroe bird is associated in my mind with the free outdoor life of the light sum-mer nights.

When we reached Sørvágsvatn, a mile from the house, Frú Hans and Frú Jógvan said *farvael*, and we started northward for the two-mile row. "I am glad that Jógvan and I could go with you," remarked Hans Kristoffer, as he dipped his oar leisurely in the water, "for you ought to see where the *huldukonur* [mountain witches] live, at Fjallavatn. The young folks of today seem to have little interest in such things."

"Did you ever really believe in huldufólk, Herr Hans?" I asked.

Hans Kristoffer smiled as he thought of past years. "Never since I was a boy," he replied, "but there are many who do still. I've heard that across the lake there once lived a large family of huldufólk who made much trouble for the people, until the bishop came and rolled a stone in front of their cave, and marked it with the sign of the cross, and that they could not pass."

"I wonder if they are there now?" I mused.

"Of that," said Hans Kristoffer, "naturally no one dares to make sure. They say that all the other huldufólk have moved away to Fjallavatn."

On reaching the head of the lake, we left the boat, and began our four-mile tramp—not an easy one—over stones, marshes, matted grass, and little watercourses running deeply in the peaty soil. At last we came to a hill above the lake.

"It is an ancient custom to rest here awhile," said Jógvan, and most gladly I observed that ancient custom.

We could see the lake from end to end, stretching somber and quiet for a mile between the fjelds, whose gray and purple cliffs rose in bold heights, six hundred to fifteen hundred feet. The water lapped on rocky shores and coarse black gravel. There was not the smallest bush or rush or water plant to rustle in the wind. One felt a hush, an emptiness in the air, though innumerable wild fowl wheeled and hovered with shrill clamor. At the north the fjelds sank lower, and there the sky gleamed cold and green. "On the other side," said Jógvan, "are the cliffs where young Jógvan is birdcatching today."

He spoke softly, lest Heini hear; for Heini's soul was bitter within him because his big brother was allowed to go, and he was thought too young.

"Jógvan loves to go to the bird crags as much as I did at his age. The boys' uncle, their mother's brother, was killed at the same place, and she is unhappy when Jógvan goes. But it is part of his lifework, and he is eighteen, and one should not forbid it. They are difficult crags. When I was a little boy, I knew two men, a young and an elderly one, who went egg hunting there. We often make the line fast above, go down by it to some good place, fasten the line to a stone, and creep along the edges, gathering eggs. This time, by some accident, the line got loose, and swung out so far that it could not be reached from the ledge on which they stood. There was no way of ascending without it. Five hundred feet below them the sea broke over jagged rocks. Their only chance was for one of them to jump out over the sea and catch the swinging rope.

"I will try it," said the older man. "You have your life yet to live. My children are grown, and will not need me."

"No," said the other, "I have no wife at home to grieve for me, and I am young and strong, and my chance of success is greater than yours would be. If I miss it, you can still try. Now, with God's help, I go." He sprang out from the ledge, caught the rope, and they were saved."

Half an hour later we stood on the shores of Fjallavatn. In three minutes Heini was fishing. Heini is sixteen, tall and slim, with strong and active legs. His nose turns up a little, and a lint-white lock curls upwards from the borders of his *húgva* or long, drooping cap. He walks with head high in air, like a fine young colt, always wears wet moccasins, and is indifferent to such trifles as cold, damp, and fatigue. A fat mitten full of worms hung from his neck, and reposed gracefully on his breast like a choice locket. It shows how fair-minded I am for a woman, that I recognize and appreciate Heini's charms, even though he scorns me (and all women), and has never, of his own free will, spoken to me.

I noticed that Heini, after he had arranged a worm on his hook, spit upon it. Now I have fished with various small boys in eight countries, and every one did the same. This subject has never, to my knowledge, been discussed by the Folklore Societies, but it surely is deserving of consideration.

"Do you always spit upon your worms, Heini?" I asked.

"Naturligvis!" [Of course] replied Heini, with crushing brevity.

Close to the lake was a *ratt*, or open inclosure of short stones, where the sheep are driven at the woolgathering, and on the lee side of the wall we made our camp. As the only woman of the party I had domestic duties to perform, and found that a *leypar* turned on its side serves admirably as a sheltered kitchen, and the top as a dining table.

After our late dinner, Hans Kristoffer and Jógvan strolled along the shore, smoking, and I rested, seated on a low mossy hillock, with my head propped up comfortably on a higher one. During dinner I had noticed a low twittering sound, and now it came again, and looking up I saw close by, on one of the stones of the ratt, six fluffy baby mouse's brothers. All in a row they sat, eyeing me with shining eyes, in the friendliest fashion. Harmless sheep they knew; also their enemies, the hooded crows and ravens; but this queer animal? Perhaps it was a new kind of sheep, and they edged closer and closer with confiding peepings, while the parent birds cried and called piteously at a little distance. I rose cautiously and drew nearer. The father bird, seeing me move, flew away; but the mother came and placed herself between me and the nearest baby. Brave little mother! Her form quivered and shrank, her dark eyes dilated, but she kept her post. I could have caught her in my hand, but it would have been too cruel, and I withdrew softly. And then the father, evidently feeling that he had cut but a poor figure in the affair, came bustling up, and proceeded to feed the babies with great show and demonstration, as though their present safety was due entirely to him.

I had come to Fjallavatn to catch a big fish, and was just getting out my tackle when Hans Kristoffer returned.

"Do you feel like walking a little way to see the huldukonur homes? The evening sun rests on them now, and you can see them well."

So along the lake shore we walked until we came in sight of two great clefts, one on each side of the lake, running deeply into the solid rock. Dark and grim, with water dripping from their depths, they seemed especially suitable as homes for huldufólk. Seated on the slope below, Hans Kristoffer told me a story of their inmates.

"There was once a shepherd of Sandavágur (the next hamlet to ours) who was cleverer than any other in the Faroes. He knew every sheep in the hagi, and he had a fine red horse that was very swift. One beautiful morning the shepherd thought he would go north to Fjallavatn to look after the sheep. Now at that time there lived here two huldukonur sisters, one in Husagjov, just above us, and the other in Tormansgjov, across the water. Both these huldukonur had dresses of scarlet cloth, and it happened that the very morning the shepherd left home the huldukona in Husagjov put out her dress to sun. A long way off the shepherd saw the bright dress with its trimming of golden buttons shining in the sun. He turned his horse to where the dress lay, took it up, and, placing it behind him on the saddle, rode away. The huldukona sat by her fire, and it occurred to her to go out and turn her dress. But when she came out, she gnashed her teeth with rage, for it was gone. She looked around the hills, and there, near her sister's house, was the shepherd riding at full speed with her dress. "Sister! Sister! Help me!" she cried. "Make long strides after him!" But her sister called back, "I cannot! Both my legs are lame!" And so the huldukona herself started in pursuit. When the shepherd came to a little stream, Vatnsoyrar, which flows in Sørvágsvatn, his horse was exhausted and could hardly go. He stopped to drink at the stream, and by that time the huldukona was close at hand. But then the horse was so refreshed that he flew on again and up the hill. "That stream was my salvation," said the shepherd, and it is called the Stream of Salvation to this day. On they went, until the horse was trembling and the sweat poured down his sides. Nearer and nearer came the huldukona, and reached him just as he came to the church wall. He threw himself from the saddle and over the wall; but the dress caught on the stones, and the huldukona seized one end. "Now I hold it!" she cried. "Hold it as you will," he answered, "there is God and the Church!" They struggled for the dress, and then it tore, and all the shepherd got was one of the sleeves; but so large was it that it made a stole for the priest, and in the Sandavágur church it is to this day.

"And here I am," added Hans Kristoffer, "taking up your time with huldufólk stories, and it's almost nine o'clock and you haven't caught a fish. Heini has a good string already."

"Herr Hans," I replied, "I am really too tired to fish now. That was a long walk here, you know. I think I'll light the spirit lamp, heat water for my hot-water bag, and sleep for a few hours. Two o'clock is the best time for fishing, anyhow, and I'll be rested by that time."

"Yes," approved Hans Kristoffer, "that's a good idea; for you will have all that way to go back again tomorrow."

A few steps above the ratt I found a cosy little hollow, soft with moss; very damp, indeed (a Faroe fjeld side is generally like a soaked sponge), but first I put down a rubber camp-sheet, then rolled myself in a pair of Jaeger blankets, pulled a soft wool hood over my head, hugged tight my hot-water bottle, and surveyed my surroundings with much satisfaction. "This is much better than a stuffy house," I said to myself, "and I never did like a puffin feather bed. It's cold, to be sure, but the air is so sweet and fresh,—and I wonder how many kinds of flowers there are right around me. Ragged robins, white bedstraw, tormentillas, wild geraniums, St. John's-wort, two kinds of heather, lady's-smock, and eyebrights close to my head; on that hillock to the right sibbaldia, lady's-mantle, butterwort, crowberry, meadowrue, and a marsh violet; on the shore silverweed, starry saxifrage, creeping buttercups, sea-thrift, and stonecrop, but all low-growing, as if they were afraid of blowing away if they grew tall. Then up on the rocky slopes I know there are nice little subalpines, at least a dozen, and possibly an Icelandic poppy. I'll climb up in the morning and see. But now it's almost ten o'clock, and I must sleep." A drowsy twittering among the stones of the ratt told me that the baby mouse's brothers were settling for the night; but on the crags across the lake the black-backed gulls laughed and screamed, and Arctic terns flashed like swallows to and fro across the quiet water. The last thing I saw, as I closed my eyes, was Heini fishing.

I awoke with a start. A large drop had plashed down on my nose. Heini was still fishing, and Hans Kristoffer stood by me with a troubled face. "I am sorry to disturb you," he said, "but we must start for home. We shall have bad weather,—cold wind, rain and fog. We are used to it, but it won't do for you to stay here in the wet. In walking it will not be so bad, you can go as slowly as you choose,—it is only eleven o'clock now,—and then by morning we shall have shelter and warm food."

I sat up, and looked about me in dismay. The fjelds opposite were half lost in dense clouds which sank lower every moment. It was bitterly chill. Alas for our "sure day!"

We packed up the leypar again and started. Hans Kristoffer and Jógvan had half a dozen good trout, and Heini all he could well carry. They ranged from one pound and a quarter to two pounds and a half. And I had not caught one.

The rain fell heavily as we left the lake, but ceased as we passed over the hills at the south. Though the dense clouds darkened the air, I could still see the golden tormentillas shining in the moss at my feet, and the heather bells heavy with rain. We were in the clouds. They swept around us, shutting out all landmarks from view. The men walked on ahead, talking in cheerful hushed tones and keeping a watchful eye on me,—holding out a helping hand at treacherous places, putting something under my head when I lay down to rest, and saying, "Now the worst is over," or "Now it will soon be day;" and once I heard a voice—was it Heini's?—saying, "We shall get to Sørvágsvatn at just the right time for fishing."

I was well knocked up by this time, and could go but a little way without stopping. Then I lay, stretched out at full length in the wet moss, while the mists drifted over my face, and scores of birds hovered and cried around me. They had shown little alarm as we passed in the morning, but they now thought that this nocturnal expedition boded no good for them. The curlews first gave the alarm; the oyster catchers and golden plover took up the cry; ravens and crows, gulls and terns, hurried from the cliffs; wrens, stonechats, titlarks, and wheatears hopped nearer and nearer, and remonstrated with me for this intrusion. Then there was a strange sound, half a whir, half a tremulous cry, like that of a lost lamb or a young child. It seemed to have a ventriloquistic quality, also; now it sounded close to my face, now at the side, now quavered downward through the air.

"Herr Jógvan," I called to him as he sat at a little distance, "I hear a cry like that of a little child. Perhaps it is a huldukona?"

"No," replied Jógvan gravely, "it is a myra-snipa" [marsh snipe].

"But I heard many myra-snipas when I was on Mykines, and they all said 'A-chik! a-chik! a-chik!'"

"That," said Jógvan, "is their good-weather cry. They always cry like this when it is stormy or foggy."

There were large dusky birds,—a dozen or more,—much bolder than any others, that swooped down at me so fiercely that instinctively I put up my hands to guard my eyes.

"Herr Jógvan," I called again, "what is this dark bird that is so bold?"

"That is a *kjóvi*; an Englishman who was here once, called it an Arctic skua. This is the smaller kind: the larger ones kill lambs, and can be dangerous to a man on the bird crags by beating his head with their strong wings. But they are rare now. I doubt if there are a dozen pairs in all the islands. The last ones here were killed a few years ago, by an Englishman, at Fjallavatn. (That was before the law protecting them was passed.) It was a fine pair, male and female, and the Englishman was very glad and proud; they were to be stuffed and sent to his home in England. Coming home he was tired and went slowly, and he told his guide to go on ahead with the skuas and take good care of them. The guide didn't understand English, but he was a faithful man, and he hurried off home. The Englishman arrived about an hour and a half afterwards. His dinner was being put on the table; his two skuas, brown and shining, served with new potatoes, and cranberry sauce."

We reached the lake at two o'clock, and I fished from the boat, using a light coachman fly, and catching fifteen good trout as the men rowed slowly homeward. A dense silvery fog was milling up from the sea. Like hoarfrost it rested everywhere, making the men's rough clothes, their hairy beards, and eyebrows, white as snow. The ends of the long oars dipped in the drifting clouds; we glided on in a still whiteness, guided only by the hushed booming of the surf against the Sorvágur sea cliffs.

At the landing I left the men to house the boat, and started on alone for the mile home stretch. The cows were sleeping by the trail. They woke, as I passed, and looked at me with wondering eyes, and a big calf arose, and followed me with blandishments, apparently thinking that the early hour might have softened my heart, and I would let him through the village gate to the longed-for infields, where he had spent the days of his infancy.

We had been gone only twenty hours, but so long seemed the time that, as the silent village came in sight around a sudden turn, it was with a vague surprise that I saw unchanged the familiar grassy roofs, the quaint weather vane on the church, the same old white whale moored out in the bay and awaiting the coming of the whaler. I stole into the house softly (we seldom lock the doors in Faroes), lest I awake Frú Hans and Frú Jógvan. My own particular mouse's brother was on my window sill. "Oh, mouse's brother," I exclaimed, as I gave him his morning crumbs, "this little room is better than a wet fjeld side, and how good, how very good, looks that bed of puffin feathers!"

Published in *Atlantic Monthly*, 89 (May, 1902), 671–676.

The Garden of Hans Kristoffer

It is a little garden of the North, far up in the sixties, at Miðvágur on one of the Faroe Isles. The years of the garden are seventy-six; those of Hans Kristoffer are eighty-four. His forebears, Norse Vikings seven centuries ago, were not garden lovers, and the chief interests of their descendants are codfish, whales, seafowl, and half-wild sheep. But the parsonage gardens of Denmark are noted, and back in the eighteenth century the daughter of a Danish pastor 'married in' to this old farm in the Ryggi section of Miðvágur. And I think that ancestral memories of faraway Danish gardens, a heritage of garden lore, have come down to Hans Kristoffer from that 'Ann Lisbit, born Svabo.' I think it is to her that he owes his garden.

One spring morning he stood, a little boy of eight years, in the doorway of his father's cottage. A mighty pile of ashes and refuse was close by; a rocky, boggy slope, a marshy bit at the bottom, where a cow stood, knee-deep. Hans Kristoffer surveyed it all, and something stirred to life in his heart. He had never seen a garden, but now he said to himself, "Here I will have a garden; here I will make things grow." And having made this resolve, he began straightway. Permission was given him to do what he chose with the land; permission, but no help. And it would be a labor of years for one small pair of arms to dig and drain it, and build a dike around it. So, to encourage himself at the very outset, he went to the wild moors, dug up violets and catchflies and little orchids, and planted them on the outskirts of the ash heap before he began the task of clearing it away. And that was the beginning of the garden.

I saw it first fourteen years ago, when I had been in the Faroes only a week. My destination was Mykines, an interesting bird island far out in the West, and a friend in Tórshavn had planned for me a short stay, midway, at Hans Kristoffer's and had written to tell him of my coming. Five hours of tumultuous seas, glimpses, through mists, of cliff islands of strange shape, with storm clouds flying from their summits, and then I was deposited on the sea rocks, cold, wet, and forlorn.

No Hans Kristoffer was visible. A curious crowd collected, faces peered at me from windows and around corners. Then a merchant appeared who spoke English, and to him I explained that I wanted to go to the King's Peasant at Ryggi. "To Hans Kristoffer's? Yes, to be sure. He was here a moment ago. Ho! Hans Kristoffer!" he called. And at the word a little old man came forward and bade me welcome. It was Hans Kristoffer, and he had been there all the time. That was my first lesson in Faroe etiquette. The stranger, it seems, must make all the advances.

Then we started for Ryggi, Hans Kristoffer paddling softly by my side in his Faroe moccasins. Not far away, I saw a long, low, grass-roofed cottage, with flowery beds half-hidden in a shrubby growth of trees. Five minutes more, and Hans Kristoffer opened a high door in a stone wall, and I passed into the garden. I had only a glimpse of yellow bands of primroses, and nodding daffodils, and then I saw the housemother, Frú Johanna Katrina, smiling a welcome in the doorway.

As I have no garden of my own, I am obliged to dig in those of other people. In my bag were some seeds and roots that I thought might be new to the Faroes; and even before Johanna Katrina brought in the coffee and kringles, Hans Kristoffer and I sat down side by side, he with a Danish-English dictionary on his knee, I with one in English-Danish on mine, for mutual enlightenment. And when we had finished the coffee and kringles, we went out and planted the roots and seeds, and have been fast friends ever since.

I went to bed that night in a little bed of puffin feathers, hearing the soft rustle of leaves close by, and the *hush-ah-hush* of surf on the strand. Later, after midnight, there were other sounds, a puzzling, yet apparently friendly presence in the garden. I peered out into the silvery twilight. It was that short hour of the Faroe summer night when the sunset glow has passed away, but the sun delays its coming. The fjelds appeared bolder and sterner, and soft wreaths of mist gathered about their summits and filled the upland hollows. The sea looked like a great brimming bowl, exactly as if it would mount higher and higher and overwhelm the land. Only a faint, far sound came from the distant bird cliffs—the wakeful kittiwakes' cry, "*Trud-lar-i! trud-lar-i!*" and Hestur and Koltur, strange shapes out at sea, seemed more than ever like sentient creatures heeding the command, "Keep silence before Me, O Islands!"

It was the hour, too, when the *Veittrir* come out, the little folk that give Christian service, and stay only where there is peace and good will. And something was stirring out among the flowers—a small brown figure, bending, lifting tenderly a bruised stalk, freeing a struggling plant from a weed, strewing a path with fine sand. Though small, it was too large to be one of the Veittrir. It was Hans Kristoffer, refreshing himself after long hours of toil in the home-fields, by tending his beloved garden.

After breakfast I went out with Hans Kristoffer, to make a closer acquaintance with the garden. In front of the cottage is a large bed of perennials with a little golden locust tree on the upper border. The taller plants are lilac and white lupines, a flowering currant, a foxglove or two, cottage lilies, yellow larkspurs, and one of bright blue monkshood, montbretia, monkey-flowers, Jacob's ladders, Shasta daisies, feverfew, mauve and white rockets, doronicums, Fair Maids of France, an oriental poppy, two peonies, and starry astrantiums. The lower plants are sweet Williams, pyrethrums, lilac and white horned violets, forget-me-nots, potentillas, Iceland poppies, a bleeding heart, Scottish bluebells, geums, catchflies, daffodils, Spanish irises, spiraeas, and wood hyacinths.

And then there is the border. First, a wonderful band of primroses. Never, no, not under Devon hedges, have I seen such a wealth of blossoms, hardly a leaf showing among them. Then comes a band of London pride, or *Saxifraga umbrosa*, or Mother of Thousands, as you choose to call it. And the inner band is Poet's narcissus. First the primroses bloom, then the Poet's narcissus, and then the Mother of Thousands.

Below the large bed is a circular grass plane, with eighteen little beds following its circumference, each just large enough to hold a clump of sweet Williams, or clove pinks, or pansies. And in the center is a tiny spruce. The garden lies on a slope facing the sea, and when the great sou'easters rage, I wonder how any mortal plant can survive. But even when mourning some damage done, I remember what charm this sharp decline gives the garden, with the lovely tints of sea, strand, and sky as a background for the blossoms. Between the laced branches of little trees are long white bars of surf and the flashing of white wings; and you should see a big clump of Grandis daffodils against the gleaming purples of the strand!

There are gravelly paths that curve and wind down the slope, as paths should do, and all are bordered with primroses and the Mother of Thousands. They pass under the tiniest trees and between the biggest currant bushes that I have ever seen, and lead to a store-house, or to a sheltered nook among elderberry bushes, where there are benches and a table, or to seats by the sea dike, or to the top of the garden with a wide view over sea and fields. And the only help Hans Kristoffer had in planning his garden was a bit of advice given him by a Danish pastor: "Don't make squares, Hans Kristoffer, make *curves.*"

Though most of the flowers are in the large bed, there are not a few in odd nooks—a Thunbergianum lily, irises, beds of vinca, sweet Williams, and several rose bushes that never bloom.

By the time I had seen everything and we sat down to rest on the bleaching grass above the garden, I had discovered that Hans Kristoffer's little trees and his primrose borders are the pride and joy of his heart. I was new to the Faroes then, and did not know that not a tree, not a shrub grows wild in the islands. But the garden bore traces of conflict: the little trees were browner than they should be, and some seemed to be perpetually blowing to the northwest, and others to the southeast, according to their exposure. And I fear they will never be much larger, much *taller,* though with the years they may learn to bow to the storms and curve low their branches within the shelter of the dike.

Indeed Hans Kristoffer reminds me of his own little trees. Small, brown, and brave, with budding hopes cut down by cruel frosts and sprouting anew in the spring. Hans Kristoffer had many questions to ask me about the trees of America, and drank in greedily all I told him about the redwoods of California, and the yellow spruces of Alaska.

"And that is far north too—Alaska," he said wistfully. "But no, they would not grow like that *here*, not if they lived to be a thousand years."

And the primroses? These bare fjelds and barren slopes did not look at all primrosy. Yet, half a century ago, Hans Kristoffer found some pale blossoms under a ledge of rock on another island—the only place where they grow in the Faroes. He brought a few roots home, and years of patient and devoted care have made these wonderful borders. As we entered the bay, I had seen them shining like golden ribbons in the wan sunlight.

The garden grew slowly in its infancy. Some native flowers, some seeds from Denmark, cuttings from a Danish official's garden in Tórshavn, little trees that voyaged adventurously in a sloop from Norway, southernwood that was once a sprig in a posy sent to a Faroe skipper's wife from a Shetland Island port; and later came contributions from a Scottish Border garden, from one in South Devon, and from bleak Aberdeen. But few survived when sent from English gardens.

During the next five years I often turned up at Ryggi, after stirring adventures by land and sea, looking like a drowned mouse, and being revived by Johanna Katrina with hot milk and a good fire of peats. Never before had such a chance to dig been mine; but I worked in ignorance, and often longed for advice, preferably from some Norwegian scientist, versed in the vicissitudes of a sub-Arctic climate in a storm center where Gulf Stream and Polar current strive for mastery. He might have told me why foxgloves, a Croceum lily, and English irises thrive here, and German irises, hollyhocks, and Madonna lilies fail. Many plants struggle along doubtfully through the alternate soakings and freezings, the pitiless downpours, and violent gales; sprout often in February and are frozen in March, sprout again and are cut down in May; get the better of their troubles, show great promise of a flowery future, and then die quietly in June.

I usually took my meals alone, with catalogues of plants, bulbs, and seeds (from Barr of Covent Garden) propped open before me. Such treasures one could get for six pence! New and improved varieties of snowdrops, crocuses, and narcissi to replace the old inferior kinds, and English wood hyacinths, pink, white, and blue—it was such an exhilarating thought that, after I had sailed away from the

Faroes, those flowers would dance down a long vista of years, and through the medium of Hans Kristoffer's many godchildren and friends, bloom in future little gardens of the seventeen inhabited islands.

There were evenings when, overweary, I have said to myself, "It's only a poor little garden. It would hardly be noticed in any other land." But I said it without conviction, and took it back again next morning. For, more than any garden I know, it is an epitome of the life of the people. In this soil during seven hundred years, honorable, hospitable, brave men and women have toiled and suffered and kept their faith. Their old-time industries I can see from the vantage point of the garden. The wind that blows over it brings messages from the home fields and the far-encircling sea and fjelds. Blindfolded, I can tell from which "airt" the wind is blowing. In the garden, years ago I heard the whale-message going like wildfire over the land. And within these precincts we welcomed the Governor, when he came, one happy day, to bring the Cross of Danebrog, bestowed by the King of Denmark on Hans Kristoffer, for good service to his fellow men.

Johanna Katrina often comes out with her knitting, and paces to

Hans Kristoffer and his wife Johanna Katrina Joensen in their garden at Miðvágur. Photograph by Elizabeth Taylor.

and fro with a mind divided between pleasure at my efforts and mortification that any guest of hers should look so bedrabbled and neglected. Johanna Katrina has a fine spirit of her own, but in all that pertains to the garden she is meekness personified. She never tries to help. She has, indeed, been sternly forbidden to give assistance of any kind. There is, of course, a reason for this. She told me, herself, the story of that fateful day when, Hans Kristoffer being absent, she thought she would help by weeding the beds in the grass plane, the little servant assisting. It was too early in the spring for flowers, and clove pinks, when not in bloom, certainly *do* look like grass, and who could have dreamed that those tufts of common-looking leaves were sweet Williams, *Hans Kristoffer's cherished dark-red sweet Williams*? The brook, close by, was in full spate, and the little maid quickly gathered up the "weeds" and threw them in the brook, and a strong west-fall tide swept them all out to sea.

But Johanna Katrina has a certain small privilege of her own—to make little posies for departing friends: a white clove pink, a sprig of southernwood, a spray of the bleeding heart, which is her special property. And of course she can gather as many primroses as she wishes.

Somewhere she has picked up the Latin name of a certain species. And I often see her nodding complacently at the primrose border and murmuring, "Primula veris! Primula veris!" as if to say, "I am not as ignorant as they think." Dear Johanna Katrina! They are *not* Primula veris; but who would have the heart to tell her so?

I was five and a half years in the Faroes without leaving the islands. Then, in the autumn of 1905, I went south to Scotland, to stay during the winter and return the next spring for another six months. When I went to Ryggi to say farewell, I found Hans Kristoffer in trouble. The spring before, he had enlarged his garden, including a strip of new land, and on it nothing would grow. Potatoes gave almost no return, carrots made only a hard disk and rootlets; flowers grew an inch tall, blossomed, and died. Something had to be done. And so, when I went to Scotland, I took a little bag of soil to be analyzed. A seeds man in Edinburgh advised me to go to the University and ask advice of the Professor of Agriculture.

In his den, in the old gray pile of buildings, the professor was finishing an important work on the domestic animals of Great Britain and contiguous islands. Only one thing was lacking,—information about Faroe sheep, and how to get it? At that moment, a knock on the door, and I appeared, carrying a bag of soil. From the moment the magic words "Faroe Islands" were uttered, my welcome was assured. Did I, perhaps, know anything about the sheep of the islands?

Did I not! I had absorbed sheeplore for more than five years. I had a personal acquaintance with scores of lambs. I knew the length of their tails, the set of their ears, the shape and color of their spots, and I had photographs and statistics. The professor was given the information and illustrations he needed.

He analyzed the soil and found it most attractive in its lacks; and when I returned the following spring, I was preceded by a beautiful present from the professor to Hans Kristoffer, of three kinds of fertilizers, the only stipulation being that they should be tried in three separate sections, and the comparative results noted. That autumn carrots and potatoes were well grown, flowers bloomed abundantly, and since then all has gone well.

And now I am back again in this month of May, 1914. I thought I was never again to see Hans Kristoffer and the garden, but a fairy godmother made it possible. Influenza and a late spring have delayed farm-work. That must come first, though the garden suffers. And *my* working powers are in abeyance. Only by making promises to an Edinburgh doctor, am I here at all, in honor bound to climb no fjelds, to have no exciting adventures, and to return to Scotland before the big storms of September.

I am in the garden now, taking notes of the changes of eight years. I weed a little, tidy up the perennials, put the refuse in a cracker box (*anglicé*, biscuit tin), replace the cover and sit on it, resting under the lee of the currant bushes. How narrow minded I was during my first years in the garden—how priggish my attitude toward these currant bushes! I thought that they should be pruned to increase their bearing, and only my ignorance of the proper methods saved them from rigorous measures that would have grieved the heart of Hans Kristoffer. He seemed to think the pruning of a bush an unkind act toward a friend. So they grow in peace, making tall leafy shrubs, pleasant to the eye, and giving shelter from the keen sea winds; and that is better than berries.

Hans Kristoffer is somewhere near. All day he has been carrying crates of seed potatoes on his shoulders, from the house attic to the fields at the bottom of the hill. It is now five o'clock, and he appeared a few minutes ago, looking a little weary (he is eighty-four years old), but in the best of spirits. He says that he thinks he has earned a little recreation. So he is crawling on all fours under the big currant bushes, scraping from the soil the thick moss that has grown there since last summer. Now and then he emerges, looking rather flushed and scratched, and all covered with fluff and dry leaves, and we chat a little until he disappears again.

"Seems to me the little spruce in the grass plane has done very well."

"The top's crooked," replied Hans Kristoffer gloomily. "It had made a beautiful green top six inches long, and one day a starling came along, nipped off the top, dropped it, and flew away. Right before my eyes he did that. *If he had only put it to some use!*" lamented he. "And then a lower shoot had to be bound up to take its place. But it was always askew. It has never looked the same."

"Did I tell you about the thrushes?" asked Hans Kristoffer on one of his brief visits. "No? Well, some little time after you went away, the currant bushes stopped bearing. I couldn't find out what was the matter. During two years we hadn't a berry. Then, in April, a great sou'wester blew a flock of red-winged thrushes onto the island's west coast. They were on their way to Iceland. I suppose they could see the trees from afar," said Hans Kristoffer with a gratified smile, "and they crossed at once to the garden. And then they couldn't go, for the storm changed to a hard nor'wester, and they never start in a hard wind. They stayed for a fortnight. We thought that there were a hundred and twenty-five in the flock. They were busy all the time among the currant bushes. Even the soil beneath the bushes looked as though it had been worked with garden tools. We were very careful not to disturb them, and went on tiptoe if we had to go to the storehouse after they were settled for the night. And we kept the cats away. You should have heard them sing. I didn't know that any birds could sing like that. I don't know what they did to those currant bushes, or what they found there, but we had a fine lot of berries that year, and since then we have had no more trouble."

It is very cold. The snow lies white on the fields, and now and then there is a sudden hissing and rattling among the currant bushes,—fine dry snow and hail,—and down-dropping veils shut in the garden.

Suddenly I remembered the primroses. I had not thought of them before. Even with this cold, they should have been in full bud now. I looked at the border nearest to me. Only the Mother of Thousands was there. Just then Hans Kristoffer appeared a few yards away. "Why, Hans Kristoffer," I cried, "where are the primroses?"

Hans Kristoffer turned a little from me and stood a moment looking over the bay. Then he came nearer, and said in a low tone, "They died."

"They *died?*" I echoed in dismay.

"Yes, they had a sickness, and it spread, and I couldn't save them. I did all I could, all that people told me to do. Oh, yes! I did my best, but nothing helped. In two years they were all gone."

I looked at Hans Kristoffer, seeing him dimly, through a mist, and I cannot say that his eyes were quite dry. For a moment I felt that I could not have it so. I would write to America, ask wealthy friends to help. My dear old friend should have his primrose borders again. But no, the distance and the difficulties are too great, and after all, the Mother of Thousands is fair to see.

But he shall have more polyanthus primroses. They will not make borders, but they are pretty in groups, and strange to say, the few that I left here eight years ago have not been affected. I have seeds with me. I will sow them tomorrow, and perhaps they may be large enough to transplant before I sail away in September.

JUNE 15, 1914

In former years the garden had few neighbors. Now there are many, and in each house are children, cats, dogs, chickens, and ducks—enemies of the garden in effect if not intention. It was not with malice prepense that two dogs had a fight yesterday among my seedlings. Nevertheless, today only five remain out of one hundred and twenty-five. And I cannot blame the hens, that they like to lie on their sides and kick in the large flower-bed. It is a pleasant place to kick in. But this cannot go on. Hans Kristoffer is growing worn with all these losses and disappointments. So I have decided to write to that kind professor in Edinburgh, who has become a friend, and ask him to get an estimate of the cost of chicken-wire to top the stone wall and the dikes around the garden. I fear it will cost too much, and I will say nothing about it to Hans Kristoffer. But I must have measurements, and I have revived an old plan we had, to make a map of the garden. And now Hans Kristoffer and I prowl about—he with a long fishing pole marked off in *alens*, and I with a dress-maker's yard-measure. We have an abstracted and solemn air, and mutter as we go, "50 by 100; 40 by 75 by 150."

AUGUST 3, 1914

Only thrice have I left the shelter of the garden for longer trips. The last time it was to a hamlet on the western coast. People were kind, and there were wonderful cliff islands, but I was homesick for little trees and encompassing walls. When I opened the high garden door, there stood a clump of beautiful English irises in full bloom. Not white, not gray were they, but like the shadow cast on white by dancing leaves. I had been in storm-swept spaces, where no fragile leaf could grow; and to see these stately flowers, their petals so fair and perfect, made the garden seem "the veriest school of peace."

Then I saw Hans Kristoffer coming toward me, and his eyes were troubled. "The Governor has sent a message," he said. "There will be war. It is thought that Denmark will be drawn in, too. People are frightened."

And now there is no more peace in the garden. The cottage is the gathering place for troubled souls. No wonder they are afraid. They remember too well the old tales of the Napoleonic wars, when the Faroes were forgotten, the yearly supply ship did not come, and chil-dren lay dead on the sea rocks where they had crawled to eat sea-weed. Four German cruisers have been seen near. There is talk about the places of refuge high up among the fjelds, where people fled from pirates in the old days. They are cunningly concealed, yet one can shelter several hundred, and a few stout men hold the entrance.

The S. S. *Tjaldur* has come in, and is anchored in the bay. The captain is called to military service in Denmark, and must take the vessel to Copenhagen. It will be crowded to its utmost capacity with Danes called to service—students, patients for hospitals, summer visitors, merchants; and there are two English officers who came for a few weeks, fishing. I have been acting as interpreter for them. They think that England *must* join the war, and they will soon be on their way to France. It is believed that Denmark will be at war before the *Tjaldur* can reach Copenhagen. It has no wireless, no cannon. The Captain's family is on board.

AUGUST 10, 1914

And now the *Tjaldur* has gone, and all is quiet again. These are dark days, made more depressing by dense fog that wraps us in like a pall. Great flights of seafowl, made bolder by the fog, gather close to the village. Their wild, raucous cries, the confused clamor, like frightened human voices, add to the sense of foreboding. And the other day, when two great creatures emerged from the mists in Nolsóyarfjordur, the people of the little capital of Tórshavn gathered on the sea rocks and awaited their fate in silence. The Dreadnoughts anchored, a flag was run up, and it was the *British* flag. Then the people said, "God be praised!" and took courage. England has joined the war.

Thrice above the sound of haymakers' voices has sounded the dull booming of cannon. Denmark has canceled all sailings. The little fleet of motor fishing boats rocks idly at its moorings. No more busy coming and going, the soft *chug-chugging* echoing along the cliffs. For there is no petroleum. Supplies are low. Denmark, England, and Norway refuse us food. There is only a little tea. This is a serious matter, and Hans Kristoffer has recalled a bit of plantlore told him long ago by a Danish pastor's wife: that the leaves of a little trailing Northern raspberry, when dried, make a good substitute for tea. With much enthusiasm we went in search of it, dried it, made a brew, and bade the family try our war tea. But the emphasis with which the proffer of a second cup was declined showed that it was not a cup that cheers.

I have been transplanting baby polyanthus primroses, each a tiny rosette of leaves. Johanna Katrina watches me with a half smile on her anxious face.

"I like to see you do that," she says. "You seem so pleased, so satisfied with your work, as though you expected that someone would be alive next spring to enjoy them."

A really delightful thing has happened. The Edinburgh professor, instead of sending me an estimate of the cost of chicken netting, has bought it himself and sent it to Hans Kristoffer as a present. Not only chicken-netting, but barbed wire, and rolls of strong-meshed netting warranted to keep out cows and sheep. But, the first surprise and joy past, Hans Kristoffer has gone about heavily, with a troubled face. "It is too much," he murmured. "I can do nothing in return. It is not right."

I saw that stern measures were necessary. "Hans Kristoffer," I said, "cannot the professor be permitted to use his own money in the way that pleases him most? Would you begrudge a kind friend a pleasure? I think you are showing a very evil spirit in this matter!"

Hans Kristoffer's face brightened. He had not looked at it in that light before. Of course, he could not deny such a kind friend a pleasure.

And then began the work of putting up the defenses. There is enough, not only for the garden itself, but for the kitchen garden and for a field of potatoes. We are nothing if not militant nowadays. And this morning Hans Kristoffer announced happily that he thought the fort was now impregnable to land forces. But only by attacks of the enemy could possible weak points in the defenses be ascertained. Nothing, he added sadly, could protect the fort from the devastations of that miserable airship—a half-time thieving crow.

AUGUST 27, 1914

Today came a cable message from an Edinburgh friend, "Advise return immediately." But I cannot return. On the Continent ambassadors and consuls must be shepherding flocks of wandering Americans, but nothing of the kind is happening to me. There is no consul, no passport, no mails, no money, no ship to the outside world. The Tórshavn bank will not cash a check. Leith has closed her port to us, and I must stay, perforce, probably the only American marooned in the far North.

We must not speak of the war to Johanna Katrina; her heart is weak, and she cannot bear tales of bloodshed and suffering. The all-too-brief bulletins are telephoned from Tórshavn and pasted on the doctor's window so all can read. When I bring home the news, Hans Kristoffer and I exchange glances, and then separately and casually retire, to meet again in sheltered paths among the currant bushes. If Johanna Katrina appears, she finds us talking loudly and cheerfully about the flowers.

SEPTEMBER 12, 1914

As the British cruisers have cleared the North Sea, the outlook seemed brighter. Two Danish boats came with supplies for the Faroes and Iceland, and if I could get permission to land at Leith, a return to Scotland seemed probable. And then the German mines began their devilish work. Disguised as trawlers and other fishing craft, and flying the flags of Norway, Denmark, and Holland, the Germans set the mines under the very noses—or bows of the British patrol. Two large Danish steamers were the first to go, and scores of other vessels, large and small, followed, most of them neutral. Of course, this is all in defiance of international law, this sowing of mines—and floating mines, too—on traffic routes of the high seas.

SEPTEMBER 21, 1914

And now the big storms of September have begun. The time has come to say farewell to the garden of Hans Kristoffer. In Eiði, far to the North, as far as one can go, lives a young Faroe-Danish house-mother, who will bid me welcome to two little attic rooms, where I can keep house during the winter. Then, the war over, the seas clear, the port of Leith open once more, I will fare away to Scotland in the spring—in the spring, if God wills it.

The potato-planting, barley-sowing, peat-cutting and drying, the fishing vessels coming and going, the curing and drying of fish, the haymaking—all these have I seen this year from the vantage ground of the garden.

And I have seen the coming of the whales!

The close of the season's work I saw years ago, one delectable October day and night—a rarely quiet day, the fjelds white with new snow, and gleaming with alternate bars of purple and gold, as the sunlight glanced across the layers of basalt. The blue peat smoke drifted across the fields from the 'Sodnhus,'—little cabins where the half-ripe barley was drying on rocks above the open peat fires; the fragrance of coffee, a snatch of an old ballad, the throbbing of flails. "*One*—two! *one*—two!" say the flails, and that emphasis tells that *three* women are down on their knees beating out the barley on the earthen floor. From the fjelds comes a confused clamor, the shouting of men, the yap-yapping of dogs, the bubbling cries of sheep, the shriller notes of frightened lambs. It is the *fjall gonga*—the "mountain-going," when sheep are driven down for slaughter. And that night many sheep are killed in Hans Kristoffer's large outer kitchen, with its floor of beaten earth, its open loft overhead, with great beams on which fishing rods, whale spears, and harpoons are laid. The air is thick with smoke and dust, and the steam from wet woollen clothes. There is a large group of sheep waiting in one corner. Others are in the adjoining cow-byre. The tired dogs are stretched at full length on the floor. The puppy, today, has made his "maiden run." His skin twitches with fatigue and his paws are red with blood. The sheep are silent except for one slight convulsive struggle as the knife pierces the throat and the vein is severed. Then comes the splashing of blood in a bucket held to receive it.

And seated below the one lamp that hangs from the rafters, where the light falls on her work and on her fair bowed head, is a slip of a girl in a faded blue cotton frock, knitting a bit of lace.

Outside, the moon shines cold and clear, and in the north, pale streamers and shafts of green and yellow dart like searchlights across the sky, or fall, wavering and shuddering, to the horizon.

Hans Kristoffer is busy bearing to the storehouse at the foot of the garden, troughs of livers and hearts, crates of heads and feet; and, later, the other men will help to hang the 'krops'—the carcases that are to dry in the salt-laden air, hanging in the open storehouses.

I remember, too, when Hans Kristoffer received the Cross of Danebrog. This is bestowed by the Danish King for some act of valor, for public services, and other reasons. The old custom is to have it given in church after service, the recipient coming up the aisle and standing before the altar. But the Governor was a man of heart. He knew what an ordeal that would be to Hans Kristoffer. And so one day the little *Pigeon Hawk* came from Tórshavn, with the Governor, his three little boys, and a learned Doctor of Divinity from Denmark. Johanna Katrina brought out her best tablecloth; there was good fare and a profusion of flowers; and, after dinner, as we sat there with coffee and little cakes, the Governor, saying only a few heartfelt words, pinned the Cross on Hans Kristoffer's homespun coat.

I know the surroundings so well that if you should blindfold me, twirl me about thrice and let me take one long sniff, I could tell you from what "airt" the wind is blowing. Is there salt sea air, fragrant grasses, a suggestion of roses and cocoanuts from delicate sea mosses? It is low tide and the wind sou'east. Infields and sea, and the pungent odor of salt cod drying?—wind in the south. Mild humid breezes, peat fields and moors, rotten cods' heads, refuse and manure?—*west, due west*. A tang in the air blowing from wild fields, wild thyme, crowberry and heather?—ah, that's the north wind, undefiled by man, and best of all when in its summer mood.

And afterward,—as if to give the garden a share in the feast, we went out and paced up and down the paths, a very gay little party, as both the Governor and the learned Doctor had special social gifts and a very pretty wit.

Published in *Atlantic Monthly*, 127 (May, 1921) 639–648.

The Northern Isles

In early June I went around Nakken in a six-man boat when the sea was quite calm, so I could be rowed near the base of those stupendous walls. The snows were melting fast. Clouds hid the summit, but looking upwards I saw waterfalls emerging from the clouds more than two thousand feet above me. Softly they seemed to fall, lightly touch here and there the basalt ledges, then make the last sheer plunge of 500 feet to the sea. The little falls never reached it. They were dispersed in veils of mist that wavered to and fro, caught in broken crags and trailed away on a passing breeze. Like a mighty cathedral was Nakken, a Rheims cathedral increased ten-fold. Portals, columns, buttresses were there. One seemed to see the figures of Prophets, Saints and Martyrs within those shadowed arches. Below, the foundations were exposed, polished and shining in gold and green, black and purple. No sea-weed there, no hand-hold whereby a drowning man could be saved. He would clutch and cling, be driven off, sucked back and buried in the rush of the swift "west fall" current, far out in the sub-arctic sea.

Elizabeth Taylor Papers, Minnesota Historical Society.

Faroe Islands Folklore

1. WHY THERE ARE RATS ON EYSTUROY

Long ago there were great swarms of rats in the Faroes. Very bad were they on the islands of Eysturoy and the six Northern Islands. Then there came from Iceland a man who was strong in sorcery, and the Eysturoy and Northern Islands men combined to seek assistance from him on how to be free from those wretched rats. He agreed to help them on condition that he should have an ox from each Parish. This they agreed to give him. So he summoned all the rats from Eysturoy and from the Northern Islands to meet him at a place on Eysturoy called Raktunga, a long point going out into the sea. And as he read aloud the summons, from all directions the rats came running, large and small, young and old.

All were now come except one unusually large old rat who lived at Eiðeskodle, north of Eysturoy. She was heavy with young, and lagged behind the others. They waited and waited and at last she came. Now all being gathered together on Raktunga, the Icelander asked the men if they were all of one mind and would keep their agreement and give him his reward. The Northern Island men said at once "Yes," but the men of Eysturoy grumbled and said that now he had brought all the rats together they could kill the rats themselves. Then the Icelander said aloud, "Eysturoy rats, fare thee each to thy hole!" And so scattered the Eysturoy rats all over the island once more. And all was as bad as before. But in the Northern Isles to this day there are no rats. They cannot live there. Eysturoy men, when they want grass sods wherewith to roof their houses come to Blankskale on Kalsoy (one of the Northern Isles) for in those grass sods no rats can live.

Later, another Icelandic sorcerer tried to drive rats from

Eysturoy, but he was not as powerful in sorcery as the first one. When he was reading the Summons and the rats were on their way, the great serpent, the Lindum on Skalasfjeld began to roar, and every rat scurried away to his home.

2. SUPERSTITIONS AND SUICIDES

This is Sunday and I have had a 2½ hour call from an elderly man whom I met carrying manure to his outfield. We engaged in a chat about oyster catchers, and I so approved of his views that I invited him to call. He has had tea and small cakes and two cigars and I have had such a fund of odd scraps of folk lore poured into my ears, that I take to writing a letter to you to ease my poor head before I take notes of it.

What nonsense to say that superstition is dead in Faroes, as the young half Danified persons claim. Here is a man, under sixty, taken at random who has a lively belief in ghosts (of course) and huldufólk and changeling babies and evil eyes and all manner of queer customs. I have learned of "unlucky days" when, if people do go to sea, the greatest precautions must be taken and one origin of the bad luck of these days is to be found in the suicide of some person on that day. Suicides are very rare in Faroes, but if one takes place, then one year from that day, and the anniversary ever after is an unlucky day.

This man's father has seen revenants. There was one day a boat at Strond "went away" with six men. The Pastor was sent for, three miles away, to come and pray with the widows. On arriving it was found that his priest's collar had been left behind. My man's father and two others were to go for it; the others were afraid to go and refused (afraid of the spirits of the lost six men) and this one man decided to go alone. Half way there he heard voices and saw a light. He stepped from the trail and the men passed him. He saw their faces distinctly. They were the dead men, their clothes streaming with sea water. He was panic-stricken, but remembered that if revenants appeared one should look away and then look again and they would disappear. This he did and they vanished and he went on his way.

The thirtieth of April is an "unlucky day." Formerly no boats ventured to sea on that day, and even now many boats do not go. Its evil repute dates from Guttorm of Muli's time, when a last day of April dawned of such serene beauty and fair promise that, contrary to custom so early in the year, the old men and young lads alike with the rest went to the fishery. Then burst without warning a terrible hurricane from the North and fifty boats went down at sea. After "that dreadful day, when a half a hundred boats went away," in many a hamlet there were only helpless old men and little boys.

Elizabeth Taylor Papers, Minnesota Historical Society.

Five Years in a Faroe Attic

Dear Helen,

When I wrote last, I was digging in the garden of Hans Kristoffer. Now I am in a remote fishing village on the northern end of Eysturoy. Eiði, as a winter residence, has but one attraction, the large family of a Danish Captain Kruse, whom I knew in past years. The youngest daughter, Amalya, and her husband, will give me shelter during the winter.

I left the capital, Tórshavn, at early dawn, on an open-decked motorboat, which was heavily laden with passengers, luggage, freight, the mail, Iceland fishermen's sea chests, three sheep, a cow, and a large cask of soft soap, which leaked badly and soon spread itself over everything and everybody on board. Later, rain fell, and mixing with the soft soap, made a fine lather. We were nine hours on the way, most of the time within the fjords, where heavy mists hid the fjelds and, falling, seemed to bar the way. The air was dank and chill, and when I at last saw Eiði in the distance, I thought happily that for seven long months I need go nowhere in a boat.

There were Kruses to meet me on the sea rocks and help me with the surf, and other Kruses, higher up, to hug me and escort me up the stony path, Kruses running down the little lanes and coming to doors to greet me, and meeting me at Amalya's threshhold, and dropping in later to bid me welcome. Other Kruses were out fishing. And so I settled down to keep house in Kvisten, which means the Attic.

You remember, of course, the story of the Three Bears and the Little Girl? Kvisten now resembles the home of the Little Wee Bear. All my life I have been bothered by chairs and tables unsuited to my height, and here was my opportunity. Joen Magnus, who is a carpenter, postman, fisherman, and a trifle of a farmer, has adapted many homes for me. His charge is six cents an hour. I pay seven, and thus the pleasantest relations are established. There are twenty-two boxes, large and small, in Kvisten's two rooms, though you would never suspect it, and all are suited to the needs of the Little Wee Bear and of me. They are *my* boxes,—mine to me,—and therein lies their charm. *I* own the kettle, the zinc pails, the frying pan, and the broom. No one has the right to invade Kvisten, and put soda in my tea, and boil it "to get the goodness out," or to add sugar and nutmeg to my potatoes. No "sweet soup" shall cross *my* threshhold! I am weary of conforming, through the years, to the ways of other people. Now I propose to have some ways of my own.

This cottage is perched high on a slope above the sea, so close that, as I sit by my packing case table, I see only sky and water and distant fjelds. In stormy weather, the great surges seem charging on to overwhelm Kvisten. They made me dizzy at first, and to get my bearings, I must rise and look down on the shore rocks and the grass-sod roofs of the Kruse trading post, and boathouses that shelter high-prowed fishing boats, Ornen, Svanen, Hvalen, Famiglien— the Eagle, the Swan, the Whale, the Family.

"I settled down to keep house in Kvisten, which means the attic."
The attic window of the Kruse home can be seen in the foreground
of this Elizabeth Taylor photograph, taken at Eiði.

The village of Eiði lies huddled along the fjord, looking south between two islands over nine miles of sea. On the north are gray, storm-bleached grass fields, rocky fjelds on either side, and a pond, which only a long dike of up-tossed boulders separated from the lonely Northern Sea. On the east, a great solemn promontory rears precipitous cliffs two thousand feet above the surf, and seems to be saying, "Thus far." I don't think it is my fancy that makes those northern waters seem sterner, more melancholy, than those of the east or west. On summer nights the glory of the sunset and the sunrise both are there; but now, in November, the sun is far away, making its shallow arc in the south.

I have been busy with preparations for winter—salting mutton and herrings, ordering supplies, filling little boxes with soil, and planting or sowing correctives of a too fishy, salty diet: chives and parsley, cress, and that best of all anti-scorbutics, the native "scurvy grass."

Amalya's quarters, called Huset, and mine, Kvisten, are on the most neighborly of terms, and often, starting to go downstairs with a little offering like a turnip or a cup of canned tomato, I meet Amalya coming up with a bit of fried fish or a pancake.

I am to have three lambs from another island. The first one came in mid-October, escorted from the landing place by a score of small boys. It was dismaying to be confronted by a whole Lamb,—intact,—but Amalya kindly officiated as mistress of ceremonies. Ole Jakob, a neighbor, was asked to kill and dress it in the cellar, I peering down fearfully from time to time through a trap door in the kitchen. Ole Jakob had half the tallow, the feet, fifty ore (about fourteen cents), and two cigars, and declared himself more than satisfied,—handsomely paid, in fact,—and sent his thanks. I replied, politely, through Amalya, that the thanks were to him.

Amalya's family has whale meat, salted, to eke out winter supplies. I have eaten fresh whale meat scores of time and found it very good—almost like beef. But it changes sadly when kept in brine, and has a curiously pervasive odor. The days when Huset has whale for dinner, Kvisten ventilates diligently, loses interest in cooking, and takes gloomy views of the war.

I find that many people think my name is Mistela. Not knowing the meaning of the word Miss, and adding it to my surname, they think it a Christian name, like Marguerite or Malene. I like it as I hear it from a group of children. "Here comes Mistela," I hear the older ones say; "now, bid good-day prettily to Mistela." And as I pass, they raise half-frightened eyes to me and say in soft chorus, "Godan dagur, Mistela."

This is the time of year when we are packed away in heavy, low-lying clouds that turn even midday to twilight. Storms and heavy rain day after day. Green slime growing on the little lanes, rocks, and cottage walls. Housework is difficult in the uncertain light. There is a feeling like black cobwebs before the eyes. While I wait for the light to brighten, the shadows deepen and the brief day has passed. A lantern is an indispensible part of Kvisten's outfit. When, in late afternoons, a bit of war news is telephoned to the doctor, he writes it on a piece of paper, and puts it in a little frame that hangs on the outer wall of a cottage. Buffeted by the storm, I make a zigzaggy progress up to that cottage, where a group of men are burning their fingers with matches and growling about the doctor's writing. Often I am kept there long, reading by the light of my lantern the message, as others join the group, and feeling very bashful about my queer pronunciation of Danish.

Am I or am I not a *Kalvakona*? That means a halibut woman, one who possesses mysterious powers that can charm a big halibut to the hook of a fisherman. But the fisherman must have promised her verbally, or in his thoughts at sea, the *beita*—a choice bit cut from the fish between the forefins. And for this beita no thanks should ever be given, though pleasure may be *indirectly* expressed. Last week, a man on the fishing bank promised me the beita, and a few minutes later he was having a sharp fight with a halibut that weighed almost two hundred pounds. When he came with the beita, Amalya, who was speaking Faroese for me, explained that, of course, Mistela understood that no *thanks* were to be given for it, but she was *awfully* glad to have it, and considered it handsomely done of him. Two days later, another man promised me the beita, and caught nothing. So what is one to think?

DECEMBER 22, 1914

A British trawler came in this morning to get supplies for the homeward run. I saw the ship's boat nearing land, and knew I would be
needed to help with the "trawler English." I found Neils already in
difficulty about "grub," "bac," and "tates," which the man had de-
manded. During the next hour I made acquaintance with plug, shag,
and cavendish, helped to make out attestations, and sent a messenger among the cottages to find potatoes. The man's face looked
drawn and heavily lined, though he was not middle-aged. I understood it when he told me that he had been in the minesweepers'
brigade. Two of their vessels had disappeared, leaving no trace of
crew or wreckage. The man expected to reach port by Christmas,
and I asked him about the homeward run—whether he followed all
the prescribed routes of the Admiralty. "Huh!" he exclaimed, with
contempt, "if we did, we'd never get any furrader. Run for it and
take yer chances. That's the only way!"

He gave me no thanks for my help, no word of farewell. He gathered up his purchases, paused in the doorway, and looked with
weather-wise eyes on land and sea. "Wind's against us," he muttered;
"everything's against us"—and so departed sadly.

Later. I have heard that his ship has been shelled and sunk, but
what became of the sad little man I do not know.

Our letters to England now go first to Copenhagen, then to
Aarhus in Denmark, then by a butter-and-bacon freighter back the
whole length of the North Sea, north of the Orkney Islands, and
down the west coast of England to Manchester or Liverpool. Time,
from sixteen to twenty-six days.

Yesterday a little deserter from Germany had tea here. Really he is
from Schleswig. He explains earnestly, "Papa, Danish; mama,
Swedish. Born in Germany, but *not* a German!" I was surprised to
find how well he speaks Danish, though Germany has done all in its
power since 1864 to suppress the language. When he tries to speak
English, he mixes it with German. His elder brother had been killed
in the first days of the war. His best friend was called to service, but
an accident delayed him. Next morning his young wife received the
message, "Two hours late. Shot." That was too much for the little
Schleswiger. He would rather be shot as a deserter than fight for

Germany. He was a meek, pallid boy, but his eyes fairly blazed as he was told of the death of his friend. Many adventures he has had, many narrow escapes, but now he has a British pass, is cook on a fishing vessel, and eventually will go to Denmark.

MARCH 7, 1915

The winter passes quickly, and it is time to think of garden plots. Kvisten has lately been deeply involved in potatoes. Food supplies are uncertain, and the Governor urges all to plant as many potatoes as possible, and new varieties have been sent from Denmark. I think my faulty Danish is responsible for the arrival from Tórshavn of more kinds, in larger numbers, than I had suspected. It has been a time of stress, looking each potato sternly in the eye, to see if it means to sprout. I have made a little collection for each family of the Kruse clan, two other friends, and myself. Nine families, and five varieties for each family, and each variety to be kept separately and correctly labeled, and I to cook, eat, work, and sleep in the midst of it all. By bedtime so many potatoes had been imprinted in my retinas that, when I closed my weary eyes, I could distinctly see potatoes, brilliantly illuminated, floating in space. And now in the dim light, under my cot-bed, my packing case table, wherever there is a place, are potatoes in shallow boxes, standing prettily in rows, making sprouts.

JULY 15, 1915

I was going to show Eiði what's what in the way of little gardens, but this is a bad ice-year in the far North. Those Greenland ice-floes will not go. They drift and pack and drift again, besieging Iceland's northern coasts, and causing ice fogs that check and blast vegetation in these islands. Those peas and parsnips, cauliflower and oyster-plant seedlings, one by one, went by the board, until only potatoes and turnips were left. Then blight attached the potatoes, dry rot and horrid white worms the turnips, and a coast-wind tore my rhubarb to bits. I have two pea plants that are doing well, but they are in a pot in Kvisten. Amalya has seen *dried* peas, and she always thought they were dug from the ground, like potatoes.

We have all felt the need of a peat fire in the *hagi*—the wild outfield. There is nothing like it as a restorer of cheerfulness. And on one of our few clear days, we went to a lake among the hills, five hundred feet above the sea. It was the coldest picnic I have ever attended, but with many attractions—kittiwakes taking fresh-water baths in the lake, black-backed gulls barking among the cliffs, and curlew chortling over the grassy slopes. *Omma* (which means grandmother) and I tended the peat fire and made large quantities of tea to restore the circulation of those who fished for trout, from boats, and we returned home at half-past nine, when the sun was still shining on the fields. Not that we wanted to, but we were so *very cold!*

JANUARY 30, 1916

Dear Helen,

In a letter received from America the writer says she thinks of me as "dreaming away the peaceful days far from turmoil and agitation." I will now tell you of one of my "peaceful days."

We knew by noon that a storm was brewing, for the sea was restless, the reefs moaning, and the rising wind hooted in a way that meant trouble to come. Darkness closed in early, and by four o'clock we were in the grip of a hurricane from the north. The house shook and groaned and strained like a laboring ship at sea. Torrents of icy rain and masses of sea water carried horizontally through the air bombarded the house, and on the northern side forced their way through every crevice and joist and crack. Under the eaves, in the sloping closets, Josefine and I crawled on all fours, with lanterns, exhuming the contents, while Omma brought sacks and mops, buckets and tubs. In Kvisten, with its thin roof of zinc, its walls of two layers of planks, the uproar was so great that we had to shout to be heard. Yet above it all sounded that high shrill crying—the *vox humana* of a hurricane.

During the worst gusts there was a curious lifting sensation, as if something had gone wrong with the attraction of gravity. It was singularly disconcerting to lose all sense of weight and stability, and feel that Kvisten might whirl away like a pack of cards. What a night that was, we thinking that the roof would go, the house be carried from its foundations, and then what would Amalya do? For in that time of fear Amalya's little son Oli was born. I had him in my charge, five minutes old,—so blue and cold he was,—and held him close in the skirts of my red wrapper, while the window frames sucked out and in, and the curtains blew in the icy drafts. Oh, poor little man—to come into the world on such a night!

I make from time to time tentative efforts to secure a passport, but they come to naught. I am in the diplomatic jurisdiction of Copenhagen; but with this troublesome heart the long and very dangerous journey to Denmark is impossible. I would venture the shorter one to Scotland, if I could get a passport. I wrote explaining fully how I was situated, that a "personal application" could not be made, and giving the best of my credentials. Such a trusting, naïve letter it was—so sure there would be some accomodation in the law for one of Uncle Sam's family, stranded in a far-away land. A few words, in reply, from a secretary, merely say that passports are issued on *"personal application."* So I remain in my island attic.

JUNE 15, 1916

We have had an anxious week. First, a rumor of the great sea fight off Jutland, and then the death of Lord Kitchener. Faroe folk, before the war, have known little and care less about the great ones of the outer world. But they knew about Lord Kitchener, and his death seems to them a personal loss, as if one more safeguard between their homes and the enemy had been broken down. And now, in another sense, they are comrades of the sea, for he has died the death that some of them will die. When the news came, I took a Kitchener photograph with me down to the Kruse store, where there is always a group of fishermen gossiping and smoking. They crowded around me eagerly, to see it, and I saw tears in the eyes of some of the older men. "A brave man, a good man," they said softly.

MARCH 18, 1917

The Tórshavn authorities announce that there is a three months' supply of grain and flour on hand, but future supplies are uncertain, and we are enjoined to use as little as possible, and to bear our coming troubles "with calm and dignity." Now we have used a seven-weeks' portion, and in all that time not one pound of food has come to the islands. I cut down on light, fuel, and food, and could have eaten less and yet carried on as usual. I will not say that I did not *want* to eat more. Queerly enough, I was more hungry in my dreams than in my waking hours. I gave little thought to *bacon* in pre-war days, but now, about once a week, I dream about it. I sit down, with joy, before a large dish of delicately browned curly bacon, when suddenly it vanishes away. Distractedly I search everywhere, mopping away my tears, see it in the distance, pursue it, and it again eludes me. My grief wakes me, and I find that real tears have made me uncomfortably damp.

Next week our rationing will begin, and on Monday there will be a house-to-house inspection. Private supplies must be declared and attestations made. The whole matter is rather complicated, and the Tórshavn powers that be have kindly tried to explain, in technical language, in many columns of the little semi-weekly paper. We get on fairly well in everyday Danish, but these explanations have made trouble. And now I see groups of excited men, waving ragged copies of *Dimmalaetting*, and hear such comments, in Faroe speech, as "Fool thou! I say thou canst not have sago!" "Death and torment! You've got it wrong!" "S death! Oatmeal *is* rationed!" "Out with thee! Thou'lt have to swear on truth and honor how many potatoes thou hast!" And I know that Eiði's menfolk are earnestly striving for comprehension before the ordeal on Monday.

15 MAY, 1917

Some supplies have come, enough to carry us through the next few weeks. In Tórshavn some employment is given on public works, and throughout the islands peasants have more food, some milk and fats, and dried mutton. But in poor fishing villages there is much undernourishment. There is an old saying, "When Eiði's fishing lines are dry, Eiði hungers." Yesterday four "six-man boats" (boats rowed by six men) were out, and a few small fish were the only returns for the hard day's work of twenty-four men. Many people have only their ration of coarse rye meal, weak tea and coffee, and wind-dried codlings. I can tell when a mother has been giving part of her scanty allowance to children or husband. There is a certain overbright eye, an exalted expression, a strained, white look of the skin over the nose and around the mouth.

A well-to-do friend in Glasgow offered help, and I wrote asking for a little fine barley meal and patent health foods for the mothers of newborn babies and for sick children. She wisely sent my letter on to London, with her application for a permit. It showed that I asked only for those in real need.

Eight Faroe cutters have been sunk on the Faroe Banks. The men could not believe that Germany would harm peaceful fishermen of a neutral land, on the grounds where their forbears had fished for a thousand years. This is a hard blow. The cutters soon would have gone to the Iceland summer fishery, and on that the people rely for help through the winter.

JUNE 20, 1917

After a cold, dark spring and early summer, we have had a week of real sunshine, such as we seldom see, and we have basked in it and become dry and warm and sunburned, and the days have been all too long and too light for one's strength. It is the time of peatwork, and a friend, Olivina, and I have had a private picnic on a promontory where she owns a peat field. She was to "set up" peats, and I to sketch and collect plants. So it was supposed, but the truth is, we had saved up flour from our ration, and in all secrecy we took the frying pan with us and made pancakes on the heights, and the full quota of work was not done that day. After the pancakes—on a day so rare—it seemed advisable to let work go, and climb to the top of the headland. There, twelve hundred feet above the sea, we looked across perhaps twenty miles of shimmering sea levels,—blue and pink and pearl—and there was no land between us and the North Pole. Puffins darted to and fro like little shuttles below us. Gulls circled with no perceptible motion of their wings. A long, lean freighter passed, probably bound for Archangel. Then, from the east, came two pretty sister ships, shining in new white paint. They kept close together, and seemed like two little children abroad on some brave adventure. Once they checked, almost stopped, and Olivina clutched my arms. "Undervandsbaden!" she quavered. But no, it was no submarine that had stopped them, only the fierce race, or current, sweeping eastward, and strongest at this phase of the moon.

12 JULY, 1917

Yesterday I was startled by the sight of seven large trawlers, all armed, swinging in from the open sea. Eiði is a lonely place. I had not seen a trawler, except far away. for more than two years. Amalya was calling me to hurry—that probably torpedoed crews were being brought to land. I found that only a slight accident to machinery had brought them in. But I could help about sending a telephone message, and soon a burly skipper and I were having a chat while awaiting an answer. He looked at me in amazement when he heard I was an American and had been in Eiði almost three years. "Good Lord!" he exclaimed, smiting his thigh in emphasis. "How have you held out in this hole?"

I replied, with spirit, that it wasn't a hole: there were many beautiful places near; I liked the people and was glad to be here. But later, looking about me, I admitted that Eiði in the fog was not looking its best that day, all dank and dripping, and the cods' heads and refuse too much in evidence.

Later, I met the young lieutenant in charge of the defenses. So trim and fit and lean he was, with clear, steady eyes. It was a credit to his discernment that he understood that this shabby old party who appeared out of the fog had a message that he must hear. To trawler captains I could not give it. No censor would pass it to the post. I looked into the eyes of that young man, and constrained him to listen; and as, for the time being, I had much dynamic force in me, he did listen, bless him, murmuring at intervals, "That is interesting"; "I didn't know that"; "I'll remember that"; "I'll do my best."

And then they sailed away, and I wandered about in much distress of mind. I was in the grip of nostalgia. The refined, clean-cut speech of the young officer, the first I had heard since April, 1914, brought to mind all that I had lost, was losing, in this exile. Out in the world the current of life was sweeping onward, full and strong, and I—what was I doing in this backwater, this futile eddy?

Then the fog lifted from the fjelds. Between two peaks the moon was rising. No stars are seen on a Faroe summer night. The pale moon casts no shadows. But a silvery radiance mingles with the daylight and the last glow of the sunset colors. Nothing is hidden, nothing obscured. The faint far fjelds show lovely tones of blue and violet. I could see the shining of the little streams as they slipped over the basalt ledges, the vivid green of their mosses, and the rich purples and reds reflected from the cliffs in the sea below.

It was so still that not the least line of white showed along the coast; but, as I looked, the whole surface of the sea rose, swelled upward and forward, and with a muffled roar, a great white surge flung itself along the cliffs' base and over the dark reefs. It swept backward, and all again was still.

So beautiful it was, Helen, so peaceful, that my own troubles seemed of little moment, the way before me easier to follow.

Four out of five salt ships from the Mediterranean, which had permission to come to the Faroes outside the "danger zone," have been forced by the cruisers to turn back into it for examination at Kirkwall, and as they came out they were torpedoed. So good ships and men are lost to England, and food that the salt would have cured; and much hardship is brought to the Faroes. For, with no salt to cure the fish, there can be no fishing. The Germans are greatly pleased to have their game hunted for them. . . . (The censor suppressed this last paragraph. I thought he would, but I couldn't refrain.)

On Suðuroy is the last port from which ships sail for lands "down below." There bands of British trawlers, homeward bound from Iceland, drop anchor, and signal to the port officials, "We have come in to sleep." Close together the ships lie, a little flock of hunted creatures, and for seven hours all is quiet on board. Then out they go, no rest for them till they reach a Scottish haven. Much suffering and many lives and ships have been spared to Britain by this little neutral group, in a waste of waters where ships can take shelter, and torpedoed crews and wounded men find help and nursing. Money cannot pay for these things, but the British Government might let us have some petroleum, and allow a ship with supplies from America to be examined at Halifax instead of at Kirkwall, in the danger zone.

15 AUGUST 1917

We think with dread of the coming darkness. No petroleum on sale, of course no gas or electric light, no coal, no candles, and only a scanty supply of peat. America, as well as England, refuses us petroleum. (I wish I could have Herbert Hoover here on a December night, in one of our worst gales!) A new odor has been added to Eiði's general fishiness. Housefathers and mothers are trying out highly unpleasant fish livers. Small boys are fishing for codlings. The old folks are praying that the Lord will send a flock of driving whales, to give food and light for the coming winter. And the smiths have gathered in all the old cans and every scrap of tin and brass, and are experimenting on little fish oil lamps. They require a reservoir above the burner, a pressure to force the oil up to the wick.

The truth is, petroleum, postal rights, and other desiderata, are denied us became the British Government is afraid that the Faroes will be used as a supply station for German submarines.

It is surprising what can be done in contriving ways and means. The soles of my felt shoes are quite worn out, and I have re-covered them with a piece of a neighboring fisherman's discarded trousers, giving in return a little flour. Anna has made a fine pair of shoes for her little girl from a fifteen-year-old felt hat. I bartered three envelopes the other day for a lamp-chimney with a broken top, a handkerchief for a small cod, and I have known a large spoonful of soft soap to be "swapped" for three hairpins.

20 OCTOBER, 1917

We have a new baby, a frail little creature, unfit to bear the coming winter. She is not six weeks old, an age when the normal child is a little pig, with unawakened intelligence. This dear baby looks from one to another with bright, questioning eyes, earnestly, sadly, and yet with a sweet composure that seems strange in such a helpless mite. We laugh at her, and tell her that she needn't put on such dignified airs, that we mean well, even if our manners are not as fine as hers. I suppose she seems older because there is no baby fat to hit the pure oval of her face and the fine lines of neck and shoulders.

We have had heavy rains and a low temperature since the middle of July. Even now, between snow squalls, haymaking is going on. Many are bearing home the half-dry hay, to spread it out in their little cellars. Wretched food it will be for the poor cows; but there is nothing else to give them.

30TH JANUARY, 1918

Eiði had a "dry Christmas" (no spirits for sale), and so, for many women and children, a happier Christmas than usual. We made a quite charming little tree from a piece of spar, with sticks inserted here and there for branches, and covered with heather and crowberry. Amalya fished out some decorations from her childhood days; there were some little toys sent in August from a Scottish friend. I made cornucopias with the colored illustrations of a Liberty rug-and-carpet catalogue (and very pretty they were), and from beeswax cast ashore from a torpedoed vessel we had little brown candles, which spluttered briskly as they burned, from the sea salt in them. We had long been saving from our flour and sugar rations, and by an elaborate system of barter and by mutual gifts in the Kruse clan, we managed to have some good Christmas food, and sugar candies and ginger nuts for the tree. It was really something like a Danish Christmas, with the singing of the Christmas songs, "Still Night. Holy Night," and "A Child is born in Bethlehem."

We are having a terrible winter. Such cold has never before been recorded in the Faroes. This long siege began on December first. I was at the window after dinner, wondering at the strange ashy-red color on the fjelds, when, with a noise like thunder on Kvisten's roof, all was blotted out, as if a gray blanket had been thrown across the window. The gale raged with hurricane force until the next morning. Seven were killed (two on this island) and many injured.

Then followed week after week of gales from the North. No fjelds, no sea, no sky, all milled up in a whirling fog of hard-cutting snow. The light in Kvisten was dim and gray, so thick was the ice on the window. I shared my wardrobe with my potatoes, yet they were frozen. The water supply gave out long ago. There is too little peat to melt much snow. The only water we have must be brought some distance, from a brackish pool near the sea. The salt water makes a sticky glaze on the skin without cleaning it. There is practically no soap in the village, no soda or other cleansing stuffs. The fish oil lamps diffuse a universal oiliness. But there is one advantage in the common plight; no one can look with disdain on his fellow man and say, "I am clean."

The pride of the family, Melrose by name, a large, half-Cheviot ram, blew away in that opening gale. His carcass was fished up three days later from the sea. This is not a time for undue fastidiousness, and Amalya has salted most of the meat, and the rest we ate with a properly thankful spirit. Only I wished that Amalya would speak of the dear departed as *mutton*, instead of saying, "Nela" (our boy's name for me), "will you have another piece of *Melrose?*"

The people miss the little visits of happier days between the cottages, the gossip over a cup of tea and coffee, and perhaps little cakes brought out to honor a guest. Now the food rations do not admit of hospitality. I admire the kindly fibbing that goes on when a neighbor comes on some necessary errand. "Now don't get anything for me. I've just had breakfast, and couldn't eat a bite more." Often I am asked wistfully, "Has the Frøkun any news of the Amerika ship—with coffee?" as if, being an American, I must possess special knowledge. But not a word have we heard.

23 APRIL, 1918

The baby, Elizabeth, died on Easter Day. The world is too hard a place now for little babies. Our boy, Oli, grieves for her; and knowing that many things are ordered from Tórshavn, he begs Amalya to write for another little sister just like Elizabeth, to be sent on at once.

30 MAY, 1918

The American schooner has come to Tórshavn, nine months from port. She must have feared she was fated to be another Flying Dutchman. Month after month of contrary gales crippled her at last, so she drifted into the danger zone and had to seek a Shetland haven for repairs. Part of the cargo is damaged, but the coffee is saved. The news passed swiftly over Eiði, called by happy voices from house to house. I saw tears of joy on one wrinkled old face, and heard a quavering voice singing the gay "Coffee Song"—a dance ballad that the singer had danced more than a half century before.

And now our only postal communication with the outer world is by one old hooker, which brings salt and some restricted wares from a British port, and takes back salt fish and fish-liver oil. To name it is forbidden, but seamen call it "The Lucky Ship." Nor can we ask when it will come or go. During more than two years the valiant old skipper, now aged seventy-four, has gone back and forth across the danger zone, having adventures that cannot be told. There is one young gunner on board, but all the crew and officers range from fifty-five to seventy years.

15 DECEMBER, 1918

All was quiet when the few-worded message came of the signing of the armistice. Of course, in a little neutral land there would be no official celebration. A crowd gathered quickly when the few-worded bulletin was put up, and some asked me, "Can it be true?" And some said, "God give it be truth!" and some wiped their eyes. And I said, "Gud ske lov" [God be praised], and went away where I could see from afar that northern shore, where now I need not dread to look, fearing what I might find there. For the seas are to be clean once more! And then I went back to Kvisten and did my housework, and that was all.

15 JANUARY, 1919

In December, for the first time since July, 1916, a real steamer entered Eiði's fjord. A shabby black old hooker, to be sure, but it was the "Lucky Ship." And now I can tell its name, the *Cromwell*, and the brave old skipper's name is Captain Gibb, of Aberdeen, and the ship belongs to the Iceland Shipping Co., Leith, Scotland. I wanted to go on board, but we are quarantined against the Spanish influenza and no one is allowed on deck. Only by going to windward can bags of salt be delivered to the freight rowboats, and oils and fish transferred to the steamer.

We fancied that after the Armies' truce we would soon be freed from the stern rule of the blockades and have mails, supplies, and steamer service as in pre-war times. But we find that little change will be made before the signing of the Peace. Leith is still a forbidden area, no mails are allowed on Danish vessels, and *Tjaldur* cannot go to Scotland where hundreds of war-bound people are trying to get a passage to Denmark. *Tjaldur* is a small vessel, and her old sea-companions, *Vesta, Ceres, Flora, Pollux, Holar, Skalholt*, and *Ingolf* are all at the bottom of the sea. In 1913 I had thirty days of Iceland-Faroe travel on four of these vessels. Of that fine ship *Ingolf* not one soul survived to tell the tale. "Sunk without a trace."

TÓRSHAVN, 2 AUGUST, 1919

The breaking up of my life in Kvisten was a hard time. I was really ill with a "near-pneumonia" cold. Storms and heavy surf swept the village front, making the launching of a boat impossible. Could I get to Tórshavn in time to go on the *Tjaldur*? Would she go to Scotland on her way to Denmark? Was my promised passage assured, when scores of passengers on the spot were clamoring to go? I dared not let myself think of the parting from those who had become so dear to me. Silence seemed the only way of getting through with it. Once I said shakily, "Amalya, you know what is in my heart?"—"Yes, Nela, I know." Then, just in time, the storm subsided.

Our boy Oli at the last would not say goodbye. "Nela was bad. Nela should not go to England. Nela should stay in Kvisten always."

It was a small party that set forth in the tiny fishing motorboat. Our housefather at the helm, a brother-in-law at the engine, two neighbors as assistants, Frú Kruse and I the passengers. The box-like pit where whelks for bait are kept had been cleaned out, and Frú Kruse and I sat down there, with our heads peering out above the rim. A piece of canvas stretched overhead kept out the rain. And so we chug-chugged southward, hour after hour, in the gently falling rain, toward Tórshavn, where I was to see a pony and a tree for the first time in five years. Part of the time we were between the islands, then on the open sea, past treacherous reefs and sucking whirlpools of the Streymoy coast, where many a boat has "gone away." Then, as we rounded a point of land, we saw on the far southern horizon a faint smudge of smoke. That was our *Tjaldur*, and she will take me south to Scotland.

Published in *Atlantic Monthly* 128 (October, 1921), 441–451.

Faroe Foods

During many years spent in the Faroes I learned to eat, with proper thankfulness, many kinds of strange foods. Puffins, razorbills, guille-mots, kittiwakes, shags, cormorants, the eggs of sea-fowl, wind cured mutton, wind dried young coal fish, and several kinds of whales: blue, humpback, fin and pilot whales.

It took a little courage, at first, to try some of these dishes, but the food was all wholesome and nourishing. [We had no seal meat, but formerly it was used, as it is now in Iceland, in places near the coast where seals are often killed. Nansen and Antarctic explorers have spoken highly of the excellence of seal-meat.]

As for the puffins and other sea-fowl the Faroe peasant house-mother stuffs them with a kind of dumpling and boils them whole, heads and all, without removing the skin. Consequently the birds have a very unpleasant fish-oil flavor. A better way is to take the breasts only, skin them carefully, and take away every particle of fat, soak them several hours in milk and water, brown them lightly in a little butter or margarine, then stew them slowly with just enough water to cover them. If the house-mother wished to add some special frills, she would put a few shreds of bacon in the frying pan, a mere suspicion of onion and a small bay leaf. Prepared in this way, they make a very appetizing dish, without a trace of "fishiness." I have eaten them prepared this way at a dinner party given by the Governor, and the most fastidious diner would have enjoyed the course.

Then there is whale meat. The best, for food, is the comparatively small pilot whale. These are never hunted by the Norwegian whalers who have stations in the islands, but are driven into the fjords by the Faroe people and killed in some bay or inlet. I have often eaten it in many forms. It looks and tastes like beef, and the heart, liver and kid-neys resemble those of other warm-blooded animals. (The whale, it should be remembered, is not a fish but is a warm-blooded mammal.) The back fin boiled, and when cold, cut in thin slices and eaten on thin slices of dry bread is quite a delicacy.

Why, indeed, should anyone object to whale meat in an undisguised form? Before the war great quantities of whale meat from the whaling stations were sent to Denmark and from there sent to Germany. Doubtless many who fancied the Bologna Sausage and other kinds of German sausage have often eaten whale meat which had been lightly salted, preserved in brine in casks and used up quickly. Probably it was quite as good as beef and better than most of the flesh of old and worn horses.

Elizabeth Taylor Papers, Minnesota Historical Society.

Elizabeth Taylor as a
Victorian Lady Traveler

by MOIRA F. HARRIS

Women travel. They always have, willingly, by choice, unhappily, reluctantly, or even by force. Throughout history women have been
emigrants, pilgrims, guides, explorers, pioneers, and wives whose
duty was to follow their spouses abroad. We know of some women
who traveled only through the words of others; but more often
women have told us in their own letters, journals, and published accounts what they saw and felt. Theirs is usually a somewhat different
view from the official male version, sometimes even the only view.

Biographies and anthologies have focused on where women traveled, from whence they came, how they traveled, and when they
went. Elizabeth Taylor belongs to an intrepid group of European
and American women who set out in the late nineteenth century to
report back from the near and far abroad, women now known as
"The Victorian Lady Travelers." Often included in this group are
Mary Kingsley, Isabella Bird, Kate Marsden, Annie Peck, Fanny Bullock Workman, Kate Field, Ethel Tweedie, Marianne North, and Ida
Pfeiffer. Some married, some didn't, but most waited to leave home,
as Elizabeth Taylor did, until they felt their domestic obligations
were complete. Most had the benefit of a small income or inheritance, but needed to supplement that pittance with funds earned by
writing or giving lectures. Those who published several books, like
Isabella Bird and Fanny Bullock Workman, were able to fund further
travel with the royalties from each best-seller.

Travel was not easy for any woman who chose a remote destination, but timing often played a significant role. Elizabeth Taylor's
Canadian and Alaskan trips were aided immeasurably by the recent
completion of railroads, both to the north and west, by 1885. She still

rode part of the way in everything from birchbark canoes to steam-boats, Red River carts and wagons, but she reached her destinations much sooner than she would have done even a decade earlier, thanks to the railroads.

Some of these ladies, like Isabella Bird, were skilled horsewomen, but Elizabeth Taylor was not. When she rode it was properly sidesaddle, sometimes precariously perched amidst baskets as she had to do in Italy, at other times in a makeshift arrangement as was the case in Iceland. After her cariole accident in Norway she would probably have preferred to walk when she was traveling on land rather than to ride in either a carriage or on horseback.

Travel, as these women wrote, meant confronting dangerous sit-uations and occasionally fierce animals. Mary Kingsley noted cheer-fully that rather than aiming a rifle, she had fled from every large African wild animal she faced. The most feared creatures Elizabeth Taylor met seem appropriate for a Minnesota-raised traveler: black flies and cows. The flies were a constant pest on her Canadian trips even if every inch of skin was covered and one wore a net head cov-ering. Cows, large horned cows, she met everywhere and, as a tiny woman, when she found a cow in her path, like Mary Kingsley, she fled.

Any traveler needs to be flexible, patient, determined, and re-silient. But the lady travelers had to believe in themselves since fami-lies were not always available, supportive or even interested in their tales of travel to unfamiliar or remote places. Elizabeth Taylor's fa-ther encouraged her art studies in New York and her travels in Canada; he facilitated them by obtaining the railroad passes and per-missions from the Hudson's Bay Company. After his death her main family link was to her sister and brother-in-law in Troy, New York, Mary and Charles Alden. They handled her finances, offered her housing on occasion, and helped ship her collections to museums. Of her St. Paul extended family, she wrote to a friend as she reached the end of her Mackenzie River trip, "Do you think that anybody wants to house an Arctic explorer?"

One of the few times any notice of her travels appeared in a local paper was in 1918 when a letter written to a friend in Georgia was shared with other relatives and eventually made its way to cousins in St. Paul. The headline read:

"ST. PAUL WOMAN MAROONED SINCE 1914
ELIZABETH TAYLOR CANNOT LEAVE OSTERO FOR U-BOATS"
(*St. Paul Pioneer Press*, March 10, 1918)

Lady travelers kept journals, took photographs, sketched, and wrote voluminous letters which could often serve later as the basis for articles. Elizabeth Taylor's most frequent correspondents were Helen Carver, a childhood friend from St. Paul; Fannie Burr from Connecticut whom she met in Abbot Thayer's art classes; and Florence Grieve from the Cheviot Hills of Scotland who was traveling in Norway that same summer of 1890 and helped her after the cariole accident. These women shared her interests, saved her letters, traveled with her, and welcomed her to their homes.

Writing travel essays for publication meant finding the appropriate magazine or newspaper and Elizabeth Taylor eagerly sought them out. Her first published works were two articles based on her trip to Fort Qu'Appelle, a Hudson's Bay Company post west of Winnipeg. She reported on mission schools for Indian children and an Indian ceremony, the Great Thirsty Dance. These articles appeared in *Frank Leslie's Popular Monthly Magazine* in 1886. The magazine eventually published six Taylor pieces about Canada, complete with illustrations based on her sketches. In an almost prophetic coincidence her first Canadian story appeared in the same issue of *Frank Leslie's Popular Monthly Magazine* as another author's account of a hiking trip in the Faroe Islands. Another early publisher of her travel accounts was *Outing* magazine. Her interest in fishing brought her writing to the pages of *Forest and Stream* and *The Fishing Gazette* while her more folkloric and literary stories about the Faroe Islands found their way to *The Atlantic Monthly* which included "The Baptizing of the Baby" in a volume of magazine classics. She also wrote for various newspapers, as her father had, in Buffalo, Brooklyn and London.

Like many other women of their time, most of these ladies were not formally educated beyond the elementary grades, but they benefited from family libraries and interests. Through study and observation they educated themselves and, through their writings, they educated and informed others. While Elizabeth Taylor was in Alaska she met Dr. Charles Gilbert who showed her ways to identify and preserve fish. The European tour she took in 1890 was led by Dr. David Starr Jordan, university president, scientist, and co-author of an important book on fish with Gilbert. Over the years she corresponded with other professors and museum curators in the United States, England, and Denmark, as she supplied them with information and materials for their collections.

In her letters and articles Elizabeth Taylor assumed that her readers would possess the same knowledge of the Bible and literature that she had so a reference to a poem would pose no problem. She wrote to her friend Fannie Burr that Oliver Wendell Holmes' poem, "The Two Great Streams," which refers to the Mackenzie River, was her longtime inspiration for that trip. When she felt she was not accomplishing any work, but merely enjoying a situation, she wrote to friends that she was like the Lotos-Eaters in Tennyson's poem. But certainly the funniest poetic reference occurs in a letter she wrote to her sister Mary Alden in 1901 after her trip to Stóra Dímun:

"I lived on Puffins with their Skins on, and milk, and little besides—and had to clench my fists and say poetry mentally with great vigor in order to distract my mind and get my Puffin down. Wordsworth's "Ode on Intimations of Immortality" was useful. 'Our birth is but a sleep and a forgetting (mouthful of Puffin) . . . Not in entire forgetfulness/ And not in utter nakedness/But trailing clouds of glory do we come' (more Puffin), etc."

The Victorian lady travelers traveled to satisfy their curiosity, to test themselves, and prove to the world that they could accomplish their goals. For some of these women, the goal was simply the freedom to travel; for others climbing mountains, painting tropical flowers, or collecting African fish were on the agenda. At a time when social mores did not permit women to enter or succeed in many fields, women could travel and write. Elizabeth Taylor chose cold places which certainly tested her survival skills, but also allowed her to write proudly, before she left on her trip to the Mackenzie River and the Arctic Ocean, that now it would be "Me and Franklin!" She relished being the first white woman or the first American to visit a place and often speculated as to what it would be like when tourists discovered that spot.

Off season was a good time to visit a place, she wrote to Dr. David Starr Jordan from Edinburgh in 1895. She had just returned from her first trip to Iceland and the Faroes and felt that:

"It was a triumph of mind over matter, for I suffered much from the cold and damp, the fare was very plain and it stormed violently nine-tenths of the time. I have a theory that, to really get the best out of a place, you should see it out of the so-called proper season. November in the Faroes would not sound promising, but I feel that that wild month was worth all the rest of the time. Such grand storms that I saw, and such effects on sea, sky, and land, such wrestlings with the winds and snow, and then there was the bringing of the sheep (to be killed) from the mountains, the Northern lights and all kinds of little happenings."

Elizabeth Taylor chose to travel and live in cold places yet the cold had always been a problem for her as she wrote in a note to herself, probably while she was in Viðareiði during her first long trip to the Faroes:

"It is my experience that one in my station of life is uncomfortable a part of the day in every country in winter."

She continued, to herself, that it had been cold in Venice, in Paris, and in New York and it obviously was going to be cold in the Faroes, certainly if fires were never lit in the dining room, but since she had asked to stay in the parsonage she needed to accept life as it was and wear mufflers and mitts.

"Wear mufflers and mitts!" As the admonition to herself suggests, Elizabeth Taylor prepared and accepted the situations in which she found herself. It was a way of life she had chosen so it was up to her to make it succeed. Her warning to herself would probably be easily understood by other Victorian lady travelers. They were not wives who dutifully accepted their husbands' new jobs—Ruths who smiled and replied, "Whither thou goest, I will pack." While they may have been early visitors to places, they were seldom the very first outsiders to arrive so their roles were not to serve as guides like Sacajawea. Rather, as a group, they were role models, who

*On her travels Elizabeth Taylor liked to botanize and fish.
Too often, as these sketches from a letter to Helen Carver show,
what she did instead was to stay inside, avoiding the rain and the cold.
Sketches by Elizabeth Taylor from Red Rock on the Nipigon River, 1889.*

found it possible to do something different and to challenge society's expectations. Like Chaucer's Good Wife of Bath, they chose the pilgrimage and had a fine set of adventures to write to the world when it was done.

Bibliography

Articles Written by Elizabeth Taylor:

I. CANADA

"The Great Thirsty Dance," *Frank Leslie's Popular Monthly*, 22:6 (December 1886), 680–3.

"The Legend of Omeshoes," *Frank Leslie's Popular Monthly*, 30:4 (October 1890), 491–495.

"Life in the Frozen North," *London Globe*, April 30, 1896.

"Ojibway Legend of Mesheka the Turtle," *Frank Leslie's Popular Monthly*, 29:1 (January 1890), 62–64.

"Out of the Frozen North," in the Contributor's Club, *Atlantic Monthly*, 79 (January 1897), 139–140.

"Quebec," *Frank Leslie's Popular Monthly*, 30:1–2 (July 1890), 17–29.

"Up the Mackenzie River to the Polar Sea. A Lady's Journey in Arctic America," *Travel*, (April 1899), 559–564.

"Up the Nepigon," *Frank Leslie's Popular Monthly*, 28:3 (September 1889), 309–316.

"A Visit to Fort Qu'Appelle," *Frank Leslie's Popular Monthly*, 22:4 (October 1886), 523–527.

"Where the Big Trout Hide on the Famous Nepigon," *New York Herald*, undated.

"A Woman in the Mackenzie Delta," *Outing*, XXV (October 1894–March 1895), 44–55, 120–132, 229–235, 304–311.

II. ALASKA

"Birds, Beasts, and Fishes. A Woman's Sport with a Fly in Alaskan Waters," unknown newspaper, undated.

"A Lady's Sea-Fishing at Sitka, Alaska," *The Fishing Gazette* (London), September 10, 1921, 189.

III. ICELAND

"A Botanist in Iceland," *Popular Science Monthly*, (March 1898), 54–55.

"Eider-Duck Farms in Iceland," *Good Words*, 38 (October 1897), 688–692.

"Mythological Relics in Iceland," *Popular Science News*, (April 1898), 83.

IV. Norway

"A Northern Berry," in The Contributor's Club, *Atlantic Monthly,*
(September 1895), 427–430.
"Over Hardanger Vidda. The Upland Summer Pastures of Norway," *Outing,* 36
(April 1900), 664–670.
"Remote Norway. A Woman's Trip Through the Upper Saeterdal," *Outing,*
(July 1899), 367–374.

V. Scotland

"A Highland Ben," *The Independent* (Boston), December 24, 1896, 1757–1758.

VI. Faroe Islands

"Absalom's Wreath," *Atlantic Monthly,* 91(February 1903), 248–254.
"The Baptizing of the Baby," *Atlantic Monthly,* 109 (February 1912), 278–283.
(Reprinted in *Atlantic Monthly Classics,* second series. Boston: The Atlantic
Monthly Press, 1918.)
"A Day in the Faroes," *Good Words,* 42 (1901), 414–419. (Reprinted in *Current
Literature,* 31 (October 1901), 452–4.)
"Five Years in a Faroe Attic," *Atlantic Monthly,* 128 (October 1921), 441–451.
"Folklore from a Faroe Praestegaard," *Chamber's Journal,* December 13, 1924,
29–32.
"The Garden of Hans Kristoffer," *Atlantic Monthly,* 127 (May 1921), 639–648.
"In the Faroe Islands," *Forest and Stream. The Journal of Rod and Gun,* March 2,
1901, 162–3; October 26, 1901, 323; October 11, 1902, 283–4; November 8,
1902, 362–3; November 15, 1902, 383–4.
"A Night with the Mouse's Brother," *Atlantic Monthly,* 89 (May 1902), 671–8.
"Odd Way to Get A Wife," *Current Literature* 32 (June 1902), 678–9. (Originally
published in *Chicago Inter-Ocean.*)
"An Out-of-the-Way Island," Buffalo, N.Y. *Morning Courier,* October 26, and
November 2, 1902.
"The Valley of the Others," *Atlantic Monthly,* 110 (December 1912), 825–832.
"Whales Aground!" *Forum,* 78 (August 1927), 214–225.

VII. Miscellaneous

"A City of Refuge," *The Interior* (Chicago), 32 (August 15, 1901), 1041–3.
"In Rugged Montenegro," *Brooklyn Daily Eagle,* (June 11, 1899), 16.
"In the Fresh Air of Ongar," *Globe* (St. Paul), May 1937, 26–29.
"Visit to Dalmatia," *Brooklyn Daily Eagle,* (June 4, 1899), 16.

About Elizabeth Taylor and Her Work

Nancy C. Alden, "The Garden of Hans Kristoffer," *Dutchess Life,* (April 1987),
12–13.
Nancy C. Alden, "Letters from Hans Cristoffer," *Dutchess Life,* (May 1988),
16–17.
Arthur G. Butler and W.F. Kirby, "List of Insects Collected by Miss Elizabeth
Taylor in Western North America in the Summer of 1892," *Annals and
Magazine of Natural History (New York),* Series 6, Vol. XII, July 1893.

James Taylor Dunn, "Elizabeth and the Far Islands. Ten Years in the Faeroe Islands," 1978. Unpublished manuscript.

James Taylor Dunn, "Nipigon Fisherwoman," *The Beaver,* (September 1949), 20–23.

James Taylor Dunn, "North Hollow Haven," *Vermont Life*, (Spring 1950), 50–3.

James Taylor Dunn, "Sitka, Salmon and Shipwreck, 1889..." *Alaska Life,* (July 1949), 4–5.

James Taylor Dunn, "To Edmonton in 1892," *The Beaver,* (June 1950), 3–5.

Oli Egilstrød, "Elisabeth Taylor," *Vardin* (Tórshavn), 50:1–2 (1983), 24–41.

Grace Lee Nute, "Down North in 1892," *The Beaver*, (June 1948), 42–46.

Grace Lee Nute, "Paris to Peel's River in 1892," *(The Beaver*, (2March 1948), 19–22.

Sverre Patursson, "Faeroerne," in *Faeroernes Naeringveie*. Kristania, Norway: Aktieforlaget Johannes Hamch, 1918, 3–12.

"St. Paul Woman Marooned Since 1914," *St. Paul Pioneer Press*, March 10, 1918.

Liv Kjorsvik Schel and Gunnie Moberg. *The Faroe Islands*. London: John Murray Ltd., 1991.

U.S. Department of Agriculture. Bureau of Biological Survey, North American Fauna No. 27. "A Biological Investigation of the Athabaska-Mackenzie Region," by Edward A. Preble. Washington, D.C: Government Printing Office, 1908.

Lady Travelers

Leo Hamalian, ed. *Ladies on the Loose. Victorian Travellers of the 18th and 19th Centuries*. New York: Dodd, Mead and Company, 1981.

Dorothy Middleton, *Victorian Lady Travellers*. London: Routledge and Paul, 1965.

Mary Morris, editor. *Maiden Voyages. Writings of Women Travelers*. New York: Random House, 1993.

Elizabeth Fagg Olds. *Women of the Four Winds*. Boston: Houghton Mifflin Company, 1985.

Jane Robinson. *A Guide to Women Travellers*. Oxford: Oxford University Press, 1990.

Catherine Barnes Stevenson. *Victorian Women Travel Writers in Africa*. Boston: Twayne Publishers, 1982.

Marion Tingling, editor. *Women into the Unknown. A Sourcebook on Women Explorers and Travelers*. Westport, Connecticut: Greenwood Press, 1989.

Other Sources

Theodore C. Blegen, "James Wickes Taylor: a biographical sketch," *Minnesota Historical Society Bulletin*, 1:4, (November 1915), 153–219.

David Starr Jordan. *The Diary of a Man,* Yonkers-on-Hudson, N.Y: World Book Company, 1922, 250, 344–353.

Ernest Thompson Seton. *Trail of an Artist-Naturalist*. New York: Charles Scribner's Sons, 1940, 284–6, 297–8.

James Wickes Taylor Papers, Minnesota Historical Society, M156 (microfilm).

List of Illustrations